MATERIALS AND METHODS IN ELT

Applied Language Studies
Edited by David Crystal and Keith Johnson

This new series aims to deal with key topics within the main branches of applied language studies – initially in the fields of foreign language teaching and learning, child language acquisition and clinical or remedial language studies. The series will provide students with a research perspective in a particular topic, at the same time containing an original slant which will make each volume a genuine contribution to the development of ideas in the subject.

Series List

MATERIALS AND METHODS IN ELT

A TEACHER'S GUIDE

Jo McDonough and Christopher Shaw

BLACKWELL
Oxford UK & Cambridge USA

First published 1993

Reprinted 1994, 1995, 1996

Blackwell Publishers Ltd
108 Cowley Road
Oxford OX4 1JF, UK

Blackwell Publishers Inc.
238 Main Street
Cambridge, Massachusetts 02142, USA

British Library Cataloguing in Publication Data
A CIP catalogue record for this book is available from the British Library

ISBN 0–631–18002–8 (hbk) — ISBN 0–631–18003–6 (pbk)

Typeset in 11 on 13pt Ehrhardt by TecSet Ltd, Wallington, Surrey

Printed and bound in Great Britain by Hartnolls Ltd, Bodmin, Cornwall

This book is printed on acid-free paper

Contents

Contents

Acknowledgements

We are grateful to the following for permission to reprint extracts from published material:

The British Council for *Teaching and Learning in Focus*, Edited Lessons vol 2, pp. 22–25. Cambridge University Press for: Unit 5.1 of G. Porter-Ladousse, *Speaking Personally*; the Table of Contents and Unit 7 of L. Jones, *Functions of English*; Table of Contents of M. Swan and C. Walters, *New Cambridge English Course*; pp. 10–11 of G. Ellis and B. Sinclair, *Learner Training*. *Colchester Evening Gazette* for 'Paying to learn: is it snobbery?'. Heinemann for permission to use p. 60 from *Integrated Skills: Intermediate* by B. Milne; and for the map of the book and Unit 3 p. 20 of E. Davies and N. Whitney, *Reasons for Reading*; pp. 34 and 35 of M. Geddes and G. Sturtridge, *Listening Links*; Unit 2 of M. Geddes and G. Sturtridge, *Reading Links*; Language Teaching Publications for pp. 16 and 17 of G. Keller and S. Warner, *Conversation Gambits*. Longman Group UK for permission to use information from *Starting Strategies* by B. Abbs and I. Freebairn; Table of Contents of R. O'Neill, *Kernel Lessons Intermediate*; Unit 11 of S. Axbey, *Soundtracks*; Unit 1 of Hopkins and Tribble, *Outlines*; Table of Contents, pp. 104 and 105 of R. O'Neill and P. Mugglestone, *The Fourth Dimension* and p. 64 of *The Third Dimension*. Macmillan, for pp. 151–5 of Forman, Donoghue, Abbey, Cruden and Kidd, *Campus English*. Oxford University Press for permission to use information from M. Underwood and P. Barr, *Listeners: Dangerous Jobs*; Unit 18 of M. Underwood, *Listen to This*; p. 96 of T. Hedge, *Writing*; pp. 59–60 of S. Sheerin, *Self–Access*. R. V. White for Unit 6 of *Writing Away* (Lingual House). Times Newspapers Ltd. for permission to use 'Nightmares that end up in death'.

We particularly wish to thank Sandra Cardew, Tricia Hedge and Keith Johnson for their careful reading of the draft manuscript and for their many perceptive comments (although they bear no responsibility for inadequacies remaining in the final version). Our thanks also to Dilly Meyer and Margaret Middleton for their most helpful efforts on manuscript and Macintosh.

Finally, our gratitude to several cohorts of practising teachers from many countries who have helped us in different ways to formulate our thinking, and particularly to those who have taken the trouble to read and comment on some of the draft chapters of this book.

Introduction

Materials and Methods in ELT: A Teacher's Guide has been written to provide teachers of English as a foreign language with an up-to-date account of major trends in ELT materials and methodology. The book has been written in the hope that it will be equally useful to teachers who are following a scheme of study in Applied Linguistics and Language Teaching Methodology in Britain or overseas as well as to classroom teachers of EFL around the world who may wish to keep abreast of current developments in the field.

The overall aim of the book is to provide a synthesis between 'principle' and 'practice' by making links between background issues in Applied Linguistics where appropriate, and at the same time looking at the practical design of materials and methods.

Each chapter has been written with this overall aim in mind and by the end of the book we hope that readers will have the necessary skills to understand the most common design principles for teaching materials, to critically evaluate the principles upon which they are based, and to assess their relevance to, and possibilities for, their own teaching context. It is our hope that readers will also gain some appreciation of materials and methods within educational frameworks that may differ from their own.

We have divided the book into three parts. The five chapters in the first part relate to the area of materials and syllabus design by looking at the *principles* on which materials and methods are based. Chapter 1 looks at the educational framework of materials and methods which is relevant to all ELT practitioners. Chapter 2 provides an analysis of the growth of the communicative approach to language teaching and the implications for materials that this approach entails. In chapter 3 we examine some critiques of the communicative approach and try to analyse some of the different 'post-communicative' trends in design principle over the last decade, notably the multi-syllabus and the process syllabus, and how these relate to actual teaching materials.

Chapters 4 and 5, on evaluating and adapting materials respectively, should be considered as a 'pair' in that the issues discussed require much cross-referencing. Chapter 4 offers a working model for teachers to evaluate materials for adoption and selection purposes. Chapter 5 follows on from this and is based on the premise that evaluating involves understanding the principles of textbook construction and is therefore concerned with how teachers, from this understanding of their learners and the materials they are working with, can adapt these materials to meet the demands of their learners in a given teaching situation.

In part II of the book we attempt to relate the principles raised and discussed in part I to each individual language skill in turn. Each chapter, 6 to 9, is organized in such a way as to show how the 'theory' related to each individual skill of reading, speaking, listening and writing has affected approaches to the design and use of teaching materials in the respective skill areas. The last chapter in this part, chapter 10, is to be seen as a final 'unifying' chapter which looks at different ways of achieving effective skills integration in teaching materials.

The third and final part of the book focuses largely on different methods of organizing the resources and management of the classroom. In selecting the different topics for this section, we decided to include only those which would relate directly to this theme. Consequently, we have not included topics such as testing, partly because it does not fit neatly into this framework and partly because it enjoys extensive coverage elsewhere. Nor have we included separate chapters on project work, whole language approaches in ESL, or curriculum support approaches in the English medium context, simply because we feel that it would have extended the present book into too many diverse areas.

The first two chapters in this section, 11 and 12, are closely linked in that they focus on classroom structures and interaction patterns – with respect to groups and pairs in chapter 11, and to the concept of the individual learner in chapter 12. The latter chapter also examines recent developments in self-access and learner training in relation to individualization.

Chapter 13 is concerned with discovering what further insights we can gain into the nature of the teaching/learning process by looking closely at language classrooms to see the kind of interaction which really takes place between teachers and learners as well as between the learners themselves. The final chapter, 14, attempts to round off all the issues raised in the previous chapters of the book, by means of a discussion of the ELT teachers' contemporary role in the classroom in relation to materials and methods. This chapter examines topic areas such as the 'good' language teacher, in-service education courses and suggestions for teacher development.

Our final goal in writing this book is to enable readers to become better informed about contemporary ELT methods and materials by providing a relatively compact reference package which incorporates practical 'operational' tasks into the text with the desired outcome that readers will have the skills to make informed judgements about their present and future classroom practice.

Jo McDonough
Christopher Shaw
Colchester
July 1992

Part I

Topics in the Design of Materials and Methods

1 The Framework of Materials and Methods

Introduction: Setting the Scene

As teachers of English as a foreign or second language (EFL/ESL), we are members of an established worldwide profession. As Richards (1985: 1) reminds us, 'the current status of English has turned a significant percentage of the world's population into part-time users or learners of English'. Wherever we work, we share many assumptions about what we do; we prepare and use teaching materials and classroom methods and techniques based on similar, or at least comparable, principles. Yet despite this commonality, it is not unusual for teachers to report a sense of isolation from colleagues in other countries, and even in different areas of their own country. Another attitude that is sometimes expressed is that the teaching situation in our country, or school, is unique, with its own special problems and difficulties. There is some justification for these feelings, of course: many teachers work in geographical isolation, and may not have access to channels of professional communication (journals, conferences, in-service training courses); different countries have widely differing educational systems and philosophies, resulting in teachers being subject to different expectations and pressures.

In this chapter, we shall take some time to look beyond our individual teaching circumstances to what can be thought of as a professional 'common core'. This has relevance to all teachers, whether we work in a Japanese high school, a Mexican university, a private language school in Spain, a Chinese polytechnic, a Turkish secondary school, a Zairean college – this list could go on indefinitely. We shall argue that the idea of a 'common core' is also useful whether our materials and methods are selected by us or specified by the educational authorities. It is, then, broadly made up of two kinds of factors: firstly, of the various wide-ranging criteria on which decisions about language teaching programmes are based, and secondly, on the *pedagogic* principles according to which materials and methods are actually designed. We shall take these two kinds of factors together and refer to them as the shared *framework*.

In what follows, this notion of a 'framework' is set out in a little more detail. We then subdivide it under the two headings of 'context' and 'syllabus', both exploring their general implications and trying to relate them as we do so to our own familiar and specific teaching situation.

The Framework: Context and Syllabus

In simple terms, the overall goals of a language teaching programme usually derive from an analysis of the reasons why a group of learners in a particular environment needs to learn English: these goals may be stated in general, educational, or very specific terms. They may, on the one hand, be set out in the large-scale categories of a national language policy with many associated implications for the development of the curriculum. The aim of English Language Teaching in Malaysia, for instance, is 'to create a society that is able to utilize the language for effective communication as the need arises, and as a key to wider experiences. For those furthering their studies, the skills learned should become an instrument with which they may cope with the necessities of using the language' (Kementerian, 1979). Alternatively, a course may be organized to address a particular learning need for, say, the identifiable professional purposes of a small group. Sandler and Stott (1981), for example, claim that the aims of their course in English for Management are to meet the needs of 'practising managers in industry and commerce who, for a variety of reasons, need to improve their performance in English. Secondly, for business studies students and management trainees who are studying for an examination in English or who are expected . . . to attain a level of proficiency in English'.

There is, then, a whole spectrum of possibilities for defining the goals of language teaching, for a country, an age group, a whole school, a class, or an individual; and whether for general educational purposes, business, scientific development, cultural appreciation or many other reasons.

Is there an explicit statement of the goals of the language programme on which you work? If so, what are its primary aims?
    If there is not such a statement, try to draft one that represents your own understanding of the goals.

To define what is meant here by 'framework' we start from the view that materials and methods cannot be seen in isolation, but are embedded within a broader professional context. This is represented in figure 1.1, which shows in a very simplified form the typical stages of planning an English language programme.
    Whether goals are stated in terms of a national language policy, or in the more restricted environment of, say, a particular school or college, the possibilities for actually implementing them will be directly related both to the learners themselves – their needs, characteristics and so on – and to the whole educational setting in which the teaching is to take place. Obviously, as we shall see in our subsequent discussion, goals need to be realistic for specific circumstances. There is little use, for example, in planning for a

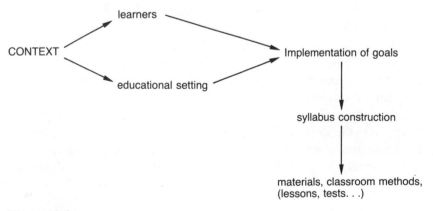

Figure 1.1

multi-media course if appropriate equipment is unavailable or unreliable, or in making too many general assumptions about classroom methodology. The statement of goals, then, related to the learners and conditioned by the setting, leads to the selection of an appropriate type of syllabus content and specification. The broad syllabus outline will in turn have direct implications for the more detailed design and selection of materials and tests, the planning of individual lessons, and the management of the classroom itself. Clearly this logical planning sequence is an idealization of what is often a less well-defined procedure, where 'set' materials may linger behind aims that have been reformulated and updated, or conversely where new syllabus types may be ill-matched to existing educational objectives. The logical sequence will nevertheless be used as a reference point for discussion, and as a starting point for the exploration of individual teaching circumstances.

This whole topic is dealt with in considerable depth by Stern who, in his *Fundamental Concepts of Language Teaching* (1983: ch. 3), proposes a very detailed 'conceptual framework', designed as a model that is intended to capture what he sees as the complexity of language teaching. After surveying a number of earlier models, he then sets out his own scheme. Its main components are (a) views of the nature of language; (b) views of the learner and of language learning; (c) views of teaching and the language teacher; and (d) the whole context, which includes the educational setting, the language context, and the language teaching background. The chief characteristics of the model are that it should be *comprehensive*, covering any type of language teaching operation; that all factors under each heading are *interdependent*, so that 'no single factor, for example the teacher, the method, the materials, a new concept, . . . or a technological device, can by itself offer a general solution to most language learning problems' (1983: 47); and that it should see language teaching as *multidisciplinary*. Stern's perspective will be evident both in this and most subsequent chapters.

The rest of this book will be concerned with the third stage of figure 1.1, the design of materials and methods. Let us now look at the most important contextual factors involved in planning, and then at the key types of syllabus from which actual courses are derived.

Contextual factors

In the preceding section, we took a broad view of 'context' and included both learners and setting under this heading. Let us examine each of these in turn in a little more detail.

Learners   It is possible to identify a number of important learner characteristics or 'variables' which, as we have suggested, influence planning decisions and the specification of goals. The relative importance of these variables, and their effect on programme design, obviously depend to a certain extent on some of the situational factors to be discussed in the next section. For example, a pupil's mother tongue may be more, or less, significant depending on whether more than one native language is represented in the classroom, or perhaps on the educational philosophy of that particular environment.

For the moment we can list here the key characteristics of 'the learner', indicating how they might affect planning and noting that they form part of our common frame of reference as language teachers, wherever we work. Some of these are characteristics of whole groups or subgroups of learners, others are individual and less open to generalization. Again, some can be known in advance and incorporated at the initial planning stage, in principle at least. Others are more appropriately assessed in the classroom environment itself, and as such are more obviously susceptible to teacher reaction and influence. They can only be outlined here, and clarified with just a short comment and example. Following Stern, they must be seen as interrelated.

We consider the learner's:

- *age*: this will particularly affect topics chosen and types of learning activity, such as the suitability of games or role play.

- *interests*: as with age, this may help in the specification of topics and learning activities.

- *level of proficiency in English*: teachers will wish to know this even where their classes are based on a 'mixed proficiency' principle rather than streamed according to level.

- *aptitude*: this can most usefully be thought of as a specific talent, in this case for language learning, as something that learners might show themselves to be 'good at', perhaps in contrast to other subjects in a school curriculum. (It can be measured by formal aptitude tests, although they are not very frequently used.) The relationship between aptitude and intelligence is not clear, and is certainly not direct.

- *mother tongue*: this may affect, for instance, the treatment of errors or the selection of syllabus items – areas of grammar or vocabulary and so on.

- *academic and educational level*: which help to determine intellectual content, breadth of topic choice, or depth to which material may be studied.

- *attitudes to learning*, to teachers, to the institution, to the target language itself and to its speakers. This is directly related to

- *motivation*, at least insofar as it can be anticipated. Obviously a whole range of factors will affect this.

- *reasons for learning*, if it is possible to state them. With school age pupils this may be less significant than with many adult learners, where it is often possible to carry out quite a detailed analysis of needs.

- *preferred learning styles*: which will help in the evaluation of the suitability of different methods, for instance whether problem-solving activities could be used, or whether pupils are more used to 'rote learning', where material is learned by heart.

- *personality*: which can affect methodological choices such as a willing acceptance of role play and an interactive classroom environment, or a preference for studying alone, for example.

Many of these factors will recur in the relevant sections of subsequent chapters.

Setting   That aspect of the context that we refer to as *setting* is to be understood here as the whole teaching and learning environment, in a wide sense: it is the factors falling under this heading which will determine whether the aims of a language programme, defined with reference to the learners' needs and characteristics, are actually feasible and realistic. In certain situations, the setting itself may be so significant that it provides the foundation for the specification of aims. This might be the case, for instance, in a country with a single political or religious ideological base, where the education system is primarily an expression of that ideology and where learner factors, although taken into account, are secondary. In the majority of circumstances, however, the setting is more likely to condition the way in which goals are carried out, and indeed the extent to which they can be.

For most EFL/ESL teachers, therefore, the following factors, in some combination and with varying degrees of significance, will influence course planning, syllabus design, the selection of materials and resources, and the appropriateness of methods:

- *the role of English in the country*: whether it is a regular means of communication or primarily a subject taught in the school curriculum, where, in turn, it may or may not be the first foreign language. This relates to the linguistic environment, and to whether English is spoken in the community outside class or alternatively never heard.

- *the role of English in the school*, and its place in the curriculum.

- *the teachers*: their status, both at national and institutional levels, their training, mother tongue, attitudes to their job, experience, expectations. This topic will be discussed in detail in the final chapter of this book.

- *management and administration*: who is responsible for what level of decision, particularly which are the control points for employment of staff, budgets, resource allocation and so on. Additionally, the position of teachers in the overall system needs to be understood, as does the nature of the hierarchy in any particular institution.

- *resources available*: books and paper, audio-visual material (hardware and software for cassette and video), laboratories, computers, reprographic facilities and so on. Design and choice of teaching materials will be particularly affected by resource availability, as will the capacity to teach effectively across a range of language skills.

- *support personnel*: administrators, secretaries and technicians, and their specific roles in relation to the teaching staff.

- *the number of pupils* to be taught and the size of classes. Overall numbers may affect the total number of teaching hours available, and the large class problem is a very familiar one in many settings worldwide.

- *time* available for the programme, both over a working year (longitudinally), and in any one week or term (intensive or extensive). Many teachers would also consider that time of day is a significant factor.

- *physical environment*: the nature of the building, noise factors, flexibility of tables and chairs, size of room in relation to size of class, heat and cold, and so on.

- *the socio-cultural environment*: this can often determine the suitability of both materials and methods. For example, some textbooks contain topics which are inappropriate to the setting, and some classroom methods require an unacceptable set of teacher and learner roles.

- *the types of tests used*, and ways in which students are evaluated: assessment procedures may, for example, be formal or informal and subjective. They may also be external, in the form of a public or national examination, or internal to the institution and the course.

- *procedures (if any) for monitoring and evaluating* the language teaching programme itself. This kind of evaluation may be imposed by 'senior management', or alternatively agreed between teachers as colleagues.

Malamah-Thomas (1987: 97) describes setting in terms of three levels in an education system – the country, the school, and the classroom. She then divides the various factors into (a) Physical (b) Temporal (c) Psycho-social and (d) Educational, showing how the three different levels may be affected by each of these. Thus, for example, psycho-social factors are related at national level to culture, politics and religion; at institutional level to school atmosphere and staff attitudes; and in the classroom to student–teacher rapport.

Teachers are affected, directly and indirectly, by all these variables. Some they may be able to influence or even control: for example, the deployment of resources and materials, or the pacing of work within an overall time-scale. Others, of course, arise from decisions taken far removed from a teacher's day-to-day professional life, perhaps at Ministry level, or at an earlier point in the country's educational history. Whatever their source, it is the teacher who is in the 'front line' – attempting to promote learning and fulfil the stated goals against the background of a complex network of interrelated factors. Not everyone will work in a situation as gloomy as that described by Gaies and Bowers (1990: 176), with large classes, low motivation, inadequate coursebooks, poorly trained teachers, lack of resources, heavy workload and the like, but we may all share their conclusion that 'by coming to grips not only with new ideas but with the evidence of what happens when they are introduced into the local context, [teachers] equip themselves with the tools for establishing an appropriate methodology that can set realistic national objectives for teacher training and education' (181).

Consider the following short case study of a fairly typical teaching environment. Note how the factors associated with the learner and the teaching situation can affect the organization of the language programme, the materials, the teachers and the methodology. For instance, most aspects are determined by decisions taken at some distance from the teacher, although teachers' views may have some effect. Again, the classes are on the whole conditioned by the examination system, but a minority of pupils are able to select classes in line with their own interests, which in turn means that teachers may be less bound by coursebooks and able themselves to be more autonomous in choice of materials and methods. In other words, there is a complex set of factors in operation, and the teacher in the classroom is the focus of a variety of pressures and influences, both direct and indirect.

> *Teacher X* works in a secondary school, with pupils ranging in age from 12 to 16. She teaches 30 periods a week, 2 of which are options selected by older pupils according to their interests. Course materials consist in the main of set text books graded according to age and proficiency level and focused heavily but not exclusively on accuracy. Materials are written by a Ministry of Education team according to Ministry guidelines, and teachers' opinions are solicited annually by an Area Language Teaching Adviser. It is Government policy to revise materials every 8 years.

Average class size is 40 pupils. The pressure of the examination system ensures satisfactory attention, though – since there is little opportunity for travel – learners do not readily perceive the relevance of learning materials to their own lives.

The school has a language laboratory, and a very small collection of books (mainly stories) written in English. Classrooms are basic but adequate. Very few supplementary English language teaching materials are available, though teachers are encouraged to make their own small-scale resource materials, and to share ideas at local teachers' centres.

This teacher has been to Britain once, on a three-week summer school. She corresponds regularly with an English school teacher.

Now examine your own teaching environment in a similar way. First list the characteristics of your learners and of the teaching situation.

Then decide which are the more significant of these, and try to plot the patterns of cause and effect that they set in motion. For example, how are your classroom materials selected? To whom are you responsible? What possibilities do you have for innovation, or for professional development?

Finally, you might like to consider what kinds of changes in your teaching situation would have the strongest effect on your role as a teacher – a change in your status? smaller groups? more time? The possibilities are many.

Try to discuss your analysis with colleagues, both with those working in the same environment and, if possible, with others from different backgrounds. Keep a note of your analysis: it will be helpful to refer to it again in subsequent chapters.

The syllabus

We can now assume that the goals of an English language programme have been set out and that the contextual factors affecting its implementation have been established and understood. The next step in the task of planning is to select a type of syllabus which is relevant to the learners for whom it is intended, appropriate to the situation, and which fulfils the aims as closely as possible.

The 'syllabus' can be seen for our purposes as the overall organizing principle for what is to be taught and learned. In other words, it is a general statement as to the pedagogical arrangement of learning content. Richards and Rodgers (1986) have proposed a useful framework for the comparison of language teaching methods which illustrates the place of the syllabus in programme planning. Their model has three distinct levels, which they term *approach*, *design* and *procedure*, and is intended to show the relationship between the theory and practice of language teaching as an 'interdependent system'. Briefly, 'approach' is the most general level, and refers to the views and beliefs – or theories – of language and language learning on which planning is based. The most obvious example here is a view of language described as a set of grammatical structures. The next level, 'design', is where the principles of the first level are converted into the more practical aspects of syllabuses and instructional materials. It is here that decisions are taken about the arrangement of content to be taught and learnt, the choice of topics, language items to be included in the programme, and so on. Finally, 'procedure' refers to techniques and the management of the classroom itself. The present book loosely follows both this model and its philosophy, by focusing on materials (design) and methods (procedure), and trying to show how they all have an explicit basis in theory (approach).

The English Language Teaching profession nowadays has available a range of different types of syllabus from which a choice will be made for a specific situation. So however diverse our teaching contexts, our courses will be based on one, or a combination of, these principles of organization. Although syllabuses typically are written and published documents, their circulation is often restricted to the particular situation for which they have been drawn up. Therefore, one of the simplest ways of surveying the types of syllabus available is to examine the contents pages of published English language teaching textbooks, because they reveal the underlying principles and assumptions on which the writers have based their material. At one and the same time, they tell us something both about the approach and the design adopted, thus bringing together principle and practice in a directly observable way.

This is not a book about syllabus design as such, and it will not be necessary or appropriate to analyse each syllabus type in depth here. References to more detailed discussion are given at the end of the chapter, and the next chapters will examine the major areas of current debate. Let us simply try to identify the key principles of syllabus organization by examining the types of contents page most often found in the materials we use, because these distinctions will be the foundation for our discussion of 'design and procedure' in the remainder of the book.

Look at the coursebook(s) that you use most frequently. With which of our samples in figure 1.2 does the table of contents in your own material compare most closely?

The first of these obviously is organized according to a list of grammatical structures, and is one that will readily be recognized by most English language teachers. The second is based on the communicative and interpersonal uses to which language is put and, in contrast to the formal structural system of the first type, highlights what people do through language. It is normally referred to as a 'functional' syllabus. This design principle is often found together with the other list of items in the same box: they are technically called 'notions', a term used to describe the rather general and abstract

<table>
<tr><td>

(1) Simple past; irregular verbs
The passive
Formation of adverbs
Type 3 conditionals
Gerunds and infinitives

</td><td>

(2a) Making suggestions
Asking for directions
Giving advice
Introducing yourself

(2b) Location
Duration
Ability

</td></tr>
<tr><td>

(3) In the restaurant
At a hotel
In the post office
At a garage

</td><td>

(4) Making notes from a talk
Reading for information
Using a dictionary
Writing an exam answer

</td></tr>
<tr><td>

(5) Space travel
Intelligence tests
Smoking
The weather

</td><td></td></tr>
</table>

Figure 1.2

categories which a language is able to express, such as concepts of time and place. For convenience – and in line with common practice – they will be placed together here, and the syllabus as a whole designated 'functional–notional'. The most important distinctions between this on the one hand and the so-called structural syllabus on the other will be taken up in the next chapter. The third sample above presents a set of everyday situations or 'settings'. The fourth focuses on language skills, and is concerned with what learners do as speakers, listeners, readers, writers. The fifth uses topics or themes as its starting point.

We can now identify five broad types of syllabus:

1   grammatical or structural
2   functional–notional
3   situational
4   skills based
5   topic-based

We comment on 'process' and 'procedural' syllabuses in chapter 3.

It is, of course, unusual to find just one of these as the only organizing principle, in isolation from others, and before leaving this discussion of syllabus types two final explanatory points must briefly be made.

First, most syllabuses are based on a combination of two or more of the types we have illustrated. Some, like this one, for example, may have a 'primary' and a 'secondary' organizing principle:

At the bank: question forms
At a garage: imperatives
At a hotel: present perfect

Indeed, many situational and topic-based syllabuses are part of a broader pattern of this kind, where a grammatical point to be taught is linked to an interesting theme or practised in a 'real-world' setting rather than learnt mechanically and outside any context. Other syllabuses are multi-layered, using several different principles which (ideally) are interwoven in a systematic way:

Talking about holidays
Requesting information

Question forms
At the travel agent
Listening and role play
Intonation practice

This deliberately is a somewhat extreme example, but it does show how topics, functions, structures, skills, situations (and pronunciation practice) can be brought together.

The second point to bear in mind here is the need to distinguish between the syllabus itself, and what we might call a 'syllabus inventory'. The inventory is simply a list of the contents to be covered in the language programme, whether that is a list of functional or grammatical items, or of skills, or of topics and situations. The 'syllabus' is the way in which that content is organized and broken down into a set of teachable and learnable units, and will include consideration of pacing, sequencing and grading of items, methods of presentation and practice, and so on. It is the latter implications that are the main focus of this book.

Examine the list below which shows a number of different types of learners and teaching situations. Work with a colleague if possible, and select two or three of them to look at in a little more detail.

Where?	*Who?*	*Why?*
China: university of technology	undergraduates	reading purposes: English is a library language
Turkey: secondary school	school pupils	part of general school curriculum
Britain: university	postgraduates in various subjects	to follow postgraduate studies after 1 year English
An English town: secondary school withdrawal class	refugees, newly arrived	language survival

Where?	*Who?*	*Why?*
France: evening class	mixed group: retired people, housewives	tourism and general purposes
London: private language school	young adults from the Middle East (male)	to do engineering in Further Education
Japan: university	undergraduates	to be tourist guides for foreign visitors
Malaysia: technical institute	post-'O'-level students	to enter higher education in Australia

First of all, try to decide what you think might be the most important factors to do with the *learners* and the *setting* for the situations you have chosen. For example, you may think that learners' proficiency levels, or attitudes to English, are significant, and that class size and resources are the key elements affecting the teaching situation.

Secondly, consider the kind of syllabus that might be selected as the most appropriate in each case, bearing in mind the stated learning purpose. It does not matter if you are not personally familiar with these kinds of teaching context. They are quite representative, and the task here is to practise applying and integrating some of the principles that we have been discussing in this chapter.

Conclusion

This chapter has discussed the background against which teaching materials and classroom methods evolve. Our professional activities as language teachers are not carried out in a vacuum and, in Richards' (1985: 11) words, 'Planning a successful language program involves consideration of factors that go beyond mere content and presentation of teaching materials'. Although we work in specific situations with specific groups of learners, according to a specified set of aims,

our work can be described along a number of shared and generalizable dimensions. These dimensions are: the characteristics of
learners; the range of factors in the teaching situation itself; and the
syllabus types available to us as a profession. The differences lie in
the relative importance of these factors, and the actual choices that
are made.

Further reading

Chapters 1 and 2 of Richards, J. C. (1985): *The Context of Language
Teaching*. Chapter 1 is entitled 'The context of language teaching'.
Chapter 2, which was written with Rodgers, is entitled 'Method:
approach, design and procedure', and is a summary of the arguments
set out in Richards and Rodgers (1986).

2 The Impact of the Communicative Approach

Introduction

In the previous chapter, we examined in very general terms the most common types of syllabus organization for English language teaching. We also noted that these syllabus types form an essential component of the framework within which objectives are specified and the details of language teaching programmes are set out. This happens, as we have seen, according to certain principles and with various possibilities for combination. It is the purpose of the present chapter to take a closer look at the approach to syllabus and materials design that has had the greatest significance world-wide for the current practice of English language teaching. This approach is most usually called 'communicative', and although other labels, particularly 'functional–notional', are sometimes taken as synonyms, 'communicative' will be used here as the cover term.

It is important for the aims of this book to understand that communicative design criteria permeate both general coursebooks and materials covering specific language skills, as well as the methodology of the classroom. In other words, there are a number of assumptions which are now an explicit or implicit part of the everyday professional lives of teachers in many parts of the world.

We shall first very briefly survey the recent history of English language teaching, emphasizing the period when dissatisfaction began to be voiced with what was then the dominant approach to syllabus and materials design. We shall then see how the gradual adoption of a communicative approach expressed itself in the claims made for the appropriacy of language teaching materials. The main section of this chapter will pick out the key implications of the concept for teaching purposes, and we shall end with an attempt to evaluate its potential advantages and disadvantages. The following chapter will contain a selective discussion of developments in syllabus and materials design in the 'post-communicative era'.

Some Background

It is neither appropriate nor possible within the scope of this book to set out all the many ramifications of 'the communicative approach': inappropriate, because our main intention is to look at its impact on teaching and learning rather than at the theory and background in themselves; not possible, because the concept covers a potentially vast area touching on many disciplines (philosophy, linguistics, sociology, psychology, even anthropology), and a full treatment would require at least one book in its own right. The 'further reading' section at the end of this chapter lists several readily available works for teachers interested in following the discussion further. For present purposes, we shall simply outline the reasons that led to the growth of a concern for 'communication' in language teaching and learning, indicating a few of the background sources from which practice has evolved.

The communicative approach is essentially a manifestation of the 1970s, in the sense that this was the decade when the most explicit debate took place, especially in the UK. By the end of the seventies it was clear that many features of the approach were here to stay. As we shall see in chapter 3, the subsequent period has been characterized by explorations of other, related possibilities for the design of materials and methods. The original 'communicative revolution' has subsided, and it has inevitably been the subject of critical comment: nevertheless, its central tenets have not been rejected, and we shall find them incorporated in a great deal of current thinking. More importantly, perhaps, teachers in many parts of the world are finding that they need to come to terms with changes in their role, as communicative principles in language teaching become central goals of their educational systems.

Towards the end of the 1960s we can discern amongst language teaching practitioners and applied linguists a growing dissatisfaction with the prevailing methodology of the time, the main emphasis of which was on the mastery of language structure. This is a generalization, but it is true to say that language learners were required, above all, to manipulate grammatical forms accurately, and that this procedure was the main measure of competence in a foreign language. All English language teachers will be familiar with the type of exercise instruction that asks (or more usually tells!) students to convert active sentences into their passive voice equivalent, or to supply the correct verb form for a given tense, or to distinguish adjectives from adverbs. A glance at many of the tables of contents of teaching materials published in the 1950s and 1960s will confirm this focus. It was argued that this kind of teaching produced 'structurally competent' students who were often 'communicatively incompetent' (Johnson, 1981), able perhaps to form correct sentences to describe the daily habits of the fictitious textbook 'Jones family', but unable to transfer this knowledge to talk about themselves in a real-life setting. In a much quoted phrase, this kind of grammatical competence has been described as 'necessary but not sufficient' (Newmark and Reibel, 1968, quoted in Johnson, 1981).

One of the indirect reasons for this dissatisfaction was undoubtedly the fact that, by the late 1960s, the world had started to shrink, in the positive sense that there were increasing possibilities for international professional cooperation and travel, whether for business, further study, or other purposes. Particularly in Western Europe, interdependence grew with the development of the European Common Market, and with it a parallel educational need for changes in the way in which the various European languages were taught (Richards and Rodgers, 1986: 65). These changes were addressed within the Council of Europe when a number of experts worked on far-reaching proposals for the establishment of a scheme to teach the languages of Europe, particularly with the needs of adult learners in mind. Wilkins (1976) was instrumental in setting out the fundamental considerations for a 'functional–notional' approach to syllabus design based on communicative criteria. More detailed specifications for courses for different languages were then developed (for English, see for example van Ek, Alexander and Fitzpatrick, 1980). Work within Europe has had an impact far beyond its original context, as we shall see in the next sections.

These educational perspectives evolved alongside, and to some extent were derived from, significant theoretical developments in linguistics and sociolinguistics. There are a number of quite well-known arguments which are clearly explained in the references given at the end of this chapter, and they will not be repeated here. We should just note – should readers wish to seek more detail – that they centre particularly on the sociolinguist Hymes' (1972) concept of 'communicative competence', and his criticism of Chomsky's view of language on the grounds that Chomsky paid exclusive attention to 'correctness' at the expense of 'appropriacy' of use in specific contexts. Again, the general relevance of this point will become clear in the next section.

We conclude this section with the observation that, although the 1970s were the years in which 'structural' design criteria started to receive widespread critical attention, the gradual shift to a more communicative methodology obviously did not take place simultaneously throughout the world. In many countries the debate is still very current, reflecting the differing and changing perceptions of the international roles and needs of education systems.

Try to characterize the approaches to materials design that the two tables of contents represent. Compare them with the textbook(s) you most frequently use: are your materials close to either of these approaches?

The Claims for Communicative Materials

During the 1970s there was, not surprisingly, a great boom in the publication of teaching materials designed according to 'communicative' principles. It is instructive to look at the kinds of claims that were being made for this 'new direction', and the following statements, taken from a number of standard published materials, are very typical (italics are ours):

i   'for students interested in *using* language rather than learning more about structure . . . students learn to use the *appropriate* language they need for *communicating in real life*'

Contents

Source: R. O'Neill, R. Kingsbury and A. Yeadon, *Kernel Lessons Intermediate, Students Book,* copyright Longman, 1971.

Contents

Source: L. Jones, *Functions of English*, copyright Cambridge University Press, 1981.

ii '... is a dynamic, *functionally-based* coursebook. It is an intensely practical book, giving the students opportunity for thorough and *meaningful* rehearsal of the English they will need for effective *communication*'

iii '... to use the language to *communicate in real life*'

iv '... teaches students to *communicate* effectively by understanding and controlling the relationship between language forms and *functions*'

v '... places emphasis on developing skills of *discourse* within a wide range of *communicative settings*. It actively trains the learner in important discourse functions ... All the language practice is presented in *real-life contexts* and related to the learner's own experience.'

It is clear even from this short selection that certain terms recur: communication, real-life, use, functions, appropriate, meaningful, context, setting and discourse. It should also be noted that in a few cases there is an either/or type of statement – 'using language *rather than* learning more about structure'. Particularly in the early days of enthusiasm for the new communicative movement, there was sometimes a tendency to regard the design of communicative materials as the only way forward, and to polarize 'functions versus grammar' as if they were somehow in opposition. A moment's thought will show that this is a very unbalanced perspective, indeed one that is entirely incorrect: it is clearly not possible to engage in purposeful communication in a language without being able to formulate the structures of that language as well. We might recall Newmark and Reibel's much wiser position, quoted earlier in this chapter, that an ability to control grammatical structure is 'necessary but not sufficient'. In other words, for most learners this ability will be part, but not the whole, of language learning. As Dubin and Olshtain (1986: 88) put it: 'There are ... prevailing misconceptions regarding the communicative approach to language learning. One such frequently expressed misunderstanding is the belief ... that it is a new methodology which has come to *replace* the structural approach ... The most significant contribution of the communicative approach is that it has brought about a more comprehensive view of teaching and learning' (italics added).

In one sense, then, the italicized terms in the numbered extracts above are labels, intended to make the materials more attractive to a potential purchaser/user. They are also much more than labels, however: they are like doors behind which is to be found a rich ground for the discussion of both the 'theory' and 'practice' of communicative language teaching. We shall pick out the key implications of these terms in the next section.

You might like to look at the claims made for the materials that you most frequently work with. In what terms are those claims expressed (if they are explicitly stated)?

Implications of the Communicative Approach for Teaching Purposes

We stated in the introduction to this chapter that the literature on the communicative approach is very large, and draws on several theoretical areas of debate. We shall restrict ourselves here to trying to show those implications that have most helped to form the kinds of teaching materials we work with and our attitudes to managing our classrooms. As we go through this section, we suggest from time to time some points for you to consider in relation to your own experience, both of language and of teaching. The seven implications discussed are:

1   'Communicative' implies 'semantic', a concern with the meaning potential of language.
2   There is a complex relationship between language form and language function.
3   Form and function operate as part of a wider network of factors.
4   Appropriacy of language use has to be considered alongside accuracy. This has implications for attitudes to error.
5   'Communicative' is relevant to all four language skills.
6   The concept of communication takes us beyond the level of the sentence.
7   'Communicative' can refer both to the properties of language and to behaviour.

The relative importance of these implications depends, for example, on the skill(s) being practised and on the nature and purpose of particular classrooms: this will be explored in the relevant chapters of parts 2 and 3.

Implication 1 In its broadest sense, the concept of 'being communicative' has to do with what a language has the potential to mean, as well as with its formal grammatical properties. The research of the 1970s laid the foundations for this view, which is particularly associated with the work of Wilkins (1976) originally carried out for the Council of Europe. Wilkins proposed two categories of communicative meaning: 'notional' (or 'semantico-grammatical') and 'functional'. The distinction between these two terms is clearly set out by Johnson (1981). 'Notions' are rather abstract concepts – frequency, duration, dimension, location, quantity and so on – which in English are closely related to grammatical categories. So, for instance, expressing 'frequency' involves tense selection and certain adverbial constructions. ('They often used to visit friends'; 'I talk to my students regularly', for example.) 'Functions', on the other hand, refer to the practical uses to which we put language, most usually in interaction with other people. Johnson suggests that, to find out the function of any particular utterance, we can simply ask 'what was the speaker's intention in saying it?' (1981: 5). For example, a short statement like 'I'll do that!' could be an offer of help, but it could also be a warning, if the speaker believes that the other person is likely to be in danger when trying to carry out some activity; while 'do you smoke?' could be a straightforward enquiry, perhaps asked during a medical examination, or it could be an indirect request for a cigarette. Other functional categories often found in teaching materials include making requests, greeting, making suggestions, asking for directions, giving advice.

For our purposes, we can note that the majority of published coursebooks for English give more emphasis to functional rather than notional categories, presumably because real-life interaction expresses itself most obviously in this way. However, it must also be pointed out that the syllabus specifications carried out within the Council of Europe and following on from Wilkins' original work go into considerable details of both notions and functions (van Ek, 1977).

The semantic criteria outlined here have obvious implications for the design and organization of teaching materials. If our coursebook is primarily aimed at mastery of the formal grammatical system, then a sentence such as 'When does the next train leave for London?' will probably occur in a Unit on 'interrogatives' or 'auxiliary "do"'. In a functional–communicative coursebook, such a sentence is more likely to be found under a heading like 'requests for information'. Similarly 'you ought to see the doctor' can be taken either as part of an exercise on modal verbs, or as one way of giving advice.

Implication 2   This is closely linked to the first, and concerns the relationship between the grammatical forms of a language and their communicative function. Let us consider a simple conversational statement like 'Give me your telephone number'. This could, of course, be an order, if spoken by a policeman to a motorist who has committed a traffic offence. However, if said, with suitable intonation, to an acquaintance, it could be a suggestion about a way of getting in touch. Or 'if you don't sit down, there'll be a problem' could be interpreted as either threatening or helpful. In other words, a grammatical structure can in principle perform a number of different communicative functions – an imperative might, for example, be a command or a suggestion, a conditional might be selected to threaten, to warn, or alternatively to give advice.

The converse relationship also holds, where a single function can be expressed in a number of different ways. To make a suggestion, for instance, we can choose to say 'You should . . .', 'You ought to . . .', 'Why don't you . . . ?', 'You'd better . . .', 'I think you should . . .', 'Have you thought of . . . ?', and undoubtedly there are several other possibilities. (In the Council of Europe's terms (van Ek, 1977), these structural items are referred to as 'exponents' of a particular function.) Figure 2.1 summarizes the relationships. For a longer list of examples, readers are directed to Wilkins (1976: 147), who shows how the imperative form can be used for suggestion, threat, instruction, direction, warning or invitation, and how the functional category 'command' can be expressed by conditional,

Communicative function

Grammatical structure

structural exponents

functional possibilities

Figure 2.1

active declarative, 'you' + verb, present continuous negative, or the future tense.

In more traditional teaching materials, this complex form–function relationship tends to be simplified, often implying a one-to-one correspondence, so that 'interrogatives' are used for 'asking questions', 'imperatives' for 'giving commands', 'conditionals' for 'making hypothetical statements' and so on. In a communicative perspective, this relationship is explored more carefully, and as a result our views on the properties of language have been expanded and enriched. However, there are a number of pedagogic problems associated with this approach to materials design, particularly to do with the sequencing of the language to be practised. We shall leave comment on this until later in the chapter.

Think of some more examples of functions in English, and the grammatical structures related to them. You could also think about comparable patterns in your own language.

How do your teaching materials handle the relationship between grammar and communicative function? For instance, is a 'function' taught together with several grammatical forms, or just one? Alternatively, is a 'function' just used as an example where the main focus is on teaching grammar?

Implication 3　It is possible for most teachers to think of classroom situations where grammar practice takes place with very little reference to everyday reality, where learners rehearse patterns simply in order to get them right rather than to express meaning. Equally, it unfortunately is just as possible for a list of language functions to be practised as ritualistically as grammar with, say, a few structural items for 'giving advice' applied in turn to imaginary people and situations. We need, then, to be a little cautious here, because there is no reason in principle why grammar practice should not be placed in a communicative context, and functional practice take place only as a list of separate and decontextualized items.

However, real-world language in use does not operate in a vacuum, and this is the third implication of the communicative approach. When we give advice, we do so to someone, about something, for a particular reason. If we are invited, it is by someone to do something, or to attend something. So in addition to talking about

a)   *Language function* and
b)   *Language form*, as we did in the previous two sections, there are other dimensions of communication to be considered if we are to be offered a more complete picture. These are, at least:
c)   *Topics*, for example health, transport, work, leisure activities, politics and so on.
d)   *Context or setting*. This may, as Yalden (1983) points out, refer to both physical and social settings, and may therefore include personal conversation and business discussion as well as the more traditional 'situations' such as travel or medical or leisure-time settings.
e)   *Roles* of people involved: whether, for example, stranger/ stranger, friend/friend, employee/boss, colleague/colleague, customer/person supplying a service.

Two short and very simple examples will serve to illustrate this:

A.   Can I have 2lbs of those red apples, and 3 lemons please?
B.   Anything else?
A.   That's all, thanks.
B.   £1.50 please.

A.   This is really good, but a bit expensive.
B.   Manchester restaurants are much cheaper.
C.   Who's paying?

   Language function and language form, then, do not operate in isolation but as part of a network of interconnected factors, all of which need to be taken into account in materials which use a communicative concept as their design principle.

Implication 4   Once we move away from the idea that mastery of grammar = mastery of a language, we are obliged at the same time to move away from evaluating our learners' proficiency on the basis of accuracy alone. It is undoubtedly desirable that their language production should be as 'correct' as possible, but we have seen that grammaticality also takes place in a wider social and communicative context. The implication here is that we should concern ourselves not only with accuracy of form, but also with appropriacy in relation to the context. This derives in part from Hymes' view of language as including 'what a speaker needs to know in order to be communicatively competent in a speech community' (Richards and Rodgers 1986: 70). The communicative approach has therefore led to a broadening of the criteria by which language proficiency is defined. We now have the concepts of appropriacy as well as accuracy, communicative as well as grammatical competence, use as well as usage (Widdowson, 1978).

For teaching purposes, these considerations clearly lead to a re-thinking of attitudes to, and the treatment of, learners' grammatical errors. For example, if a learner tries to buy a train ticket by saying 'Give me a ticket to London (please)', or writes to a college for information with the phrase 'Send me your prospectus', he may show satisfactory mastery of language form, but he is offending certain forms of sociolinguistic behaviour. We may say 'What?' to a friend we have not understood, but we would be advised to say 'Pardon?' to the boss; 'Shut the door, will you?' may be appropriate within the family, but 'Excuse me, would you mind closing the door?' for a stranger on the train (example from Littlewood, 1981: 4). We can also look at 'error' from another perspective, and ask whether to prefer *'Please could you to send me your prospectus?' or *'Can I have 6 air letter, please?' to the choice of an imperative form. (* is a symbol used to denote grammatical inaccuracy.)

We can see from this that the notion of error is no longer restricted only to incorrect grammar or perhaps choice of vocabulary. If 'being communicative' includes also paying attention to context, roles and topics, then it is logically possible to make an error at any of these levels. It is even possible – though this can only be mentioned in passing – to make 'cultural' errors: an English person's way of thanking someone for a present is to say 'You really shouldn't have done that', readily interpretable as a reprimand by a giver who is not familiar with the normal response. (See also Cook, 1989: 123–5 for other examples.)

The extent to which error types are significant depends very much on particular teaching situations, and on the objectives of specific programmes. It is certainly not possible to make generalizations, and what may be tolerated in one case may be unacceptable in another. But even a partial acceptance of communicative criteria will allow for a certain amount of creativity and exploration in language learning, and this will inevitably extend the framework in which errors are evaluated.

Implication 5   Particularly in the early phase of the 'communicative revolution', it was sometimes assumed – mistakenly – that the approach was only really valid for teaching the spoken language, when learners needed to make conversation in English. The assumption is an understandable one, since face-to-face interaction is the most obvious kind of communication with other people, and learners were and are increasingly felt to need oral skills, given the greater opportunities for travel and for communication with English speakers visiting their countries.

It is important to realize that 'communicative' can in fact refer to all four language skills. We can look at this in two different ways. Firstly, we can divide the 'four skills' into 'productive' (speaking and writing) and 'receptive' (listening and reading) and practise them separately. It is possible to do this successfully from a communicative perspective, as we shall see in part 2 of this book. However, treating the skills discretely can also lead to a concern for accuracy in production and an emphasis, in comprehension, on the grammatical characteristics of written and spoken material. More usefully, we can group together the oral/aural skills of speaking and listening, and the 'paper skills' of reading and writing. In both cases, we have a giver and a receiver of a message, and the ways in which the information in the message is understood by the receiver is an integral part of the communication. This is true whether we think of a brief exchange, a letter, a book, or an extended discussion. Possibilities of this kind for exploring the four skills, and integrating them with each other, will be examined in more detail in part 2.

How do you interpret the idea of 'communicating in English' for your own learners? What, in other words, are their particular 'communicative needs', and to what extent are each of the 'four skills' important?

Implication 6   Materials based on an approach to teaching that takes mastery of the formal system of a language as its major objective are likely to use the grammatical concept of the sentence as the basis for exercises. We may find, for example, the instruction 'Put the verb in infinitive form into the present perfect' or 'Join each pair of sentences with a relative pronoun', followed perhaps by ten numbered sentences. Not much real-life communication proceeds strictly according to such fixed patterning. A letter to a friend, for instance, is unlikely to be only a string of sentences:

I went to the USA.
I went to New York.
I saw the Statue of Liberty.
I flew by Concorde.

Nor does this conversation sound natural although, like the letter, it practises some useful verb structures, and the questions and answers are at least related:

Where did you go for your holidays? I went to New York.
What did you do? I saw the Statue of Liberty.
How did you travel? I flew by Concorde.

A concept of communication does not have to be based on sentence-level criteria, and it can allow language to be described, and language learning to take place, over longer stretches. In principle it can handle whole conversations, or paragraphs, or even longer texts. In recent years, a number of categories for describing language have been developed that are not based on sentence-level criteria, but on the broader notion of 'discourse'. There is a large and growing background literature on 'discourse analysis', and a detailed explanation of these categories is outside the scope and intention of this book. Essentially, the notion gives us the possibility of showing how different parts of a text or a conversation or any stretch of language are interlinked. This may be, for example, by cross-referencing with pronoun use or definite articles; by semantic links across items of vocabulary; by markers of logical development ('however', 'therefore', 'so', 'because' and the like); by ellipsis in conversation (the short answers' of coursebook practice); and by substitution ('this is my book, yours is the other one'). Alternatively, a 'text' in this sense may be described in terms of its intention and its thematic coherence. (Readers who wish to follow these ideas further are referred to the work of Halliday and Hasan (1976) and Widdowson (1978)).

Implication 7 Finally, the term 'communicative' itself has been used in relation to teaching in two distinct though related ways, and this apparent ambiguity has sometimes been a source of confusion. Firstly, as we have seen from a number of the implications outlined in this section, the concept can refer to a view of the nature of language, leading to the procedures that have been detailed for a 'functional' analysis of language. In other words, language is seen to have inherent communicative as well as grammatical properties.

Secondly, a communicative approach also implies a concern with behaviour, with patterns of interaction as well as linguistic content. Morrow (1981) makes a simple and useful distinction between the 'what' – the contents of a language programme – and the 'how' – the ways in which that content might be learned and taught. This behavioural 'how' would cover the kinds of activities we carry out and the tasks we perform, such as writing a letter, or an essay, or talking to a friend, at a meeting, to a stranger and so on. We shall see in the next two parts of the book how such activities can be implemented in the classroom (a) in terms of the framework of skills and activities that we use for language practice and (b) in the various possibilities available for structuring and managing the classroom itself.

Conclusion: Possibilities and Problems

There are a number of reasons why a communicative approach is an attractive one, providing a richer teaching and learning environment. It can:

- include wider considerations of what is appropriate as well as what is accurate

- handle a wider range of language, covering texts and conversations as well as sentences

- provide realistic and motivating language practice

- use what learners 'know' about the functions of language from their experience with their own mother tongues

At the same time, there are other questions which are still not fully resolved, answers to some of which depend on the nature of the particular situation in which we teach. Some of the more important of these issues are:

- Having selected appropriate language functions, and having 'filtered out' the most useful grammatical exponents, on what basis should we take decisions about sequencing and grading? It is unlikely that all grammatical items can be taught at the same time, so there is a problem of systematicity. We might refer back here to the structurally different ways of making a suggestion noted in the second implication, above.

- Is the approach a useful one for all proficiency levels, particularly for beginners? Do beginners perhaps require an initial one-to-one correspondence between a function and a form?

- Is is equally appropriate in all teaching contexts, regardless of objectives, location, ages of learners, length of course, mother tongue of teachers and so on? For example, it has been argued that a more grammatically-oriented syllabus is to be preferred in a context where English is a foreign language and where learners are unlikely to be exposed to it. Again, some teachers whose mother tongue is not English claim to have little confidence when working with communicative materials.

- Does it always matter if the 'real world' is not being practised in the classroom?

There is much in the approach, then, that is still open to debate and, as the next chapter will show, more recent materials have reacted in various ways to and against the communicative movement of the 1970s. However, the main principles, with varying degrees of change and modification, have had a lasting impact on materials and methods that should not be underestimated.

1   Look at the syllabus guidelines for your own situation, if they are available. Are claims made there for 'communicative' objectives? Since it is the teacher who has to interpret them, how are the general objectives translated into your everyday classroom reality?

(If you are working in a group of teachers from different backgrounds, you might like to compare your observations with those of others.)

2   The Unit on pp. 37–42 is taken from a popular and representative coursebook written during the 1970s. Look at the Unit carefully and consider the following points (some of which will be taken up again in the chapters on the evaluation and adaptation of teaching materials):

a)   What is the role of grammar in the Unit?

b)   What language skills are practised?

c)   To what extent does the Unit deal with (i) communicative functions as properties of language (ii) communicative behaviour and activities?

d)   How large are the stretches of language that learners are asked to deal with? How much of the language practice is concerned with the manipulation of sentence structure?

e)   Do learners have any freedom to 'create' meanings and language for themselves? Can they in any sense 'be themselves', and talk about their own interests, wishes, needs?

f)   Would these materials be suitable for your learners? If not, how would you wish to change them? (With this question we are anticipating chapter 5.)

Further reading

1   Johnson, K. and K. Morrow (eds) (1981): *Communication in the Classroom* This is a useful collection of articles which relates communicative principles to teaching materials and to classroom techniques.

2   Littlewood, W. T. (1981): *Communicative Language Teaching*. A standard introductory text on the communicative approach, illustrated with many examples.

7 Offering to do something, asking permission, giving reasons

7.1 Conversation

Richard: Well, that was delicious! Thanks very much indeed ... I didn't know, you're a really good cook, aren't you?
Brenda: Thank you.
Richard: If you like, I could do the washing-up.
Brenda: No, don't bother, I can do it myself later.
Richard: Alright ... er ... do you mind if I smoke?
Brenda: Yes, go ahead!
Richard: Oh, I've lost ... left my cigarettes in the hall.
Brenda: Shall I get them for you?
Richard: Er ... no, no ... oh look, it's alright – I ve got another packet here.
Brenda: Let me get you an ashtray.
Richard: Thanks.
Brenda: Would you like me to make coffee now?
Richard: Yes! Thanks! Um ... look, I wonder if I could possibly use your phone?
Brenda: Oh, I'm sorry, that's not possible. You see, it's out of order again.
Richard: Oh, n ... er ... well, it's rather complicated, but you see I promised to phone a colleague before nine and I see it's now about five to ... um ... er ... would you mind very much if I went down the road to the phone box?
Brenda: Oh, it's about ten minutes' walk away. If you like, I could drive you there.
Richard: Oh, would you? Thanks!
Brenda: Yes, certainly.
Richard: Thanks!
Brenda: I'll make coffee later, when we get back.
Richard: Right!

7.2   Presentation: offering to do something

When something needs to be done you can ask someone else to do it, or offer to do it yourself or just do it without saying anything. If someone else is doing something, you can offer to help.
Here are some useful ways of offering to do something:

Let me get it for you.
Shall I get it for you?
Any point in my getting it for you?
How about my getting it for you?
Would you like me to get it for you?
If you like, I could get it for you.
Can I help you with that?

We might accept such offers with answers like:

That's very kind of you, thanks.
Oh would you? Thanks.
Thanks a lot.

Or refuse them by saying:

No, don't bother, I can do it myself.
No, it's alright, I can manage.
Thanks ever so much, but it's alright, really.

Decide when you would use each of the expressions.

7.3   Practice

Talk to your teacher and make some helpful offers to cope with his or her problems. Your teacher is bored, ill, lonely, thirsty, depressed, unfit, hard-up, hungry, and over-worked. If you have time, do this with another student, too.

7.4   Communication activity

Work in pairs. You will be offering to help each other with various difficulties. One of you should look at activity 91, and the other at activity 63.

7.5 Presentation: asking permission

Sometimes you need to do more than just offer to do something – you may need to ask permission to make sure you are allowed to do it. The expression to use depends on:
a) The type of task you want to do and the trouble you may have getting permission to do it.
b) Who you are and who you are talking to – the role you are playing and your relationship.

Here are some useful ways of asking permission. The expressions get more and more polite as you go down the list:

I'm going to . . .
I thought I might . . .
I'd like to . . .
Alright if I . . .?
Anyone mind if I . . .?
D'you mind if I . . .?
Is it alright if I . . .?
Would it be alright if I . . .?
Would you mind if I . . .?
I wonder if I could possibly . . .?
I hope you don't mind, but would it be at all possible for me to . . .?

We tend to give permission in just a short phrase, like:

OK.
Yes, go ahead.
Yes, I suppose so.
Oh well, alright.

And we refuse permission like this:

That's not a very good idea.
No, please don't.
I'd rather you didn't if you don't mind.
I'm sorry, but that's not possible.

Decide when you might use each of the expressions. Give examples of each expression in use.

7.6 Practice

Make a list of five things you would like to do, but which you have to get your teacher's permission for. Ask for permission to do them – watch out, your teacher may ask you *'Why?'*! Later your teacher will change roles and play the role of the head of the school, so you may then need to change the way you ask.

7.7   Presentation: giving reasons

When you ask someone for permission, he or she is likely to ask you *'Why?'*. Here are some useful ways of explaining your reasons:

Well, you see . . .
The reason is . . .
Well, the thing is . . .
My reason for asking is this . . .
It's because . . .
It's rather complicated but you see . . .
. . . and that's why I'd like to . . .
. . . and that's my reason for asking if I can . . .

Decide how you would give reasons using these phrases. Imagine you want to borrow various things from your teacher. What would you say?

7.8   Practice

Build conversations like this from the prompts below:

A: Would it be alright if I left the room for a moment, you see I have to make a phone call?
B: I'd rather you didn't if you don't mind, you see this is a very important part of the lesson.
A: Oh, alright, I see.

leave room
smoke my pipe
borrow car
take day off
open window
have coffee break
borrow umbrella
use phone
watch TV
borrow book

Imagine that you are talking to an acquaintance, rather than a close friend.

7.9   Communication activity

Work in pairs. You will be playing several different roles during this activity. One of you should look at activity 11, and the other at activity 56.

11

Your partner is going to play three different roles – boss, friend and teacher – while you ask for permission in an appropriate way. Make these requests *in this order* and if necessary explain why you want to do them:

1 Ask your boss to let you change your holiday from next week to the week after.
2 Ask your friend if you can borrow his or her dictionary.
3 Ask your teacher to let you go and make a phone call now.
4 Ask your boss again. This time you want to take the Friday off before your holiday begins. Say why this is necessary.
5 Ask your friend again. This time you want to keep the dictionary over the weekend. Say why.
6 Ask your teacher to let you go to the bank immediately. Say why it is so urgent.
7 Now, ask your boss to let you change your holiday *back* to next week now. Say why.
8 Now, ask your friend to let you borrow his or her grammar book as well as the dictionary over the weekend. Say why.
9 Now, ask your teacher to let you go to the bank *again*. Say why.

When you have finished, go to activity 84.

56

Your partner is going to ask you for permission to do certain things. In each conversation you switch from one role to another. Your partner will make the requests in this order, so follow these instructions.

1 You are the boss. Your partner is one of your most reliable workers.
2 You are a friend. You are on good terms.
3 You are the teacher. Your partner is a student who often misses lessons.
4 You are the boss again. Ask your employee why he or she didn't say this before.
5 You are a friend. You have to write an essay over the weekend.
6 You are the teacher again. This lesson is a very important one.
7 You are the boss again. You are getting tired of your employee's changing his or her mind.
8 You are a friend. Your class has a grammar test on Monday.
9 You are the teacher. You want everyone in the class to be present during this very important lesson.

When you have finished, go to activity 114.

63

First listen to your partner's problems and offer to help him or her with each of them. Then tell your partner your own problems and see if he or she offers to help you:

1 You have a terrible headache.
2 You have to phone your boss to say you're ill, but you're afraid to do it yourself.
3 You're dying for a cigarette.
4 Your watch has stopped.
5 A button has come off your shirt (or blouse) and has to be sewn back on.
6 You feel like a cup of tea.
7 You've written a letter which needs typing.
8 You're very nervous about a date you have this evening.

When you have finished, discuss what you did with the rest of the class.

91

Tell your partner about the following problems you have and see if he or she offers to help you with them. You can decide whether to accept the offer or refuse it politely:

1 You have a difficult essay to write, and you don't know how to approach it.
2 You meant to get a newspaper this morning and don't have enough time to get it now.
3 You feel like a cup of coffee.
4 You're short of money – £5 would be enough.
5 You can't get your car to start.
6 A button has just come off your coat, but you can't find it.
7 You've written a letter which needs posting.
8 You have a sore throat and can't stop coughing.

Now listen to your partner's problems and offer to help with each of them.

Source: L. Jones, *Functions of English*, Unit 7 and activities, copyright Cambridge University Press, 1981.

3 Current Approaches to Materials Design

Introduction

The previous chapter identified the most significant factors within the broad concept of the 'communicative approach'. We noted in particular the shift in focus towards the 'real-world' use of language along the dimensions of context, topic, and roles of the people involved. Alongside this there is often a stated requirement for 'authenticity' – a term which loosely implies as close an approximation as possible to the world outside the classroom, in the selection both of language material and of the activities and methods used for practice in the classroom. The issue of 'authenticity' has been somewhat controversial, and there is no space here to go into the complexities of the argument: for readers who wish to do so, Clarke (1989) offers an interesting discussion on the relationship between communicative theory, teaching materials, and the concept of authenticity. We also looked at the re-definition of the place of grammar in language learning, at different attitudes to error and error correction, and by implication at the possible perspectives on teaching and learning, teachers and learners, suggested by the approach. These themes will all reappear in different ways throughout this book.

The present chapter uses a selection of courses produced over the last five to ten years – in other words, as the main communicative debate began to die down – in order to examine the design perspectives that they demonstrate. We shall take some fairly popular courses available on the general market, partly on the argument that if a course is used frequently, then its users probably find it relevant and appropriate. It is not the intention to carry out an evaluation of their inherent quality, but rather to follow through developments and identify trends. Readers will again be invited to contextualize the discussion by commenting on materials familiar to them. We shall concentrate particularly on organization and coverage, and on views of learners and learning underpinning current materials. Towards the end of the chapter we shall look briefly at how some recent ideas in syllabus design have led to rather novel views on the nature of materials.

New Beginnings?

An obvious question, when discussing developments in materials design over the last decade or so, is whether a new 'movement' can be detected – at least in the sense in which proponents of communicative methodology took up a strong position on (even against) the status of grammar as the basis for teaching. We need, then, to ask to what extent current materials represent a radical departure from the kinds of criteria set out in chapter 2.

One writer who has taken an explicitly critical view of some of the more extreme forms of the communicative approach is Swan. Much of his argument is directed against the ideas that syllabuses and materials can be based on *either* function *or* form, that meaning can be accounted for *only* on two levels, and that learners do not know how to use the functions of language unless they are taught to do so – as if they had no 'experience and commonsense'. 'Normal students,' he claims, 'know what they want to say more often than they know how to say it', since 'unfortunately, grammar has not become any easier to learn since the communicative revolution' (1985: 11, 78). He makes several other specific criticisms. His general view is expressed in the following terms: 'What has happened . . . might be called the "new toy" effect. A limited but valuable insight has been over-generalized, and is presented as if it applied to the whole of language and all of language teaching . . . The "new toy" effect is leading us to look at everything in functional terms . . .' (1985: 7, 81). And finally, 'the Communicative Approach, whatever its virtues, is not really . . . a revolution. In retrospect, it is likely to be seen as little more than an interesting ripple on the surface of twentieth century language teaching' (1985: 87).

Swan is of course right to remind us of the need for teachers to take a critical, or at least a questioning, view of any new movement or set of beliefs claiming to revolutionize our profession. However, much of his criticism is levelled against the more simplistic interpretations of the term 'communicative', and he deliberately overstates his case in order to reinforce his points. In fact the 'retrospect' that Swan invites, taken in the 1990s, shows that current materials do not constitute a rejection of the 'communicative approach', and no major new movement can be identified. Certainly the bases outlined in chapter 2 have not yet been matched by a new set of theories. Some of the rejection has stemmed from criticism of the false polarization of language form and language function, and the 'phrase-book' approach to materials, where a certain use of language (perhaps 'Requesting a service') is offered along with a fixed set of grammatical expressions.

Many of the key principles of the approach have been incorporated into materials, although not necessarily directly. We shall see, for example, how certain aspects have come into more central focus, how others have been re-interpreted depending on teaching objectives, and how more recent insights into the nature of language and language learning have come to join them.

Some Claims for Current Materials

In the last chapter, we saw that the kinds of statements made in relation to materials by their writers and publishers can serve as a helpful indicator of the principles on which those materials are based.

Look back at those claims, and compare them with the following, taken from some standard coursebooks of the last few years. Note particularly the terminology used to describe the materials, and compare it with our list in chapter 2.

  i 'carefully structured multi-syllabus approach . . . systematic development of all 4 skills . . . emphasis on pronunciation, study skills and vocabulary learning ... authentic and semi-authentic reading and listening practice ... language for immediate communication'

ii 'thorough, communicative practice of grammatical structures ... coverage of all the 4 skills ... comprehensive coverage of the English tense system'

iii 'plenty of practice in 'core' grammatical structures and deals with language at a deeper level ... covers all the 4 skills ... makes students think about the language they are using'

iv 'proven multi-syllabus approach ... careful pacing ... allowance for different learning styles and teaching situations ... authentic reading and listening material ... motivating range of up-to-date topics'

v   'focuses on the real English students will encounter and need to use in today's world ... regular Grammar sections focus on important grammatical areas at sentence level and above ... wide cross-section of real texts promotes reading for pleasure, as well as developing functional reading skills ... word study ... encourages students to be selective in their vocabulary building'

It is not difficult to identify some mainstream communicative themes in this selection – real English, authenticity, the sentence *and above*, communication. At the same time there clearly are a number of further elements here. We find more explicit statements about the place of grammar practice; much reference to language skills, including 'study skills'; specific comment on vocabulary learning and pronunciation; and mention of 'styles' in learning. For convenience we shall now divide these claims into two broad and related areas: content and learning. Several of them come together in the phrase 'the multi-syllabus approach', which we shall explore in the first of the next two sections.

Organization and Coverage

Multi-syllabus

Teaching materials following a traditional structural approach typically appear as an ordered list of grammatical items – perhaps

1   Simple present active
2   Present continous
3   Simple past

and so on. There is here a single organizing principle which provides the material to be taught and learned in each unit or section of the course. However, it is likely that learners will not only be expected to formulate rules and manipulate structures in a vacuum; they will probably be given a situation or a topic as a context for practice. In other words, even traditional materials may have a *primary* organizing principle (structures) and a *secondary* one (topics, or situations) – see the discussion of syllabus in chapter 1. We might, say, teach the present perfect by asking our students about things they have done or places they have visited; regular activities and habits are often used to teach the simple present. In chapter 2 we saw how the development of the communicative approach not only consolidated a two-tier arrangement (functions and structures), but also opened up the possibility of the principled inclusion of other 'layers' of organization (functions, structures, roles, skills, topics, situations), although, with some exceptions, this was not fully explored in the materials of the time. It is really in the last ten years or so that the idea of a multi-layered syllabus has begun to be more explicitly and systematically addressed.

The table of contents on pp. 48–9 – referred to as a 'Map' – is a good illustration of a typical multi-syllabus approach. Look back at the 'communicative' contents page reproduced in chapter 2 on p. 24, and note down some of the similarities and differences you find between the two approaches illustrated.

Swan justifies this approach in the following terms: 'When deciding what to teach to a particular group of learners, we need to take into consideration several different meaning categories and several different formal categories. We must make sure that our students are taught to operate key *functions* . . . to talk about basic *notions* . . . to communicate appropriately in specific *situations* . . . to discuss the *topics* which correspond to their main interests and needs . . . At the same time, we shall need to draw up a list of *phonological* problems . . . of high priority *structures*, and of the *vocabulary* which our students will

Map of Book 1

Grammar

Students will learn these grammar points

Phonology

Students will work on these aspects of pronunciation

1 to 4

Present tense of *be*; *have got*; *a* and *an*; noun plurals; subject personal pronouns; possessives; possessive *'s* and *s'*; predicative use of adjectives; questions (question word and yes/no); *be* with ages; prepositions of place; *this*; *any* in questions.

Word and sentence stress; rhythm; linking; intonation; consonant clusters; /θ/ and /ð/; /ə/; pronunciation of *'s*; weak form of *from*.

5 to 8

Simple Present tense; *there is/are*; imperatives; *was* and *were* (introduction); countable and uncountable; *some/any*, *much/many* and other quantifiers; *the*; omission of article in generalisations; object personal pronouns; attributive use of adjectives; frequency adverbs; adverbs of degree; prepositions of time, place and distance; omission of article in *at home* etc.; *-ing* for activities; *be* with prices.

Word and sentence stress; rhythm; linking; intonation, including polite intonation; weak forms, /ɪ/ /θ/ in ordinals; pronunciations of *the*.

9 to 12

Have got; Present Progressive tense (introduction); more Simple Present tense; Simple Past tense; past tense of *be*; *I'd like* + noun phrase / infinitive; *when*-clauses; demonstratives; *be* and *have*; *both* and *all*; *a . . . one*; prepositions of place; *say* and *tell*; *ago*; *What (a) . . . !*

Linking; sentence stress; weak forms; hearing unstressed syllables; rhythm and stress in questions; rising intonation for questions; high pitch for emphasis; stress in negative sentences; stress for contrast; spelling/pronunciation difficulties; /h/; voiced *s* in verb endings; Simple Past endings; strong form of *have*.

13 to 16

Can; Present Progressive tense (present and future meanings); *be* with ages and measures; difficult question structures; comparative and superlative adjectives; structures used for comparison; *a bit / much* before comparative adjectives; *good at* + noun/gerund; *look like* + noun phrase; *look* + adjective; *What is . . . like?*; prepositions in descriptions; prepositions of time.

Stress and rhythm recognition and production; decoding rapid speech; hearing unstressed syllables; pronunciations of the letter *a*; pronunciations of the letter *e*; pronunciations of the letter *i*; /ə/ and stress; weak and strong forms of *can* and *can't*; weak forms of *as*, *than* and *from*; /θ/ in ordinals.

17 to 20

Present Perfect tense; more Simple Past tense; verbs with two objects; *Could you*, *Why don't we*, *Let's* and *Shall we* + infinitive without *to*; question words as subjects; elementary reported speech; reply questions; *So . . . I*; *say* and *tell*; *for* and *since*; *How long . . . ?*; *no* = *not any*; *some* and *something* in offers and requests; article and prepositional usage; sequencing and linking words; *both . . . and*; *neither . . . nor*; *Do you mind if . . . ?*

Decoding rapid speech; linking with initial vowels; contrastive stress; pronunciations of the letter *u*; /iː/ and /ɪ/; polite intonation for requests; rising intonation in reply questions; weak forms of *was* and *were*.

21 to 24

Going to; *will*-future; infinitive of purpose; imperatives; conditional structures; structures with *get*; adverbs vs. adjectives; adverbs of manner; paragraph-structuring adverbials; position of *always* and *never* in imperatives.

Spellings of /ɜː/; 'long' pronunciation of vowel letters before (consonant +) *e*; pronunciations of the letter *o*; /w/; /iː/ and /ɪ/; 'dark' *l* in Future tense contractions; recognition and pronunciation of *going to*; pronunciation of *won't*.

Functions

Students will learn to

Greet; introduce; begin conversations with strangers; participate in longer conversations; say goodbye; ask for and give information; identify themselves and others; describe people; ask for repetition; enquire about health; apologise; express regret; distinguish levels of formality; spell and count.

Ask for and give information, directions, personal data, and opinions; describe places; indicate position; express likes and dislikes; tell the time; complain; participate in longer conversations; express politeness.

Ask for and give information; describe people and things, and ask for descriptions; talk about resemblances; greet; make arrangements to meet; ask for information about English; make and reply to offers and requests; narrate; shop; make travel enquiries and hotel bookings; change money.

Compare; ask for and give information and opinions; describe and compare people; speculate; make and reply to requests; invite and reply; describe and speculate about activities; plan; count (ordinals); telephone.

Request and reply; borrow; suggest; agree, disagree and negotiate; invite and reply; narrate; report what people have said; ask for, give and refuse permission; show interest; compare; ask for and give information and opinions; distinguish levels of formality; ask for information about English; start conversations; make arrangements to meet; order food *etc.* in a restaurant.

Talk about plans; make predictions; guess; make suggestions; express sympathy; give instructions; give advice; predict; warn; announce intentions; raise and counter objections; narrate.

Topics and notions

Students will learn to talk about

People's names; age; marital status; national origin; addresses; jobs; health; families; physical appearance; relationships; numbers and letters; approximation; place.

Addresses; phone numbers; furniture; houses and flats; work; leisure occupations and interests; food and drink; prices; likes and dislikes; preferences; things in common and differences; days of the week; ordinal numbers; existence; time; place; relative position; generalisation; countability; quantification; degree; frequency; routines.

People's appearances; clothing; families; colours; parts of the body; relationships; physical and emotional states; clothes; places; prices; sizes; people's pasts; history; poverty; happiness; racism; childhood; growing up; resemblance.

Abilities; physical characteristics and qualities; weights and measures; numbers (cardinal and ordinal); ages; personalities; professions; names of months; future plans; the weather; holidays; places; travel; time; similarities and differences; temporary present and future actions and states.

Holidays; going out; food and drink; daily routines; historical personalities; people's careers; interests and habits; likes and dislikes; contrast; sequence; past time; frequency; duration up to the present; similarity.

Houses; seasons; holidays; places; plans; health and illness; sports; machines; horoscopes; danger; purpose; intention; manner; the future.

Skills

The Student's Book and Practice Book between them provide regular practice of the basic 'four skills'. Special skills taught or practised at Level 1 include decoding rapid colloquial speech, reading and listening for specific information, writing longer sentences, writing paragraphs, writing formal letters, writing friendly letters and notes, and filling in forms.

Vocabulary

Students will learn 900 or more common words and expressions during Level 1 of the course.

Source: H. Swan and C. Walters, *New Cambridge English Course*, pp. iv and v, copyright Cambridge University Press, 1990.

need to learn. In addition, we will need a syllabus of *skills* . . .' (1985: 79).

At first sight this is a complex, if rich, view of materials design, because several (in this case, eight) syllabus possibilities are in play. Not only do the details have to be specified for each individual organizing principle, but the principles themselves then have to be linked in a systematic way that does not leave the learner faced with a number of separate lists of items. A more straightforward way of looking at this kind of multi-syllabus is to see it in terms of a merging of two broad approaches. One of these is concerned with a view of language in use, and includes categories of function, context and language skill. The other is a version of a more formal linguistic syllabus, and is comprised of elements of grammar, pronunciation, and vocabulary. Obviously these two approaches are not mutually exclusive: pronunciation and vocabulary, for instance, can both be practised in a context of use, or alternatively can be rehearsed in isolation. What a multi-syllabus does is to build on a range of communicative criteria at the same time as acknowledging the need to provide systematic practice in the formal properties of language.

In passing we can recall the earlier argument that current approaches have grown out of those immediately preceding them, and have not on the whole developed from a complete break with the past. Elements of the multi-syllabus idea can be traced in some of the explicitly 'communicative' writing of the 1970s. Johnson, for example (1982, though written before this date), uses the terms 'uni-dimensional' and 'multi-dimensional' to denote types of syllabus, and discusses three possible dimensions of organization – functions, settings, and notions. The focus here was certainly on semantic criteria: nevertheless, the teaching materials derived from this perspective (Morrow and Johnson, *Communicate*, 1980) have both communicative and formal elements, and include work on functions, settings, roles, and grammar.

The lexical syllabus

In the approach to materials design that has been discussed here, we have seen that the two general headings of 'semantic' (or 'language in use', or 'functional', or 'pragmatic') and 'formal' are broken down into a number of component parts, each one of which can generate a set of syllabus items. Thus 'topics' might include talking about class members and their families; interests and hobbies; different countries; world news; weather and so on. Pronunciation (or 'phonology') can cover individual sounds, minimal pairs, sentence stress, weak forms, intonation, and several other features. While some coursebooks have taken the whole spread of organizing principles, others have chosen to give particular emphasis to specific areas. One area that has recently received considerable attention is that of vocabulary, or lexis.

The teaching of vocabulary is a very large topic, and we shall restrict ourselves here to commenting briefly on its role in some current coursebooks. (For more discussion, see Willis, 1990.) Most of us – whether as learners or teachers – have experience of classrooms where practising vocabulary means learning lists of words, not always in relation to a real-world context and sometimes in the form of two columns, with a mother tongue equivalent for the foreign language word. We have probably noticed that vocabulary approached in this way is not always efficiently remembered and re-used. It is typical of many current coursebooks that they are concerned (a) to rationalize vocabulary as content, in other words, to establish a principled framework and a set of contexts within which vocabulary development can take place, and (b) to base teaching on an understanding of the psychological mechanisms whereby people learn and remember lexical items. We shall comment on the background to the second of these in the next section. As far as the first point is concerned, we can note that it is unusual to find merely a list of words to be learned by rote: the multi-syllabus concept means that vocabulary is selected according to the other dimensions on which the materials are built. For example, *Signature* (Phillips and Sheerin, 1990) takes three large-scale categories in sequence, and then subdivides each, linking the vocabulary practice directly to the sub-topics, as follows (only a few examples are given under each heading):

1 *People*:
   nationalities
   languages
   personal information
2 *The world around us*:
   travel

    medicine
    house and home
3 *Past, present, future*:
    education
    the media
    the world of the future

As with a number of other courses, this is linked to work in grammar and pronunciation, and involves different language skills.

For most of us, of course, 'vocabulary' also means using a dictionary. 1987 saw the publication of a new dictionary for learners of English. The dictionary is called COBUILD, which stands, rather technically, for the 'Collins [Publisher] – Birmingham University International Language Database'. It is based on an extremely large corpus of language of many millions of words, stored on a computer database. Sources of data are both the spoken and written language, and include magazines, books, broadcasts, conversations and many more. The philosophy of the dictionary is to provide 'above all a guide to ordinary everyday English', and frequency of occurrence is a key criterion for inclusion. It focuses particularly on the most common 2,000 to 3,000 words, the 'powerhouse of the language', and the examples given in the dictionary entries are taken from the source material. Both the philosophy and the database of the dictionary have led to an approach to materials design that is usually termed the 'lexical syllabus'. One current course based directly on the COBUILD work covers about 2,500 words over the three levels of the course (Collins, 1989). Its central claim is that the lexical database provides 'a rich input of *real* language', thus giving authenticity and context to the tasks and exercises. Each Unit has a set of lexical objectives, so that by the end of Unit 15 ('Newspapers') of the third level, for example, students should have learned 44 new words, making a cumulative total of 625 for this level so far. (In this particular Unit, items include 'arrest', 'bomb', 'criticize', 'explode', 'explosion', 'headline', 'identity', 'target', 'violence' etc.).

In this section, we have discussed the principle of the 'multi-syllabus', and have shown how some coursebooks have highlighted and developed one particular area of design-vocabulary. In the next section we shall turn our attention to ways in which current approaches view the learners themselves.

Learners and Learning

There are a number of ways in which current coursebook design is concerned in general terms with a perspective on 'the learner', as well as with the language material itself. These ways can be grouped as follows:

1   Although the majority of learners study in the environment of a whole class, and often in a large one, an analysis of the characteristics of learners as individuals can offer a helpful view on the construction of materials and methods.
2   Learners will naturally need to engage in the process of both comprehending and producing language. In doing this they use a range of strategies that are probably shared by all language users, whether learning a foreign language or using their mother tongue.

The first of these perspectives is normally characterized by the concept of 'individual differences'; the second is studied under the heading of 'language acquisition'. Skehan (1989) points out that the one is a view of *differences*, the other of *similarities* and *universals*. Both perspectives have come into some prominence as factors affecting materials design, and we shall briefly survey each of them in turn.

Learners

In the previous section on the organization and content of current materials, we did not discuss in any detail the selection of topics for language practice, whether for discussion, or comprehension, or writing. We have chosen to start this section with them because they are the most obvious way in which learners' needs and interests can be taken into account. The possibilities for topic choice are potentially so wide that a meaningful classification is difficult. Themes may or may not be drawn from a source of 'authentic' language data; they may come from the field of world affairs, or medicine, or sport, from social and family life, from everyday topics, and from other areas too many to enumerate. Here is a small selection of themes taken from some of the coursebooks used as examples in the preceding section. You might like to consider whether such topics would be relevant for your own learners, and whether learning context determines topic choice. For instance, materials appropriate for students in an English-speaking environment – social situations, travelling, everyday 'survival' – may not be applicable in other educational settings, and vice-versa:

Travelling	Clothes	Historical people
Dangerous animals	Music and singing	Driving
Food and drink	Health and illness	The environment
Dreams and fears	Television	The role of
Money	Racism	computers
Relationships	Education	Leisure time
		Getting old

Topics in this form are listed as content, as material to be covered. Some coursebook writers, however, even if they themselves make the initial selection, prefer to help learners develop their language proficiency by devising techniques for personalizing these topics. One set of materials (*Third Dimension* and *Fourth Dimension*) has made this into a design principle. The authors define the term 'dimension' rather differently from the way it was used in the previous section to designate a component of a multi-syllabus. Their 'dimension' is what they call 'expressivity'. It goes beyond the other (important) dimensions of accuracy, fluency and intelligibility: 'expressivity means not only the ability to say and write things fairly clearly, accurately and fluently but also to express what you really want to express and to give some real depth to that expression. Depth comes from a knowledge of choices in language' (O'Neill, 1989). Expressivity, it is claimed, helps learners to 'take off', and to achieve independence and personal involvement in their use of language. The aim of personalization is linked directly to grammar practice and vocabulary building across all the language skills. Techniques include interpreting pictures introducing the theme of a Unit, imagining one's own thoughts and actions in certain situations, commenting on one's own culture, advising others, finishing a story, and many more.

What kinds of topics could you personalize in this way with your own students? The materials just discussed include loneliness, honesty, friendship, success and failure, love, sport and violence. Are these appropriate for your own classroom?

Topics, of course, are by no means the only way in which attention can be paid to the learners themselves. Although for most teachers, especially those faced with big classes, the goal of large-scale individualization of instruction is not a very realistic one, some differences between learners can be taken into account in a limited way. The third part of this book will explore the possibilities in more detail. Here we shall simply highlight the 'individual differences' that appear to be significant in current materials.

Researchers in the psychology of second language learning have investigated a number of learner characteristics that have implications for the language classroom. An understanding of such characteristics, or 'variables', can make it possible for teachers and materials designers to adjust and vary certain aspects of the classroom to allow for the different individuals in it. Skehan (1989) and McDonough (1986), for example, suggest the following key learner variables:

- *Personality*: learners may be quiet, or extrovert, for instance

- *Motivation*: learners may have chosen to learn; they may be obliged to take a course or an examination; they may or may not perceive the relevance of material

- *Attitude*: learners have attitudes to learning, to the target language, and to classrooms

- *Aptitude*: some people seem more readily able than others to learn another language

- *Preferred learning styles*: some learners are more comfortable in a spoken language situation, others prefer written material

- *Intelligence*

We are not concerned here with the relationships between these factors. This is an interesting and complex issue, which readers can follow up in the references provided.

Some of the dimensions along which individuals vary, particularly intelligence, do not have an obvious effect on language learning potential. Others are difficult to measure, and certainly to change: it is not normally considered part of a teacher's role to try to adjust students' personalities. Yet others, such as motivation, can more obviously be affected by the learning environment. What we should note, in other words, is that some individual differences can have an influence on language instruction, and others can be influenced by it. A distinction also needs to be made between the possible effects of the coursebook and those of the structure and management of the classroom itself.

Several of the English language teaching materials now available attempt to incorporate some consideration of learner characteristics into their methodology. As far as variables differentiating between learners are concerned, mention is made most frequently of differences in learning styles. The pedagogic response to this is to allow in a principled way for variety, especially in content and in language skills, and to build in suggestions for variability in pacing – the speed at which learners are able to work through the material. Pacing, in turn, implies a concern for aptitude, a factor that interests all teachers even if no formal measurement of aptitude is available. We also find reference to the importance of understanding learners' attitudes. As one coursebook puts it, 'Students have their own ideas about language learning. Up to a point, these must be respected ... however, learners sometimes resist important and useful activities which do not fit in with their preconceptions, and this can hinder progress' (Swan and Walter, *New Cambridge English Course*, 1990: viii). In other words, students may have expectations, perhaps about the role of correction, or about pronunciation, and ignoring them will certainly have an adverse effect on motivation.

As mentioned earlier, most of the teaching we do is to learners in a class with others, so all materials necessarily have to be a compromise, as do teachers' interpretations of materials.

Taking the individual differences discussed in this section, to what extent do you think they influence your own teaching, and how far can you, as a teacher, influence them? Compare your observations if possible with someone who works in a different educational environment.

Learning and language processes

Some readers will be familiar with the terms 'learning' and 'acquisition'. Except to note that, in the psychological literature, they conventionally distinguish more conscious and logical processes from the spontaneous nature of acquisition, particularly by children (McDonough, 1986: 95), we shall not make use of the distinction here and shall continue to refer to 'learning'. The purpose of this short section is only to introduce what is arguably the most significant approach to materials design of recent years. The details are the subject of the whole of part 2 of this book.

This can be considered as typical of an earlier approach to reading comprehension:

Text

Questions

1.
2.
3.

where the text might, for example, be about the life of a famous person, and the questions are there to find out whether the text has been understood. ('Mr X was born in Edinburgh in 1835'. Question: 'When was Mr X born?'). Such a format is more like a *test* of comprehension, and does not itself *teach* the learners any strategies for understanding the passage. Alternatively, learners were often required to *translate* the English text into their mother tongue. Despite new ways of analysing and describing language material, it took some time for our profession to turn its attention to the psychology of learning, particularly in relation to the comprehension skills of reading and, subsequently, listening. A 'test' or 'translation' method clearly tries to check that learners have understood a particular piece of language, but does little to develop techniques that can be transferred to other texts. Currently, then, there is a growing concern to ensure that practice is given in activating these generalizable skills that are believed to represent underlying (even universal) processes for all language users. Thus the reading skill, for instance, as we shall see in chapter 6, is seen in terms of a number of different 'sub-skills', such as reading for general information, scanning, skimming and so on. These sub-skills or strategies can then be used as the basis for specific tasks and exercises in a lesson. It is important to note that 'comprehension' is therefore no longer just a way of doing more grammar practice using a text, but opens up a perspective on psychological text-processing mechanisms.

Let us look at how some current materials make use of this perspective. The sub-skills of comprehension most frequently found are:

1　Reading/listening for the general idea, or 'gist'. In relation to reading, this is sometimes referred to as 'skimming'.
2　Looking for specific items of information (or 'scanning' for details).
3　Predicting, or anticipating what is coming next.
4　Making inferences or deductions when a 'fact' cannot simply be identified.

These skills are practised through a number of exercises and techniques. For example, we find various activities to be carried out before reading; activities that require different groups in the class to share different information; questions in the middle of a text to help with anticipation; and true–false questions that require learners to combine two or more parts of a text before they can answer. Overall we can observe that different kinds of texts and different reasons for reading or listening can be allowed for in the methodology used. The aim is not primarily to ensure that every word and every grammatical structure are understood – there are more efficient ways of doing this – but to equip learners with useful and transferable skills.

Finally, we should comment on a further dimension of the concept of a 'skill'. The kinds of strategies discussed above have developed from general work in the psychology of language processing which need not necessarily be applied to questions of language *learning*.

Most teachers are also concerned with the *conscious* skills their students need in order to learn as efficiently as possible. With this in mind, we find that increasing attention is being paid to two related areas. The first of these is usually referred to under the heading of 'Study Skills', the second of 'learner strategies'.

Study skills can be thought of as a range of learnable and practical techniques that help students to adopt more effective methods of study. In the area of English language teaching known as English for Specific Purposes (ESP) the concept is very well developed, particularly for students studying their own specialism through the medium of English where a mastery of a large number of academic-related skills is very important. In terms of general English coursebooks, study skills have a more restricted scope. The most frequently practised skill is that of using a monolingual dictionary. Learners are taught, for example, to understand the different parts of a dictionary entry, to select relevant information from a longer entry, and to recognize the significance of word parts, especially prefixes. Other skills include keeping a vocabulary book containing definitions and examples in English as well as (or instead of) the mother tongue equivalent, and sometimes the wider reference skills involved in using the different sections – contents page, index and so on – of a textbook.

The second area – learner strategies – owes much to research which analyses the components of successful language learning and offers definitions of a 'good language learner'. 'Success' is thought to be based on such factors as checking one's performance in a language, being willing to guess and to 'take risks' with both comprehension and production, seeking out opportunities to practise, developing efficient memorizing strategies, and many others. (For a detailed discussion, see Wenden and Rubin, 1987; Skehan, 1989: ch. 5.) Some current materials draw on this research, and incorporate explicit practice in 'good learner' strategies. One coursebook (*Fourth Dimension*) has an accompanying Study Book: activities include reading a text about language learning and identifying sentences giving key advice (such as 'I think, in order to learn, you mustn't be afraid of making mistakes'); and using this advice to make decisions about useful strategies. Another book (*Signature*) invites students to assess themselves with reference to a list of 'good language learner' strategies.

There has only been space here to look briefly at approaches to materials design drawn from various aspects of the literature on the psychology of language learning. We conclude the chapter by commenting on a rather different focus altogether.

The 'Process' Syllabus

This final short section is really concerned with an approach to syllabus rather than materials design, and much though not all of the work is as yet experimental. The most common labels attached to this kind of syllabus design proposal are 'process', 'task-based', and 'procedural' (we shall not discuss the internal distinctions here). The essence of all of them is described by Breen: 'One of the major sources of impetus for the recent interest in alternative methodologies has been an intensified theoretical and research focus upon the language learning process and, in particular, the contributions of the learner to that process' (1987: 159). In other words, the focus is on 'how' rather than 'what'. This is obviously true (up to a point) of the discussion in the preceding section, but the 'process syllabus' concept takes the claim further. Most importantly, it contains the far-reaching implication that syllabuses cannot be fully worked out in advance but must evolve as learners' problems and developing competence gradually emerge. The idea of project work, for example, where only the outline of the task is specified, is based on this view. Course design is therefore more likely to start with a 'bank' of possible tasks rather than a tightly controlled set of contents, whether that content is based on linguistic or psychological criteria.

This approach to syllabus design has been worked out in detail by Prabhu (1987), whose 'procedural' syllabus was based on a classroom experiment in India (the so-called 'Bangalore Project'). He lists three categories of problem-solving task:

1 Information-gap activities, for example, where each person in a pair has only part of the required information
2 Reasoning-gap activities, for example making a decision or an inference based on given information
3 Opinion-gap activities, for example taking part in a discussion of an issue, or completing a story

'Materials' from this point of view then become sources for the development of tasks and are only loosely, not fully, pre-constructed: Prabhu refers to this as a 'simple', not a 'sophisticated' syllabus. He regards tightly structured materials as restrictive, and is particularly critical of the 'multi-syllabus', and indeed of any approach to syllabus that is 'materials-driven'. These are challenging ideas, which potentially give teachers more responsibility in classroom decision-making and which arguably involve them more directly in the learning development of their students.

Conclusion

This chapter has discussed two important growth areas in materials design since the 'communicative revolution' of the 1970s: first the concept of a multi-syllabus, where a number of components are interwoven, and secondly, the increasing interest in various areas of the psychology of language learning and language use, both in the characteristics of individuals and in underlying processes. Clearly not all coursebooks incorporate all the elements that have been covered here, and it would probably not be appropriate for them to do so. They are design principles, and cannot have equal and universal applicability: as we have seen, different teaching situations have different requirements and expectations. The final two chapters in this part of the book will discuss procedures for evaluating and adapting general design criteria for specific contexts.

Consider again Swan's eight headings for the divisions of a syllabus: Grammar, Functions, Notions, Situations, Pronunciation, Skills, Vocabulary, Topics. In your own teaching situation, are all of these equally relevant?

When you have decided which headings you would include/exclude, list a few items under each category, and sketch out some ideas for how you might relate them to each other. For example, you may decide to select Functions, Grammar, Skills, Vocabulary. You might then include:
    Giving advice (functions)
    Modal verbs (grammar)
    Conversation (skill)
    Topic areas (education, health, i.e., vocabulary)

Further reading

1   Cook, V. J. (1991): *Second Language Learning and Language Teaching*. Relates various aspects of learning processes to the classroom context.

2   Johnson, K. (1982): 'Units of organization for a semantic syllabus'. Chapter 4 of *Communicative Syllabus Design and Methodology*. This is a useful analysis of some of the possibilities for constructing a 'multi-layered' syllabus.

3   Willis, D. (1990): *The Lexical Syllabus*. Although this describes one particular course in detail (the COBUILD English Course), it offers the only detailed discussion to date of this kind of syllabus and its associated materials design.

4   Evaluating ELT Materials

Introduction

The ability to evaluate teaching materials effectively is a very important professional activity for all EFL teachers and in this chapter we shall examine the reasons why teachers need to evaluate materials in the first instance. We shall then move on to discuss the criteria that can be used to evaluate materials by suggesting a working model which we hope will be an effective one to use for teachers working in a variety of contexts. The model that we suggest is based on the view that it is useful for us as teachers to perform an external evaluation of materials first of all in order to gain an overview of the organizational principles involved. After this we move on to a detailed internal evaluation of the materials to see how far the materials in question match up to what the author claims as well as to the aims and objectives of a given teaching programme.

The Context of Evaluation

Let us look at why we need to evaluate materials in the first place. Cunningsworth (1984) suggests that there are very few teachers who do not use published course materials at some stage in their teaching career. Many of us find that it is something that we do very regularly in our professional lives. We may wish at this stage to make a distinction between teaching situations where 'open-market' materials are chosen on the one hand, and where a Ministry of Education (or some similar body) produces materials which are subsequently passed on to the teacher for classroom use on the other.

The nature of the evaluation process in each of these scenarios will probably differ as well. In the first type of situation, teachers may have quite a large amount of choice in the materials they select, perhaps being able to liaise freely with colleagues and a Director of Studies/ Principal with respect to this material. However, there are many situations around the world where teachers in fact get a very limited choice or perhaps no choice at all, and this second scenario mentioned above may well obtain for teachers who are 'handed' materials by a Ministry or a Director and have to cope as best they can within this framework. This situation will more than likely involve teachers in an understanding of why the materials have been written in such a way and how they can make effective use of them in the classroom. For the vast majority of teachers working in the first situation that we have just mentioned, that of having a good deal of choice in the selection of appropriate materials, writing their own materials can be very time consuming and not necessarily cost-effective; hence the need to be able to discriminate effectively between all the coursebooks on the market. Today there is a wealth of EFL material available. Sheldon (1988) mentions figures for the United States alone, where 28 major publishers now offer 1,623 ESL textbooks between them. Brumfit (1980) writes about how there is no 'Which' (a British magazine which reviews consumer products) for textbooks, and that putting a book on the market implies that the book has been cleared of basic faults. However, this is not always the case.

Another fairly typical factor to consider is that teachers/course organizers are often under considerable professional and financial pressure to select a coursebook for an ELT programme which will then become *the* textbook maybe for years to come. Added to this pressure is the fact that in many contexts materials are often seen as being the core of a particular programme and are often the most visible representation of what happens in the classroom. Even though some practitioners may take issue with O'Neill's comment that 'no other medium is as easy to use as a book', (1982: 107), the reality for many is that the book may be the only choice open to them. The evaluation of current materials therefore merits serious consideration as an inappropriate choice may waste funds and time, not to mention the demotivating effect that it would have on students and possibly other colleagues.

For some teachers the selection of a good textbook can be valuable, particularly in contexts where the assimilation of stimulating, authentic materials can be difficult to organize. Other teachers working with materials given to them by a Ministry or similar body will clearly have some different issues to contend with. They may, for example, be having to work with materials which they find very limiting, and will probably need to resort to adapting these materials as best they can to suit the needs of their particular context. (Please see the next chapter for a full discussion of materials adaptation.) Even though such teachers will not have to evaluate to adopt materials, they may well be interested in evaluation as a useful process in its own right, giving insight into the organizational principles of the materials and helping them to keep up with developments in the field. This in turn can help the teacher to focus on realistic ways of adapting the materials to a particular group of learners where pertinent.

We have assumed that as teachers we all use published teaching materials. What do you feel are the reasons for this? What are teaching materials expected to achieve and how might they do it? Could we ever teach a foreign language without published materials? Is it ever possible for everything we need for a course to be contained in one textbook?

No textbook or set of materials is likely to be perfect and even though 'it is clear that coursebook assessment is fundamentally a subjective, rule-of-thumb activity, and that no neat formula, grid or system will ever provide a definite yardstick' (Sheldon, 1988: 245), we nonetheless need some model for hard-pressed teachers/course planners that will be brief, practical to use and yet comprehensive in its coverage of criteria, given that everyone in the field will need to evaluate materials at some time or other. We hope to do this by offering a model which distinguishes the purpose behind the evaluation – be it to 'keep up-to-date with current developments' or to adopt/select materials for a given course.

In the first instance, teachers may be interested in the evaluation exercise for its own sake. For example, we may wish to review all the materials which have come out during a given period of time and require some criteria with which to assess these materials. In doing this, we may of course find materials which may be suitable for adoption/selection at some future date. For teachers wishing to select, however, this distinction is clearly important since there is no point in doing a full evaluation for selection purposes if a preliminary evaluation can show that those materials will be of little use for a particular group.

We thus examine criteria in two stages; an external evaluation which offers a brief 'overview' of the materials from the outside (cover, introduction, table of contents), which is then followed by a closer and more detailed internal evaluation. We cannot be absolutely certain as to what criteria and constraints are actually operational in ELT contexts worldwide and some teachers might argue that textbook criteria often are very local. We may cite examples of teachers who are actively involved in the evaluation process. One teacher from a secondary school in Europe is able to 'trial' a coursebook with her students for two weeks before officially adopting it. Some secondary school teachers in Japan team-teach their classes with native speakers and are able to evaluate materials jointly with them. However, as we pointed out in chapter 1, we are attempting to look at areas where our professional framework shares similar interests and concerns, and with this in mind the criteria that we shall examine here will be as comprehensive as possible for the majority of ELT situations on a worldwide basis. Of course the evaluation process is never static; when materials are deemed appropriate for a particular course after a preliminary evaluation, their ultimate success or failure may only be determined after a certain amount of classroom use (summative evaluation).

In chapter 1 we looked at the educational framework in which we all work. With reference to this, you might like to think about who actually evaluates materials in your educational system; i.e., what is the role of published materials and therefore the role of evaluation? Do teachers do it (by themselves, jointly with other teachers/students?), or does the Ministry of Education choose or write the materials for you?

You might also like to think about the criteria that you used to select the ELT materials that you are using at the moment. Or, if you did not select the materials, think about the criteria that you would use. Discuss your answers with a colleague if at all possible. Did you select the same criteria? Note down your answers because we shall refer to them again at the end of this chapter to see how far the criteria you mention overlap with ours.

The External Evaluation

In this central stage of the model we have included criteria which will provide a comprehensive, external overview of how the materials have been organized. Our aim is basically that of examining the organiz-ation of the materials as stated explicitly by the author/publisher by looking at:

- the 'blurb', or the claims made on the cover of the teachers/ students book

- the introduction and table of contents

which should enable the evaluator to assess what Cunningsworth (1984: 2) has termed 'what the books say about themselves'. We also find it useful to scan the table of contents page in that it often represents a 'bridge' between the external claim made for the materials and what will actually be presented 'inside' the materials themselves. At this stage we need to consider why the materials have been produced. Presumably because the author/publisher feels that there is a gap in the existing market that these materials are intended to fill: so we shall have to investigate this further to see whether the objectives have been clearly spelt out. To illustrate what we mean, here is an example of one such 'blurb' taken from a well known EFL textbook from the 1970s:

> . . . for upper-intermediate and more advanced students inter-ested in *using* language rather than learning more about struc-ture. Students at these levels often have a very good knowledge of English structure and vocabulary but cannot apply their knowledge to communicate effectively . . . introduces the major communicative functions for which language is used and pro-vides stimulating presentation and practice material.

It appears therefore that this textbook is aiming at the higher proficiency student who has a very good 'usage' background but needs a course which will activate language use. Later, when the evaluator investigates the organization of the materials he or she will have to ascertain whether or not this is really the case.

Let us see the types of claim that can be made for materials in the introduction. The following example is part of the introduction taken from a recent EFL series. We have put certain terms and key concepts which we feel need further investigation in italics:

> This book is intended for *good intermediate level* students who have already got a *basic knowledge of grammar*. The *aims* of the book are to:
>
> – expose students to a variety of *authentic written and spoken language*, and to give them confidence in coping with it.
> – provide plenty of *opportunities for oral fluency*, from *discussion* activities to full-scale *role plays*.
> – expose the students to *language in use*, with *opportunities to revise areas of grammar or functional language* which may still be causing problems.
> ... these *themes* have been chosen as ones which are likely to *interest and motivate the average learner*, and which are *generative* in terms of *useful vocabulary areas*.

We can deduce from this that the claims made for the materials by the author/publisher can be quite strong and will need critical evaluation in order to see if their claims can be justified. From the 'blurb' and the introduction we can normally expect comments on some/all of the following:

- *The intended audience.* We need to ascertain who the materials are targeted at, be it teenagers aged 13 and upwards or adults, for example. The topics that will motivate one audience will probably not be suitable for another.

- *The proficiency level.* Most materials claim to aim at a particular level, such as false beginner or lower intermediate. This will obviously require investigation as it could vary widely depending on the educational context.

- *The context in which the materials are to be used.* We need to establish whether the materials are for teaching general learners or perhaps for teaching English for Specific Purposes (ESP). If the latter, what degree of specialist subject knowledge is assumed in the materials?

- *How the language has been presented and organized into teachable units/lessons.* The materials will contain a number of units/lessons and their respective lengths need to be borne in mind when deciding how and if th*:*y will fit into a given educational programme. Some materials will provide guidelines here such as '... contains 15 units, providing material for 90–120 hours of teaching'. In other words, the author expects that between 6 and 8 hours will be required to cover the material.

- *The author's views on language and methodology* and the relationship between the language, the learning process and the learner.

In many cases the date of publication of the materials will be of importance here. For materials written over the last decade or so designed to fit into a multi-syllabus or process syllabus, we might expect the author to make claims about including quite a large amount of learner involvement in the learning process. This will require investigation. For example, the materials may claim to help the learner in an understanding of what is involved in language learning and contain various activities and tasks to develop this.

Look at the 'blurb' and the introduction to the materials that you typically use. Also look back at the 'blurbs' that we examined in chapters 2 and 3. What kinds of information do they give you?

To give an overview of some typical 'blurbs', we have selected a range of examples taken from EFL coursebooks. We may notice how certain 'key' words and expressions come up time and time again.

As you are reading them, note down some of the claims that are made for the materials that you would want to investigate further in the next (internal evaluation) stage.

1 '. . . is a beginners course in English for complete or near beginners . . . has a careful structural progression with specific communicative aims.'

2 '. . . is a new beginners course for students aged 14 and over. It presents a totally new approach to language learning as it takes account of basic communication needs as its first priority.'

3 '. . . systematically covers the notional, functional and grammatical areas that are important to students at this (intermediate) level. In each unit, students are taught the relationship between structures and meaning and learn how to use structures in a communicative context.'

4 '. . . focuses on the real English students will encounter and need to use in today's world. Book 1 is for false beginner adult learners. Fifteen units will provide about 100 hours of class work, at the end of which students will be able to cope confidently with a very wide range of straightforward situations.'

When evaluating materials it is useful to keep a note of these claims which we can then refer back to later in the process. There are also some other factors that we believe it necessary to take into account at this external stage as follows:

- Are the materials to be used as the main 'core' course or to be supplementary to it?

This will help to evaluate their effectiveness in a given context as well as the total cost. It may be that sheer economics will dissuade the evaluator from selecting these particular materials, especially if they are not going to be the core part of the course.

- Is a teacher's book in print and locally available?

It is also worth considering whether it is sufficiently clear for non-native speaker teachers to use. Some teachers books offer general teaching hints while others have very prescribed programmes of how to teach the material including lesson plans. Non-availability of the teacher's book may make the student edition difficult to work with.

- Is a vocabulary list/index included?

Having these included in the materials may prove to be very useful for learners in some contexts, particularly where the learner might be doing a lot of individualized and/or out-of-class work. Some materials explicitly state that they are offering this. '. . . student's book with an introductory unit, forty double-page units, four self-check units, . . . an interaction appendix, a vocabulary appendix with phonetic spelling, a list of irregular verbs, and a listening appendix', and the claims made are worthy of investigation.

The table of contents may sometimes be seen as a 'bridge' between the external and internal stages of the evaluation and can often reveal useful information about the organization of the materials, giving information about vocabulary study, skills to be covered, functions and so on, possibly with some indication as to how much class time the author thinks should be devoted to a particular unit. Consequently, it is often useful to see how explicit it is.

Look at the example on p. 72. What information does it give us about the materials?

- What visual material does the book contain (photographs, charts, diagrams) and is it there for cosmetic value only or is it actually integrated into the text?

In recent years there has been a tendency to use glossy prints in some materials to try and make the book appear more attractive. It is worth examining if the visual material actually serves any learning purpose; i.e., in the case of a photograph or a diagram, is it actually incorporated into a task so that the learner has to comment on it/interpret it in some way?

- Is the layout and presentation clear or cluttered?

There are some textbooks which are very well researched and written but are so cluttered with information on every page that teachers/learners find them practically unusable. Hence, a judicious balance between the two needs to be found. The potential durability of the materials is another important factor in teaching contexts where materials may be selected for several groups over a period of years. Factors such as paper quality and binding need to be assessed.

Source: R. O'Neill and P. Mugglestone, *Fourth Dimension,* copyright Longman, 1989.

- Is the material too culturally biased or specific?

- Do the materials represent minority groups and/or women in a negative way? Do they present a 'balanced' picture of a particular country/society?

It is possible that the content of some materials will cause offence to some learners. The investigation by Littlejohn and Windeatt (1988) into teaching materials shows how textbooks may be 'biased' in subtle, and in some cases not so subtle, ways in their representation of class, ethnic background and reference to smoking and drinking.

- The inclusion of audio/video material and resultant cost. Is it essential to possess this extra material in order to use the textbook successfully?

- The inclusion of tests in the teaching materials (diagnostic, progress, achievement); would they be useful for your particular learners?

During this external evaluation stage we have examined the claims made for the materials by the author/publisher with respect to: the intended audience, the proficiency level, the context and presentation of language items, whether the materials are to be core or supplementary, the role and availability of a teachers' book, the inclusion of a vocabulary list/index, the table of contents, the use of visuals and presentation, the cultural specificity of the materials, the provision of audio/video material and inclusion of tests.

After completing this external evaluation, and having funds and a potential group of learners in mind, we can arrive at a decision as to the materials' appropriacy for adoption/selection purposes. If our evaluation shows the materials to be potentially appropriate and worthy of a more detailed inspection then we can continue with our internal or more detailed evaluation. If not, then we can 'exit' at this stage and start to evaluate other materials if we so wish, as figure 4.1 illustrates:

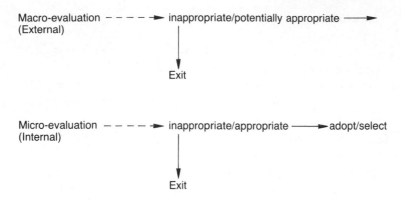

Figure 4.1

The Internal Evaluation

We now continue to the next stage of our evaluation procedure by performing an in-depth investigation into the materials. The essential issue at this stage is for us to analyse the extent to which the aforementioned factors in the external evaluation stage actually match up with the internal consistency and organization of the materials as stated by the author/publisher – for, as we saw in the previous section, strong claims are often made for these materials. In order to perform an effective internal inspection of the materials, we need to examine at least two units (preferably more) of a book or set of materials to investigate the following factors:

● The presentation of the skills in the materials

We may want to investigate if all the language skills are covered, in what proportion, and if this proportion is appropriate to the context in which we are working. Are the skills treated discretely or in an integrated way? The author's presentation and treatment of the skills may conflict with the way in which we wish to teach – if the skills are presented too much in isolation, for example. If they are integrated, is this integration natural? (See chapter 10 for a discussion of integrated skills.)

- The grading and sequencing of the materials

This criterion is an important one and merits some investigation as it is not always patently clear what the principle is. Some materials are quite 'steeply' graded while others claim to have no grading at all.

In this example the materials are based on a lexical frequency count: 'The course is in three levels, each covering about 100 hours of classwork, and each level is complete in itself. Together they cover the most useful patterns of 2500 of the most frequently used words in English. Book 1 covers the first 700 of these . . .' Sometimes the grading of the materials will be within the unit, other materials will be graded across the unit allowing a progression of difficulty in a linear fashion. Other materials claim to be modular by grouping a set of units at approximately the same level. In cases where there is virtually no grading at all – 'Most of the units do not have to be taught in any particular order . . .' – we have to investigate the extent to which we think this is true, and how such a book would suit our learners.

- Where reading/'discourse' skills are involved, is there much in the way of appropriate text beyond the sentence?

As teachers we sometimes find that materials provide too much emphasis on skills development and not enough opportunity for students to practise those skills on extended reading passages.

- Where listening skills are involved, are recordings 'authentic' or artificial?

We need to ascertain whether or not dialogues have been specially written, thereby missing the essential features of spontaneous speech.

- Do speaking materials incorporate what we know about the nature of real interaction or are artificial dialogues offered instead?

- The relationship of tests and exercises to (a) learner needs and (b) what is taught by the course material.

Where these are included as part of the materials, we need to see if they are appropriate in context.

- Do you feel that the material is suitable for different learning styles; is a claim and provision made for self-study and is such a claim justified?

With the growth of interest in independent learning and learner autonomy, many materials will claim that 'self-study modes' are also possible. From the knowledge that we have of our learners, we will need to assess this particular claim.

- Are the materials sufficiently 'transparent' to motivate both students and teachers alike, or would you foresee a student/ teacher mismatch?

Some materials may seem attractive for the teacher but would not be very motivating for the learners. A balance therefore has to be sought. At this stage it is also useful to consider how the materials may guide and 'frame' teacher-learner interaction and the teacher-learner relationship.

In the internal evaluation stage we have suggested that as evaluators we need to examine the following criteria: the treatment and presentation of the skills, the sequencing and grading of the materials, the *type* of reading, listening, speaking and writing materials contained in the materials, appropriacy of tests and exercises, self-study provision and teacher-learner 'balance' in use of the materials.

The Overall Evaluation

At this stage we hope that we may now make an overall assessment as to the suitability of the materials by considering the following parameters:

1 *The usability factor.* How far the materials could be integrated into a particular syllabus as 'core' or supplementary. For example, we may need to select materials which suit a particular syllabus or set of objectives that we have to work to. The materials may or may not be able to do this.
2 *The generalizability factor.* Is there a restricted use of 'core' features which make the materials more generally useful? It

may be that not all the material will be useful for a given individual or group but some parts might be. This factor can in turn lead us to consider:

3   *The adaptability factor.* Can parts be added/extracted/used in another context/modified for local circumstances? There may be some very good qualities in the materials but, for example, we may judge the listening material or the reading passages to be unsuitable and in need of modification. If we think that adaptation is feasible we may choose to do this. (Again, please refer to chapter 5 for a full discussion of materials adaptation.)

4   *The flexibility factor.* How rigid is the sequencing and grading; can the materials be entered at different points/used in different ways? In some cases materials which are not so steeply graded offer a measure of flexibility which permits them to be integrated easily into various types of syllabus.

The following remarks illustrate the type of comments that teachers have made to us regarding the suitability of certain published ELT materials for their teaching situations:

'There is a wide variety of reading and listening material available but the speaking material is not very good and is too accuracy based. I would therefore have to add something in terms of fluency. The book is usable and could be adapted, but given the cost factor I would prefer to look for something else.'

'The materials are very good. I was looking for something that would present the skills in an integrated way and would make a connection with the real lives of my students. I checked the 'blurb', the table of contents and made a detailed inspection of several units. On the whole the author's claims are realized in the materials. Consequently I could use this as a core course with very few adaptations.'

Thus, when all the criteria that we have discussed have been analysed we can then reach our own conclusions regarding the suitability of the materials for specified groups or individuals, as the aim of this final stage is intended to enable the evaluator to decide the extent to which the materials have realized their stated objectives.

Even after the internal evaluation we still have the option of *not* selecting the materials if we so wish. (Please refer back to figure 4.1.) This is usually avoided, however, if we undertake a full and thorough internal inspection of the material as we have outlined above. But once materials have been deemed appropriate for use on a particular course we must bear in mind that their ultimate success or failure can only be determined after trying them in the classroom with real learners.

At the beginning of the chapter we asked you to note down some criteria that you would use to evaluate materials. Now refer back to those criteria. How far do they match up with the ones that we have mentioned? Are there any which are different?

Now take a coursebook or set of ELT materials which are unfamiliar to you and put into operation the criteria that we have examined in this chapter.

Conclusion

In this chapter we have suggested that materials evaluation can be carried out in two complementary stages which we have called the external and internal stages. We then outlined and commented upon the essential criteria necessary to make pertinent judgements with reference to ELT materials in order to make a preliminary selection. We suggested that this particular model should be flexible enough to be used in ELT contexts worldwide, as it avoids long checklists of data and can operate according to the purpose the evaluator has in evaluating the materials in the first place. We also suggested that materials evaluation is one part of a complex process and that materials once selected can only be judged successful after classroom implementation and feedback.

Further reading

The following contain useful information on materials evaluation:

1   Cunningsworth, A. (1984): *Evaluating and Selecting ELT Teaching Materials.*

2   Sheldon, L. E. (ed.) (1987): *ELT Textbooks and Materials: Problems in Evaluation and Development.*

3   Sheldon, L. E. (1988): Evaluating ELT Textbooks and Materials. *ELT Journal*, 42/4: 237–46.

5   Adapting Materials

Introduction

The main concern of all the chapters in this part of the book has been to examine the principles on which current teaching materials and classroom methodology are built. This final chapter in part 1 looks at some of the factors to be considered in the process of adapting teaching materials within particular classroom environments where there is a perceived need for change and manipulation of certain design features. There is clearly a direct relationship between evaluating and adapting materials, both in terms of the reasons for doing so and the criteria used: this chapter can therefore usefully be seen as forming a pair with chapter 4. We shall first set the scene for a discussion of adaptation by looking at ways in which the concept can be understood. We shall then try to enumerate some of the reasons why teachers might need to adapt their teaching material. Finally, in the main part of the chapter, these reasons will be examined in terms of the procedures typically used in adaptation.

The Context of Adaptation

A straightforward starting point for considering the relationship between evaluation and adaptation is to think of the terms 'adopting' and 'adapting'. We saw in the previous chapter that a decision about whether a particular coursebook should be used in a specific teaching situation can be taken on the basis of a number of evaluative criteria. These criteria, formulated as a set of questions to ask about the materials, provide answers that will lead to acceptance or perhaps rejection. For instance, typical questions concerned aspects of 'skills', different ways in which language content is handled, and the authenticity of both language and tasks. However, a decision in favour of adoption is an initial step, and is unlikely to mean that no further action needs to be taken beyond that of presenting the material directly to the learners. It is more realistic to assume that, however careful the design of the materials and the evaluation process, some changes will have to be made at some level in most teaching contexts. Adaptation, then, is a process subsequent to, and dependent on, adoption. Furthermore, whereas adoption is concerned with whole coursebooks, adaptation concerns the parts that make up that whole.

An important perspective on evaluation – though of course not the only one – is to see it as a management issue whereby educational decision-makers formulate policy and work out strategies for budgeting and for the purchasing and allocation of resources. In this sense, teachers do not always have direct involvement: they may well influence decisions about whole textbooks only if they are part of a Ministry of Education team concerned with trialling or writing materials, for example. Others, perhaps, may be invited to make suggestions and comments as part of a corporate process of materials selection, but even then the final decision will be taken at a managerial point in the school hierarchy. A far more widespread, and necessary, activity among teachers is therefore that of adaptation, because the smaller-scale process of changing or adjusting the various parts of a coursebook is, as we shall see, more closely related to the reality of dealing with learners in the dynamic environment of the classroom.

This said, let us remind ourselves of another major and persuasive reason for evaluating textbooks even in a context where teachers have little direct say in decision-making. Evaluation as an exercise can help us develop insights into different views of language and learning and into the principles of materials design, and is something we do against the background of a knowledge of our learners and of the demands and potential of our teaching situation. It is difficult to see how the dependent activity of adaptation can take place without this kind of understanding – how can we change something unless we are clear about what it is we are changing?

With this wider perspective in mind, and as a starting-point for thinking about the process of adaptation, it will be useful to extend a little the criteria put forward in chapter 4 under the headings of 'external' and 'internal'. External factors comprise both the overt claims made about materials and, more significantly for the present chapter, the characteristics of particular teaching situations. Internal factors are concerned with content, organization and consistency. Thus:

External (what we have)   *Internal (what the materials offer)*

Learner characteristics   Choice of topics
Physical environment   Skills covered
Resources   Proficiency level
Class size   Grading of exercises

To adapt materials is to try to bring together these individual elements under each heading, or combinations of them, so that they match each other as closely as possible. The horizontal lines indicate only a very small number of the possibilities for cross-referencing. For instance, we may be unable to use the full range of listening skills practised in a coursebook because of resource limitations; and the link between a stated proficiency level and that of our own learners is an obvious one. Madsen and Bowen refer to this matching as the principle of 'congruence': 'Effective adaptation is a matter of achieving "congruence" . . . The good teacher is . . . constantly striving for congruence among several related variables: teaching materials, methodology, students, course objectives, the target language and its context, and the teacher's own personality and teaching style' (1978: ix). With an emphasis on materials, Stevick talks of bridging a gap: 'the teacher must satisfy the demands of the textbook, but in ways that will be satisfying to those who learn from it' (1972). (Even if we agree with Prabhu's (1987) critique of 'materials-driven' classes referred to at the end of chapter 3, we must recognize that the great majority of teachers work with coursebooks, so Stevick's comment is entirely realistic.) In general, then, teaching materials may be internally coherent but not totally applicable in context; alternatively, they may be largely appropriate at the same time as they show signs of an inconsistent organization.

The final point to be made in this section is one that is frequently overlooked, perhaps because it is so much a part of our everyday professional practice that we are unaware of its implications. Adaptation tends to be thought of as a rather formal process in which the teacher makes a decision about, say, an exercise that needs changing, and then writes out a revised version for the class. In fact, although the concept of adaptation clearly includes this kind of procedure, it is also broader than this. Adapted material does not necessarily need to be written down or made permanent. It can be quite transitory: we might think of the response to an individual's learning behaviour at a particular moment, for instance when the teacher re-words – and by doing so adapts – a textbook explanation of a language point that has not been understood. The recognition of the short-term needs of a group may similarly require teachers to 'think on their feet' by introducing extra material, such as a grammatical example or some idiomatic language, from their own repertoire in the real-time framework of a class. Madsen and Bowen make the point clearly: 'the good teacher is constantly adapting. He adapts when he adds an example not found in the book or when he telescopes an assignment by having students prepare "only the even-numbered items". He adapts even when he refers to an exercise covered earlier, or when he introduces a supplementary picture . . . While a conscientious author tries to anticipate questions that may be raised by his readers, the teacher can respond not merely to verbal questions . . . but even to the raised eyebrows of his students' (1978: vii). To focus only on these kinds of activities would obviously not give us a complete picture of the concept of adaptation, because it would be necessary at some stage to extend and systematize its possibilities. Nevertheless, it is worth noting that the task of adapting is not an entirely new skill that teachers must learn.

Before you read on, consider the materials that you use most frequently: to what extent do you feel that they need, in principle, to be adapted? Try to note down the main aspects of change or modification that you think are necessary or at least desirable.

It will also be useful to think about adaptation from the point of view of the *source* of your materials. Are they commercially produced and widely used internationally; are they designed at national level by your

Ministry of Education; or are they perhaps more localized, produced by a team of teachers for a particular area or school?

If possible, share your comments with other teachers. You could also discuss the scope that you have for adapting materials – do you have time? Is it acceptable to do so in your teaching situation? Are you actually required to adapt?

In this part of the chapter, we have tried to show that adaptation is essentially a process of 'matching'. Its purpose is to maximize the appropriacy of teaching materials in context, by changing some of the internal characteristics of a coursebook to better suit our particular circumstances. We shall now look in more detail at possible reasons for adaptation, and at some of the procedures commonly used.

Reasons for Adapting

We have just asked you to consider your reasons for needing to make modifications to your own materials, and some of the changes you would wish to make. These reasons will depend, of course, on the whole range of variables operating in your own teaching situation, and one teacher's priorities may well differ considerably from those of another. It is certainly possible that there are some general trends common to a large number of teaching contexts: most obviously there appears to be a widespread perception that materials should aim to be in some sense 'communicative' and 'authentic'. Nevertheless, it is worth bearing in mind that priorities are relative, and there is no absolute notion of right or wrong, or even just one way of interpreting such terms as 'communicative' and 'authentic'. It is also the case that priorities change over time even within the same context. For instance, decontextualized grammar study is not intrinsically 'wrong' in a communicatively-oriented class, just as role-play is not automatically 'right'. Nor does a need to adapt necessarily imply that a coursebook is defective.

It will be useful to compare your own reasons with those in the following list. The list is not intended to be comprehensive, but simply to show some of the possible areas of mismatch ('noncongruence') that teachers identify and that can be dealt with by adapting.

- Not enough grammar coverage in general

- Not enough practice of grammar points of particular difficulty to these learners

- The communicative focus means that grammar is presented unsystematically

- Reading passages contain too much unknown vocabulary

- Comprehension questions are too easy, because the answers can be lifted directly from the text with no real understanding

- Listening passages are inauthentic, because they sound too much like written material being read out

- Not enough guidance on pronunciation

- Subject-matter inappropriate for learners of this age and intellectual level

- Photographs and other illustrative material not culturally acceptable

- Amount of material too great/too little to cover in the time allocated to lessons

- No guidance for teachers on handling group work and role play activities with a large class

- Dialogues too formal, and not really representative of everyday speech

- Audio material difficult to use because of problems to do with room size and technical equipment

- Too much or too little variety in the activities

- Vocabulary list and a key to the exercises would be helpful

- Accompanying tests needed

Undoubtedly much more could be added to this list, but it must serve as an illustration of some of the possibilities. All aspects of the language classroom can be covered: the few examples above include (a) aspects of language use (b) skills (c) classroom organization and (d) supplementary material.

Principles and Procedures

The reasons for adapting that we have just looked at can be thought of as dealing with the modification of content, whether that content is expressed in the form of exercises and activities; texts; instructions; tests and so on. In other words, the focus is on what the materials contain measured against the requirements of a particular teaching environment. That environment may necessitate a number of changes that will lead to greater appropriacy. This is most likely to be expressed in terms of a need to personalize, individualize or localize the content. We take 'personalizing' here to refer to increasing the relevance of content in relation to learners' interests and their academic, educational or professional needs. 'Individualizing' will address the learning styles both of individuals and of the members of a class working closely together. 'Localizing' takes into account the international geography of English language teaching and recognizes that what may work well in Mexico City may not do so in Edinburgh or in Kuala Lumpur. Madsen and Bowen (1978) include a further category of 'modernizing', and comment that not all materials show familiarity with aspects of current English usage, sometimes to the point of being not only out of date or misleading but even incorrect.

In this section we shall now look at questions of procedure – at the main techniques that can be applied to content in order to bring about change. There are a number of points to bear in mind. Firstly, this can be seen as another kind of matching process or 'congruence', where techniques are selected according to the aspect of the materials that needs alteration. Secondly, content can be adapted using a range of techniques; or, conversely, a single technique can be applied to different content areas. For example, a reading passage might be grammatically simplified or its subject-matter modified, or it can be made shorter or broken down into smaller parts. The technique of simplification can be applied to texts, to explanations and so on. Thirdly, adaptation can have both quantitative and qualitative effects. In other words, we can simply change the amount of material, or we can change its methodological nature. Finally, techniques can be used individually or in combination with others, so the scale of possibilities clearly ranges from straightforward to rather complex. All these points will be raised again in the discussion of individual techniques.

The techniques that we shall cover are as follows:

> Adding, including expanding and extending
> Deleting, including subtracting and abridging
> Modifying, including re-writing and re-structuring
> Simplifying
> Re-ordering

Each one will be briefly introduced, and a few examples given. There are implications for all of them in parts 2 and 3 of this book where we consider language skills and classroom methodology. Readers interested at this stage in more detailed examples of procedures for adaptation are referred to the 'Further reading' at the end of this chapter. The first references have broadly similar lists of techniques, and offer a large number of worked examples.

When you have finished reading through the discussion of techniques, select one or two of them and consider their application to any materials with which you are familiar.

It will be useful at this stage to work on a small scale, taking single content areas, such as an an exercise, a text, or a set of comprehension questions.

1　*Adding*

The notion of addition is, on the face of it, a very obvious and straightforward idea, implying that materials are supplemented by putting more into them, while taking into account the practical effect on time allocation. We certainly can add in this simple quantitative way by the technique of *extending*. We might wish to do this in situations such as the following:

● The materials contain practice in the pronunciation of minimal pairs (bit/bet; hat/hate; ship/chip) but not enough examples of the difficulties for learners with a particular L_1. Japanese speakers may need more l/r practice, Arabic speakers more p/b, Spanish speakers more b/v, and so on.

- A second reading passage parallel to the one provided is helpful in reinforcing the key linguistic features – tenses, sentence structure, vocabulary, cohesive devices – of the first text.

- Our students find the explanation of a new grammar point rather difficult, so further exercises are added before they begin the practice material.

The point to note here is that adding by extension is to supply more of the same. This means that the techniques are being applied *within* the methodological framework of the original materials: in other words, the model is not itself changed.

Another, more far-reaching perspective on addition of material can be termed *expanding*. Consider these possibilities:

- The only pronunciation practice in the materials is on individual sounds and minimal pairs. However, this may be necessary but not sufficient. Our students need to be intelligible, and intelligibility entails more than articulating a vowel or a consonant correctly. Therefore we decide to add some work on sentence stress and rhythm and on the related phenomenon of 'weak' and 'strong' forms in English. A further advantage is that students will be better able to understand naturally spoken English.

- If there is insufficient coverage of the skill of listening, the reading passage provided may also be paralleled by the provision of listening comprehension material, using the same vocabulary and ideas but presented through a different medium, making sure that it is authentic in terms of the spoken language.

- Although the new grammar material is important and relevant, the addition of a discussion section at the end of the unit will help to reinforce and contextualize the linguistic items covered, particularly if it is carefully structured so that the most useful points occur 'naturally'.

These kinds of addition are not just extensions of an existing aspect of content. They go further than this by bringing about a qualitative as well as a quantitative change. Expanding, then, as distinct from extending, adds to the methodology by moving outside it and developing it in new directions, for instance by putting in a different language skill or a new component. This can be thought of as a change in the overall system.

Finally in this section, it is worth pointing out that additions do not always have to be made onto the end of something. A new facet of material or methodology can be introduced before it appears in the framework of the coursebook. For example, a teacher may prepare the ground for practice in an aspect of grammar or communicative function determined by the syllabus through a 'warm-up' exercise involving learners talking about themselves and their everyday lives.

2   Deleting or omitting

Deletion is clearly the opposite process to that of addition, and as such needs no further clarification as a term. However, although material is taken out rather than supplemented, as a technique it can be thought of as 'the other side of the same coin'. We saw in the previous section that material can be added both quantitatively (extending) and qualitatively (expanding): the same point applies when a decision is taken to omit material. Again, as with addition, the technique can be used on a small scale, for example over part of an exercise, or on the larger scale of a whole unit of a coursebook.

We shall refer to the most straightforward aspect of reducing the length of material as *subtracting* from it. The following kinds of requirements might apply:

- Our pronunciation exercises on minimal pairs contain too much general material. Since our students all have the same mother tongue and do not make certain errors, quite a lot of the exercises are inappropriate. Arabic speakers, for example, will be unlikely to have much difficulty with the l/r distinction.

- Although a communicative coursebook has been selected as relevant in our situation, some of the language functions presented are unlikely to be required by learners who will probably not use their English in the target language environment. Such functions as 'giving directions' or 'greetings' may be useful; 'expressing sympathy' or 'ordering things' may not.

Deletion in these cases, as with extending, does not have a significant impact on the overall methodology. The changes are greater if material is not only subtracted, but also what we shall term *abridged*:

● The materials contain a discussion section at the end of each unit. However, our learners are not really proficient enough to tackle this adequately, since they have learnt the language structures but not fluency in their use. The syllabus and its subsequent examination does not leave room for this kind of training.

● Students on a short course are working with communicative materials because of their instrumental reasons for choosing to learn English: some of them wish to travel on international business, others plan to visit a target language country as tourists. The lengthy grammatical explanations accompanying each functional unit are therefore felt to be inappropriate.

Addition and deletion often work together, of course. Material may be taken out and then replaced with something else. Where the same kind of material is substituted, as for instance one set of minimal pairs for another, the internal balance of the lesson or the syllabus is not necessarily altered. The methodological change is greater when, for example, grammar practice is substituted after the omission of an inappropriate communicative function, or when a reading text is replaced by a listening passage. This takes us directly into the next section.

3 Modifying

'Modification' at one level is a very general term in the language applying to any kind of change. In order to introduce further possibilities for adaptation, we shall restrict its meaning here to an *internal* change in the approach or focus of an exercise or other piece of material. It is a rather important and frequently used procedure which, like all other techniques, can be applied to any aspect of 'content'. It can be sub-divided under two related headings. The first of these is *re-writing*, when some of the linguistic content needs modification; the second is *re-structuring*, which applies to classroom management. Let us look at some examples of each of these in turn. You will undoubtedly be able to think of many more.

Re-writing   Currently the most frequently stated requirement for a change in focus is for materials to be made 'more communicative'. This feeling is voiced in many teaching situations where textbooks are considered to lag behind an understanding of the nature of language and of students' linguistic and learning needs. Re-writing, therefore, may relate activities more closely to learners' own backgrounds and interests, introduce models of authentic language, or set more purposeful, problem-solving tasks where the answers are not always known before the teacher asks the question. The first two readings listed at the end of this chapter also contain substantial discussion and examples for making textbooks more communicative, as does chapter 9 of Cunningsworth (1984).

It is quite common for coursebooks to place insufficient emphasis on listening comprehension, and for teachers to feel that more material is required. If accompanying audio material is either not available, or cannot be purchased in a particular teaching context, then the teacher can re-write a reading passage and deliver it orally, perhaps by taking notes from the original and then speaking naturally to the class from those notes.

Sometimes new vocabulary is printed just as a list, with explanatory notes and perhaps the mother tongue equivalent. We may wish to modify this kind of presentation by taking out the notes and writing an exercise that helps students to develop useful and generalized strategies for acquiring new vocabulary. Equally, a text may have quite appropriate language material for a specific group, but may not 'match' in terms of its cultural content. For example, a story about an English family, with English names, living in an English town, eating English food and enjoying English hobbies can in fact be modified quite easily by making a number of straightforward surface changes.

A last example here is that of end-of-text comprehension questions. Some of these are more like a test, where students can answer by 'lifting' the information straight from the text. These questions can be modified so that students have to interpret what they have read or heard, or relate different sections of the text to each other. Chapter 6 looks at these kinds of tasks.

The point was made in the introduction to this chapter that content changes are not always written down. Adaptation of linguistic content may just require re-wording by the teacher as an oral explanation.

Re-structuring   For many teachers who are required to follow a coursebook rather strictly, changes in the structuring of the class are sometimes the only kind of adaptation that is realistically possible. For example, the materials may contain role-play activities for groups of a certain size. The logistics of managing a large class (especially if they all have the same L_1) are complex from many points of view, and it will probably be necessary to assign one role to a number of pupils at the same time. Obviously the converse – where the class is too small for the total number of roles available – is also possible if perhaps less likely.

Sometimes a written language explanation which is designed to be read and studied can be made more meaningful if it is turned into an interactive exercise where all students participate. For instance, it is a straightforward matter to ask learners to practise certain verb structures in pairs (say the present perfect: 'Have you been to/done X?'; or a conditional: 'What would you do if . . . ?'), and it can be made more authentic by inviting students to refer to topics of direct interest to themselves.

Modifying materials, then, even in the restricted sense in which we have used the term here, is a technique that has a very wide range of applications. It refers essentially to a 'modality change', to a change in the nature or focus of an exercise, or text, or classroom activity.

4   Simplifying

Strictly speaking, the technique of simplification is one type of modification, namely a 're-writing' activity. Since it has received considerable attention in its own right, it is considered here as a separate procedure. Many elements of a language course can be simplified, including the instructions and explanations that accompany exercises and activities, and even the visual layout of material so that it becomes easier to see how different parts fit together. It is worth noting in passing that teachers are sometimes on rather dangerous ground, if a wish to 'simplify' grammar or speech in the classroom leads to a distortion of natural language. For example, over-simplification of a grammatical explanation can be misleadingly one-sided or partial: to tell learners that adverbs are always formed by adding '-ly' does not help them when they come across 'friendly' or 'brotherly', nor does it explain why 'hardly' cannot be formed from 'hard'. A slow style of speech might result in the elimination of the correct use of sentence stress and weak forms, leaving learners with no exposure to the natural rhythms of spoken English.

However, the main application of this technique has been to texts, most often to reading passages. Traditionally, the emphasis has been on changing various sentence-bound elements to match the text more closely to the proficiency level of a particular group of learners. Thus, for instance, we can simplify according to:

a) Sentence structure. Sentences are reduced in overall length, or a complex sentence is re-written as a number of simpler ones, for example by the replacement of relative pronouns by nouns and pronouns followed by a main verb.

b) Lexical content, so that the number of new vocabulary items is controlled by reference to what students have already learned.

c) Grammatical structures. For instance, passives are converted to actives; simple past tense to simple present; reported into direct speech.

These kinds of criteria form the basis of many of the published graded 'simplified readers' available for English language teaching.

Simplification has a number of further implications. Firstly, it is possible that any linguistic change, lexical or grammatical, will have a corresponding stylistic effect, and will therefore change the meaning or intention of the original text. This is particularly likely with literary material, of course, but in principle it can apply to any kind of text where the overall 'coherence' can be affected. Widdowson (1979) goes into these arguments in more detail. Secondly, some teaching situations require attention to the simplification of content when the complexity of the subject-matter is regarded as being too advanced. This could be the case for some scientific explanations, for example, or for material too far removed from the learners' own life experiences. Thirdly, simplification can refer not only to content, but also to the ways in which that content is presented: we may decide not to make any changes to the original text, but instead to lead the learners through it in a number of graded stages. We shall come back to this notion of 'task complexity' in the chapters on reading and listening comprehension.

5   *Re-ordering*

This procedure, the final one discussed in this section, refers to the possibility of putting the parts of a coursebook in a different order. This may mean adjusting the sequence of presentation within a unit, or taking units in a different sequence from that originally intended. There are limits, of course, to the scale of what teachers can do, and too many changes could result, unhelpfully, in an almost complete re-working of a coursebook. A re-ordering of material is appropriate in the following kinds of situation:

- Materials typically present 'the future' by 'will' and 'going to'. However, for many learners, certainly at intermediate level and above, it is helpful to show the relationship between time reference and grammatical tense in a more accurate way. In this particular example, we would probably wish to include the simple present and the present continuous as part of the notion of 'futurity', perhaps using 'Next term begins on 9 September' or 'She retires in 1995' as illustrations.

- The length of teaching programme may be too short for the coursebook to be worked through from beginning to end. It is likely in this case that the language needs of the students will determine the sequence in which the material will be taken. There is little point in working systematically through a textbook if key aspects of grammar, vocabulary or communicative function are never reached. For instance, if the learners are adults due to study in the target language environment, it will be necessary to have covered several aspects of the tense system and to have introduced socially appropriate functions and frequently used vocabulary.

- Finally, 're-ordering' can include separating items of content from each other as well as re-grouping them and putting them together. An obvious example is a lesson on a particular language function which is felt to contain too many new grammar points for the present proficiency level of the learners.

A Framework for Adaptation

There are clear areas of overlap among the various techniques discussed in this section, but it would be beyond the scope of this chapter to try to cover all the combinations and permutations. The intention here has been to offer a workable framework into which the main possibilities for adaptation can be fitted (not to offer some 'how to do' recipes, which are well covered elsewhere). Figure 5.1 shows how the considerations on which the principle of adaptation is based fit together.

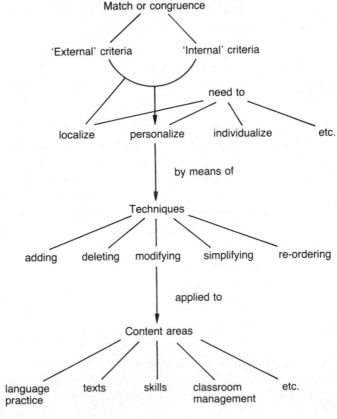

Figure 5.1

Choose some materials with which you are familiar, or any others that you would like to work with. (If you do not have any to hand, look back at the unit re-printed at the end of chapter 2.) Decide on any features of the material that you would like to change because it is not entirely suitable for your own teaching situation. Referring as much as possible to the techniques we have been discussing, draw up some suggestions for how to adapt the material to achieve greater 'congruence'. If possible discuss with other colleagues the reasons for your decisions and your chosen procedures.

Conclusion

At one end of the scale, adaptation is a very practical activity carried out mainly by teachers in order to make their work more relevant to the learners with whom they are in day-to-day contact. It is, however, not just an exercise done in self-contained methodological isolation. Like all our activity as teachers, it is related, directly and indirectly, to a wider range of professional concerns. Adaptation is linked to issues of administration and the whole management of education, insofar as it derives from decisions taken about material to be adopted. Further, the need to adapt is one consequence of the setting of objectives in a particular educational context. Finally, adaptation can only be carried out effectively if it develops from an understanding of the possible design features of syllabuses and materials.

This chapter completes our discussion of the principles on which materials and methods are based. In part 2 we hope to show how some of these principles have been expressed in relation to the concept of language skill.

Further reading

1   Grant, N. (1987): *Making the most of your textbook.*

2   Madsen, K. S. and J. D. Bowen (1978): *Adaptation in Language Teaching.*

Both of these references include a discussion of the principles of adaptation, illustrated by a large number of examples. Grant's book is particularly practical, and focuses on making material developed for the various language skills more communicative.

Part II

Teaching
Language Skills

6   Reading Skills

In part I of this book we examined in detail the issues involved in principles of materials design. In this second part of the book, we devote a chapter to each language skill in turn with a final chapter which examines the concept of integrating language skills in the classroom. The division of each language skill into separate chapters is intentional and is *not* intended to reinforce the notion of the skills being taught in isolation, but rather is a way of devoting sufficient space to each one to further our original intention throughout the whole book – that of linking key principles to instances of actual classroom practice. Cross-referencing (both explicit and implicit) occurs often within this part of the book.

Introduction

We shall begin this chapter by thinking about the different types of material that we read and how these are linked to the purpose that we have in reading. After this, we attempt to show how advances in our conceptual knowledge about the reading process have changed some of our approaches to designing and using materials for the teaching of reading. The final part of the chapter is devoted to looking at different ways of providing feedback to learners on their reading.

As a skill reading is clearly one of the most important; in fact in many instances around the world we may argue that reading is *the* most important foreign language skill, particularly in cases where students have to read English material for their own specialist subject but may never actually have to speak the language; such cases are often referred to as 'English as a library language'. Even though we are looking at each language skill independently in these chapters, there is clearly an overlap between reading and writing, in that a 'text' has to be written down before we can read it. In many societies literature is still seen as the prime example of writing and therefore one of the first things a student is asked to do is to read. In classroom terms one of the reasons for this is partly practical: it is often thought to be easier to supply a written text to be read than a spoken one to be understood. Much of the current thinking on reading tends to focus primarily on the purpose of the activity; even if reading is done for pleasure it is still purposeful.

Williams (1984) usefully classifies reading into (a) getting general information from the text; (b) getting specific information from a text; and (c) for pleasure or for interest.

Think about all the materials that you have read during the last week, both in English and in your own L_1 if it is different. Make a list of them. You may wish to reflect on how your reading of them could be classified according to Williams' categories outlined above. How many of these different types of reading material would you find in your teaching textbook?

The list that you have drawn up may well include a newspaper, letters (personal and formal), booklets, leaflets, advertisements, labels on jars, tins and packets, magazines, the telephone directory, train timetables and so on. However, if this list could be said to be representative of *actual* reading material, ELT materials in some contexts still have virtually none or very little in the way of newspaper articles, labels or advertisements for students to read, but contain many examples of what we might call more 'traditional' types of text, especially longer stretches of narrative and descriptions. We shall look at the implications of this later in the chapter.

Rivers and Temperley (1978: 187) list the following examples of some of the reasons that L_2 students may need or want to read:

- to obtain information for some purpose or because we are curious about some topic

- to obtain instructions on how to perform some task for our work or daily life

- to keep in touch with friends by correspondence or to understand business letters

- to know when or where something will take place or what is available

- to know what is happening or has happened (as reported in newspapers, magazines, reports)

- for enjoyment or excitement

Think about your own students' reading purposes in relation to the ones outlined above. Which ones are similar/different?

Changes in the Concept of Reading Skills

We have looked at some of the purposes and reasons for reading which we may wish to develop with our learners. Let us now look at how the concept of reading as a skill has evolved in recent years and how this in turn has come to be reflected in the types of ELT materials available.

The traditional way of organizing materials in a unit is generally to begin with a piece of specially written material which is then 'read' by the student. Such an arrangement essentially focuses on items of grammar and vocabulary which are then to be developed during the unit. This is clearly inadequate if we are attempting to teach reading skills, as students are not being exposed to the variety of styles that we would expect with a variety of texts – a scientific report is not written in the same way as a personal letter or instructions on a medicine bottle.

Hence, in reading classes we sometimes have a confusion of aims: often the students are not being taught reading and how to develop reading abilities *per se*, but rather a written text is being used as a vehicle for the introduction of new vocabulary and/or structures. It is fairly common for such texts to begin along the following lines:

It is eight o'clock in the morning. Mr Smith is in the dining-room of their house. Mr Smith is sitting at the table reading his newspaper. He is waiting for his breakfast. Mrs Smith is in the kitchen cooking breakfast for Mr Smith, her husband, and their two children. John and Mary . . .

The text would then continue in a similar way.

Clearly, as reading material it seems artificial because the intention is to draw learners' attention to items of structural usage rather than the authentic features which are characteristic of 'real' text, or what makes texts 'hang together'. Many teachers, however, still work with this type of material. In this particular passage the sentences are strung together in isolation with little attempt at coherence. The same structures are repeated several times in a rather contrived way, making the whole text feel awkward and inauthentic. Another problem associated with these specially prepared texts, when it comes to the choice of topic, is that the learners are either presented with over-familiar material which does not focus on what they can bring to the text, or the content is inconsequential for them. No real interaction takes place between writer and reader as the artificiality of the text means that no real message is being communicated. As we shall see later in relation to the overfamiliarity issue, comprehension questions on a text can sometimes be answered without having to look at the text at all! The essential purpose of all reading generally is to get new information and/or for pleasure, not to go over what is known already or what is inconsequential to the reader in the first place.

A good many of the so called 'traditional' reading materials do not really provide learners with useful texts or effective strategies to improve their reading abilities, and if we are to improve the teaching of reading skills then research into the reading process may well be of some use. However, research tends to show that we know more about what skilled readers can do, rather than how they do it with any real degree of certainty.

Traditionally, and this is borne out in many of the materials, the reader was seen as the 'recipient' of information or as an 'empty vessel' who brought nothing to the text. This notion of 'text as object' (figure 6.1) is now frequently discredited in reading circles as readers are not entirely passive.

This 'text as object' viewpoint regards the reader as having nothing to contribute to the reading process as such; the writer provides information for the reader who is seen as an 'empty vessel' which

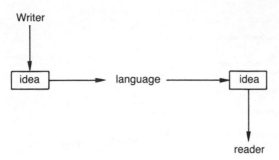

Figure 6.1

merely receives information. We may liken this to a one way traffic system in which everything flows in one direction only.

In recent years, however, an increasing number of ELT materials which profess to develop reading skills have moved from the 'text as object' viewpoint shown above, to that of the 'text as process', by encouraging close interaction between the reader and the text (figure 6.2).

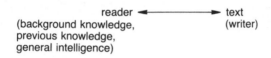

Figure 6.2

Types of Reading Skill

It is generally recognized now that the efficient reader versed in ways of interacting with various types of text, is flexible, and chooses appropriate reading strategies depending on the particular text in question. Pugh (1978) shows how efficient readers 'switch' styles according to the type of text they are reading. We therefore have to match reading skill to reading purpose. We do not, for example, read seventeenth-century poetry in the same way as we read the television page in our newspaper. Skilled readers scan to locate specific information in a text and skim to extract general information from it.

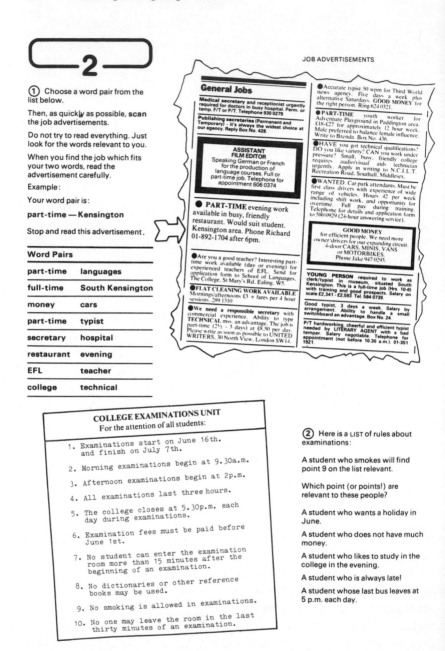

2

① Choose a word pair from the list below.

Then, as quickly as possible, **scan** the job advertisements.

Do not try to read everything. Just look for the words relevant to you.

When you find the job which fits your two words, read the advertisement carefully.

Example:

Your word pair is:

part-time — Kensington

Stop and read this advertisement.

Word Pairs

part-time	languages
full-time	South Kensington
money	cars
part-time	typist
secretary	hospital
restaurant	evening
EFL	teacher
college	technical

JOB ADVERTISEMENTS

General Jobs

Medical secretary and receptionist urgently required for doctors in busy hospital. Perm. or temp. F/T or P/T. Telephone 930 0279

Publishing secretaries (Permanent and Temporary) - it's always the widest choice at our agency. Reply Box No. 428.

ASSISTANT FILM EDITOR
Speaking German or French for the production of language courses. Full or part-time job. Telephone for appointment 606 0374

● **PART-TIME** evening work available in busy, friendly restaurant. Would suit student. Kensington area. Phone Richard 01-892-1704 after 6pm.

● Are you a good teacher? Interesting part-time work available (day or evening) for experienced teachers of EFL. Send for application form to School of Languages, The College, St Mary's Rd, Ealing, W5.

● **FLAT CLEANING WORK AVAILABLE** Mornings/afternoons £3 + fares per 4 hour sessions. 289 1310

● We need a **responsible secretary** with commercial experience. Ability to type part-time (2½ - 3 days) at £8.50 per day. Please write as soon as possible to UNITED WRITERS, 30 North View, London SW14.

● Accurate typist 50 wpm for Third World news agency. Five days a week plus alternative Saturdays. GOOD MONEY for the right person. Ring 624 0321.

● **PART-TIME** youth worker for Adventure Playground in Paddington area. £18-£27 for approximately 12 hour week. Male preferred to balance female influence. Write to Brenda. Box No. 436.

● HAVE you got technical qualifications? DO you like variety? CAN you work under pressure? Small, busy, friendly college requires audio/visual aids technician urgently. Apply in writing to N.C.I.L.T. Recreation Road, Southall, Middlesex.

● WANTED. Car park attendants. Must be first class drivers with experience of wide range of vehicles. Hours 42 per week including shift work, and opportunity for overtime. Full pay during training. Telephone for details and application form to 580 0929 (24-hour answering service).

GOOD MONEY for efficient people. We need more owner/drivers for our expanding circuit. 4-door CARS, MINIS, VANS or MOTORBIKES. Phone Jake 947 0293.

YOUNG PERSON required to work as clerk/typist in museum, situated South Kensington. This is a full-time job (Hrs. 10-6) with training and good prospects. Salary on scale £2,341 - £2,593. Tel. 584 0739

Good typist, 3 days a week. Salary by arrangement. Ability to handle a small switchboard an advantage. Box No. 24.

P/T hardworking, cheerful and efficient typist needed by LITERARY AGENT with a bad temper. Salary negotiable. Telephone for appointment (not before 10.30 a.m.). 01-351 1921.

COLLEGE EXAMINATIONS UNIT
For the attention of all students:

1. Examinations start on June 16th. and finish on July 7th.

2. Morning examinations begin at 9.30a.m.

3. Afternoon examinations begin at 2p.m.

4. All examinations last three hours.

5. The college closes at 5.30p.m. each day during examinations.

6. Examination fees must be paid before June 1st.

7. No student can enter the examination room more than 15 minutes after the beginning of an examination.

8. No dictionaries or other reference books may be used.

9. No smoking is allowed in examinations.

10. No one may leave the room in the last thirty minutes of an examination.

② Here is a LIST of rules about examinations:

A student who smokes will find point 9 on the list relevant.

Which point (or points!) are relevant to these people?

A student who wants a holiday in June.

A student who does not have much money.

A student who likes to study in the college in the evening.

A student who is always late!

A student whose last bus leaves at 5 p.m. each day.

Source: E. Davies and N. Whitney, *Reasons for Reading*, p. 20, copyright Heinemann, 1979.

These skills are quite widely practised in many contemporary ELT reading skills courses at present. The example from a textbook on p. 106 is one of many.

Skimming and scanning are clearly useful strategies for learners to operate; however there is arguably a limit to their usefulness in the context illustrated above, in the sense that the learner scans for particular information and then does not actually have to do anything with it. All that we have mentioned thus far tends to confirm the now generally accepted view that efficient readers are not passive and do not operate in a vacuum; they react with the text by having expectations (even though these might in fact have nothing to do with the content of the text), and ideas about the purpose of the text as well as ideas about possible outcomes.

Efficient readers also interrogate materials of all types by looking for 'clues' in titles, sub-titles and within the passage itself. Pre-reading questions can be useful because they focus learners' attention on the types of information that they are about to read.

Classroom teachers often complain that students view reading as tedious and therefore low priority simply because they do not feel challenged or involved in the text. This can be overcome if they can be encouraged to 'dialogue' with the writer by expecting questions to be answered, reflecting on expectations at every stage, anticipating what the writer will say next, and so on. Efficient readers appear continually to interrogate the text, forming expectations at every stage.

Getting the learner to interact with different types of text as outlined above does not necessarily mean that learners will have to understand the whole text immediately. They may, for example, be able to understand and to extract specific information from the text as in the example on p. 108.

Schema Theory

Another major contribution to our knowledge of reading, with many implications for the classroom, is provided by Schema theory. Bartlett (1932) first used this particular term to explain how the knowledge that we have about the world is organized into interrelated patterns based on our previous knowledge and experience. These 'schemata'

30 Looking Forward

1 Some science fiction writers were recently asked what their predictions were for the 21st Century. The article below is about what one person thinks life will be like.

Life in the 21st Century

As for daily life, I think that we will be able to order most of our shopping by computer and this will be delivered to our homes, so in fact there won't be any need to go out to the shops. I'm sure that most of our homes will have a video telephone so we will be able to see the person we are talking to. We will also be watching 'holovision' which will give you threedimensional life-size pictures on your screen – this will replace television. Because of improved technology, there will be no more road accidents. Cars will be guided by computers so people will not have to do any more driving.

I think most of our food will be in the form of pills and liquids which will have all the vitamins and protein that we need for a balanced diet. Only when we go out for social eating will we eat the same food as today, but we will no longer be eating meat.

About once a year our bodies will go into a health centre for a service in much the same way as a car has to be serviced. So, for example, our veins will be cleaned out, our blood purified, our muscles toned up and so on. Any part that is worn out could be replaced by a new plastic part. We will all be much healthier by then anyway, because there will be more leisure time for us to use for exercise. Also a safe medicine will have been discovered which will allow people to lose or put on weight as they need. One exciting development will be the possiblity of being deep frozen for a period of time and then waking up some years later. I would be interested in that myself!

A lot of our wildlife will be conserved in parks but unfortunately I think we will have lost the rhinoceros, the tiger and the panda and a few other species because of ruthless hunting by man. However, most of our energy problems will have been solved by developments in the use of solar energy and safe nuclear energy.

Because of improved media technology, all cultures will become similar and, indeed, everybody will be speaking an international language (English) by 2020.

There will be more women in politics than men – and the world will be a more peaceful place because of this. In fact, women will also be able to run the Marathon faster than men.

2 Write a list of the points you agree with and another list of the points you disagree with.

Agree	Disagree
Shopping by computer	Videophones in homes

Source: B. Milne, *Integrated Skills: Intermediate*, Unit 10, p. 60, copyright Heinemann, 1991.

also allow us to predict what may happen in a future context. This theory takes our idea of the interactive reading process a stage further by proposing that efficient readers are able to relate 'texts' to their background knowledge of the world. Brown and Yule (1983) provide a comprehensive account of how this background knowledge can guide and influence the comprehension process. Clearly it can sometimes be based on previous knowledge of similar texts. For example, if we are reading a newspaper, we know from previous experience about the typeface, the layout, the order in which the information is presented, and so on. We share cultural background material with others. The word 'wedding' in a British context could engender a complete schematic framework to accompany it; i.e., 'last Saturday', 'Registry Office', 'Best Man' and so on. This is why reading something written by someone in a language with different cultural assumptions can be difficult. Overseas teachers and students sometimes complain that reading literature in an L_2 is problematic not just because of the language, but also because shared assumptions or different schemata do not always match up.

In many cases an efficient reader appears to use what are called 'top-down' and 'bottom-up' strategies. This means that the reader will not just try to decipher the meaning of individual lexical items but will also have clear ideas about the overall rhetorical organization of the text. The essential features of the bottom-up approach are that the reader tries to decode each individual letter encountered by matching it to the minimal units of meaning in the sound system (the phoneme) to arrive at a meaning of the text, whereas with the top-down approach, the interaction process between the reader and the text involves the reader in activating knowledge of the world, plus past experiences, expectations and intuitions, to arrive at a meaning of the text. In other words, the top-down process interacts with the bottom-up process in order to aid comprehension (figure 6.3).

We might further illustrate this by looking at a speaking/listening analogy first of all. If someone asks us 'Have you got a light?' and we get stuck at the level of the bottom-up process by working out each individual word, then clearly we are missing the top-down request, that the speaker is in fact asking for a match.

Let us look at an extract from a newspaper about education in Britain in order to see how some of these principles may operate in reality.

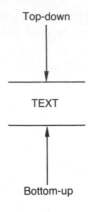

Figure 6.3

From the title, can you predict what the passage will be about? As you are reading the text think about how you are reading it.

Paying to Learn: Is It Snobbery?
The British social system is probably the most snobbish in the world but that does not necessarily mean – since it is perfectly natural for parents to wish to give their children the same or a better education than they themselves received – that those who choose to educate their children privately are all snobs. Thus, many upper class families who were forced to send their children to boarding schools at the height of the British Empire because they were often out of the country for years, naturally wish to continue the tradition, although nowadays it involves great financial sacrifices. Even today many pupils in boarding schools are still opting out of what may be the best state education system in the world. Some of these are obviously doing this for snobbish reasons – believing that to have been educated privately is to be socially 'one-up' and that children thus educated, whatever their ability, will have an advantage over their state educated contemporaries. The less said about this type of parent the better. Fortunately, most parents who choose private education have very good reasons for doing so.

A good start to a child's education is vital and, since the war, classes in many primary schools have been very large so that nervous children or those of average or below average ability could easily get lost in the crowd and miss out on education altogether. This explains the popularity of the small private preparatory school in which a child has more individual attention and help with particular difficulties. Some children of very good ability certainly do not *need* to be educated privately: my own children have all been educated in the state system and have all gone on to higher education.

However, this is a free country and parents who wish to pay for education are perfectly entitled to do so – they could spend their money much less wisely. There are, nonetheless, two great dangers in having a private system running alongside the state system. One is the development of a privileged class, with the result that people get the top jobs not on the basis of ability but of who they are and where they went to school. If this country is to survive, we must educate our best brains to the highest possible standard – irrespective of their social and financial standing. The other is that we shall need a highly skilled and adaptable workforce capable of dealing with the advanced technology of the future and this will require an efficient state system of education possessing all the necessary advanced equipment.

Where did you look on the line; did you skim/scan; did you go backwards/forwards? Did you stop to look at every word; did you stop to think at all?

As teachers we may want to offer our learners one effective reading strategy, which might be to approach this text by noting the title first of all. This clearly points ahead to what the writer will be saying and how the argument develops at various stages in the text itself, when the author is giving approval and disapproval to various types of parent. The reader may also put 'schematic' knowledge into operation: in other words an understanding of the background to the British education system; the state versus private education debate; the British Empire; the class system. This 'top-down' processing would interact with the text as would the 'bottom-up' processing at the lexical level. The reader may also get through the passage by means of what are sometimes referred to as the discourse signposts in the text: expressions such as 'However', 'fortunately', and 'there are, nonetheless', which are meant as a useful guide for the reader.

Implications

It is useful for us as teachers to provide students with a purpose for reading with materials which stimulate their interest and which do not have an over-familiar content. Of all the language skills reading is the most private, and there is a problem in getting feedback on a private process. The notion of privacy in reading can sometimes be related to learner needs; a learner may need material of a different level and topic to other learners in the group which may involve the teacher in the provision of some individualized reading in the programme. Reading practised with reading laboratories and/or self-access centres may well be more pertinent to some learners' needs. (For a full discussion of individualization and self-access systems see chapter 12.) We also have to be able to assess the difficulty of the materials for our own particular learners and to grade them according to familiarity of topic, length and complexity of structure and possible number of unfamiliar words/expressions, as overloading learners with too much may well involve them in decoding vocabulary at the expense of reading for meaning. We can also develop and foster appropriate skills according to reading purpose, for example by encouraging students to read quickly when it is appropriate to do so. Timed activities or 'speed reading' can be related to the private nature of the reading process that we mentioned earlier. In other words, reading quickly with good overall comprehension does not necessarily have to be made competitive with other students as the individual student and/or the teacher can keep a record of how long it takes to extract information from a given source. Consequently, the transferability of principled flexible skills to different types of reading material is one of the most effective things to develop in the reading skills class.

Classroom Practice and Procedure

On a worldwide level, the format of teaching reading skills may well vary according to local circumstances. Many teachers consider dividing reading into intensive, classroom based work with an adjunct extensive reading programme to give further out-of-class practice. Some classes will be called 'reading' and will therefore focus primarily on the development of reading skills. Sometimes teachers include reading skills as part of another class either for reasons of expediency – because there is only one timetabled period for English – or for reasons of principle – because they believe that reading is best integrated with the other skills such as writing.

White (1981) makes some suggestions about the stages and procedure of a reading lesson which may help us (a) to put the skill into a classroom context, and (b) to see some of its possible relationships with the other language skills:

Stage 1   Arouse the students' interest and motivation by linking the topic of the text to their own experience or existing knowledge. Give some pre-reading/focusing questions to help them to do this.

Stage 2   Give them points to search for in the reading text, or ask the students to suggest the points.

Stage 3   After reading, encourage a discussion of answers.

Stage 4   Develop into writing by using the information gained for another purpose.

Look at the reading passage, 'Paying to learn', that we examined above. How could you develop it within the framework outlined above?

Beaumont (1983) has developed a scheme for achieving goals and objectives in a reading lesson which may be summarized as follows:

1   Text structure – how is it linked together, how can we work out unfamiliar words?

2   Text purpose – what is the text for? Who is it written for? What does it do? How does it fulfil its purpose?

3   Reading for information – what are the topic and the main ideas? What are the supporting ideas? How can we distinguish between the main and the supporting ideas?

4   Interpretation – what are the opinions of the writer; how can we tell what the writer feels?

Now let us look at a range of ways for developing reading skills in the classroom and the principles behind each of them:

1   Practising specific strategies such as skimming/scanning with a particular text. The idea behind this is to enable the learner to read and select specific information at the expense of other (redundant) information.

2   One effective way of developing reading skills which gives the learner a reason for reading is to use the information gap principle often associated with communicative language teaching. Some reading materials, such as those devised by Geddes and Sturtridge (1982) use this principle. In these materials, the information required for the completion of a target task is distributed among two or more sources. Each sub-group only has *part* of the information required to complete the task. The sub-groups consequently have to exchange their information so that the information gap is filled and the target task completed. This activity clearly links reading with other forms of communication, eg. speaking/discussion or listening/writing, and can thus provide a reading-driven integration of the language skills.

3   Several of the more recent materials for reading contain what are sometimes referred to as 'text scrambling' activities. The principle behind this type of material is that students can be taught to have an awareness of the discourse or cohesive features of reading materials. If a passage is clearly written then it can be 'scrambled' and reassembled in the correct order if the learner can recognize the discourse patterns and markers in the text.

4   Some reading materials are constructed along the lines that the learners bring not only background knowledge to reading but also emotional (affective) responses as well, and will want to talk about their reactions to various texts. We saw in chapter 3 how O'Neill (1989) in *The Fourth Dimension* discusses ways of developing the notion of 'expressivity' with texts that are designed so as to tease out learner reactions to different passages (talking about themselves, past experiences, health, distant relatives and so on).

Examine your own materials for reading. To what extent do they incorporate these principles – which ones are different?

Decide which type of reading skills you could develop with the following materials. Start with the nature of the text and then look at what kind(s) of skills could come from it.

1)

13 The Uncle I Hardly Knew

Questions

1 What kind of person do you think lives in this room? What do you learn about his or her tastes simply by looking at it?

2 Describe some of the things you think go on in this room at different times of the day.

3 Suppose you could walk around the house or building this room is in. What are some of the other rooms you would find? What do you think you would find in them?

4 Imagine you could design a room like this for your own use. Describe the furniture you would put in it and how you would decorate it.

The person who designed this room and now lives in it has written a short text about the story behind it.
Read it on the next page.

READING

I hardly knew him. But what he did for me has helped to change my life. Perhaps I had better explain.

My name is Bruno Caselli. I was born here in London but my parents both came from Italy. My father died when I was nine. It's strange, you know, but for a time I felt as if he had somehow let me down, as if it were his fault that he had a bad heart. Children can be like that. They often behave as if their parents had only one purpose in life, and that was to be their mothers and fathers. They don't see them as real people.

I'm an only child. My mother and I were very poor for a time. She had a brother, who lived in Australia. His name was Eduardo. Uncle Eduardo came to London several times to see us. He was very fond of me and took me for walks in Hyde Park. But Australia is a long way away and we didn't see very much of him.

I went to Art School when I was eighteen but what I really wanted to study was architecture. However, it is a difficult profession to get into, and requires long training. I worked for a time as a technical illustrator but didn't make very much money from it. I even did office work for a time. When I got up to go to work in the mornings, I felt as if I were going to prison. That's how much I hated it.

One day, nine years ago, when I was twenty-two, I got a letter from a lawyer in Australia. He told me that Uncle Eduardo had died and that he had some other important news for me. He refused to say what it was until he came to London personally to see me. We met in a hotel in London a few weeks later. The news was that Uncle Eduardo had made quite a lot of money in Australia and had left it all to me. I could hardly believe it. I felt like jumping up and down for joy. But I didn't, of course.

I gave part of the money to my mother. I used the rest to study architecture and then to start my own business. I specialise in converting old factories and warehouses into living accommodation. The room in the photo opposite is an example. There's plenty of space and light. Even on a dull day you don't get the impression that the room is dark and gloomy. The business is doing well. I have lots of contracts. But none of this would have been possible if it hadn't been for Eduardo, the uncle I hardly knew.

Explain and describe

1 Which of these adjectives do you think best describes how Bruno felt when his father died?

a sad
b sad and angry
c confused
d desperate

2 Now explain why you chose the adjective that you did.

3 Explain why Bruno says he 'hardly knew' his Uncle Eduardo.

4 Describe the various things Bruno did between the ages of 18 and 22.

5 Describe how he felt when the lawyer told him about his Uncle Eduardo.

6 Explain how his life has changed since that day.

Discussion and interpretation

1 Can you imagine the exact words of the letter from the lawyer in Australia? This is the way it began.

> *Dear Mr Caselli,*
> *I am writing to you on behalf of your uncle, Mr Eduardo Gatto, who died in Sydney in December of last year.*

The rest of the letter was fairly short. What do you think it said?

2 What do you think
a the lawyer actually said to Bruno when they met in the hotel in London?
b Bruno said to the lawyer when he had given him the news?

3 Discuss what you would do if you had just inherited a very large sum of money (say $1 million) from a relative. Find out what others in your class would do, as well.

Source: R. O'Neill and P. Mugglestone, *Fourth Dimension*, pp. 104–5, copyright Longman, 1989.

Unit 2 A Treasure Hunt

Stage 1 Introduction

Part 1 People have always dreamed of finding buried treasure. It is not only the hope of finding gold and precious stones which excites them but the search itself – following the clues and piecing together the information. Some people seem to enjoy hiding treasure as much as others enjoy seeking it.

Read the newspaper report. What did the millionaire bury? Did he leave any clues?

Eccentric Millionaire Buries Treasure

It was confirmed by lawyers yesterday that eccentric millionaire Harry Evans who died last month had buried the priceless Hadley jewel. They said that Mr Evans, who had no family himself, felt that the jewel from his private collection should go to 'someone who wanted it enough to search for it'. He left a number of verses as clues to the whereabouts of the buried treasure. The Hadley jewel consists of a gold chain and pendant which contains two miniature portraits. Apparently Mr Evans buried the piece in a water-proof container somewhere beyond the range of metal detectors.

Experts yesterday described the piece as 'unique' and expressed anxiety for its safety.

Just watch these 'sm...

Part 2 Below is an entry from an exhibition catalogue describing the jewel. Why is it called the Hadley jewel?

Chain and pendant (The Hadley Jewel)   *Cat. no. 157*

Gold and enamelled in black, white, pale blue and red. Set with table-cut rubies, emeralds and pearls.

Height: 6.8 cm.

Condition: the gold suspension ring on the chain is not original and the replacement is 18th century.

History: the Hadley Jewel is so called because it was given as a marriage gift to Catherine Linton on the occasion of her wedding to John Hadley in 1580. It belonged to the Hadley family from Elizabethan times until the twentieth century. The gold miniature case contains portraits of a man and a woman. The lid has floral decorations set into the gold and the whole case is surrounded by a broad band set with gems. Three large irregular pearls hang at the base of the pendant.

Stage 2 Jigsaw Reading Tasks

Read the texts for your group (Group 1 p. 29, Group 2 p. 39, Group 3 p. 49):

1 You have only *some* of the clues that Harry Evans left – read yours carefully!

2 Name as many things as you can on the map.

3 In the table below make short notes about the buildings and monuments you have marked on the map.

Building or monument	Date	What it looks like

Stage 3 Discussion

1 Find out what the other two groups have named on their maps.

2 Which buildings and monuments have they found out about?

3 Put all your clues together, making sure you begin with the first clue.

4 Mark on the map the exact place where the Hadley Jewel is buried.

5 What happens in your country when someone finds buried treasure?

Unit 2 A Treasure Hunt

Harry Evans buried the Hadley Jewel somewhere in the Ashton-Hadley Hall area.
Here are some of the clues he left:

> Whether it rains or whether it shines
> These are the last of the precious lines.
>
> Now you must look for the leaves of the vine
> Because what you are seeking is buried under time.

Here is an extract from *A Guide to Country Walks.*

Walk 2: Ashton and Hadley Hall (3 miles)

The visitor can leave his car at Ashton picnic area
where there are car parking and toilet facilities as well
as wooden tables and benches enabling people to
picnic in comfort. He can then follow the rough path
south and past the ruins of an old castle on his right.
This is known as Alfred's castle and is said to have
belonged to the old king. The grassy hill commands a
fine view of the valley below. Little remains of the
castle now because the stone was taken to build the
stately house set in the magnificent park that can be
seen in the village to the south west. This is Hadley
Hall, built about 1690 for the Earl of Swinley.

Hadley Hall may well surprise the visitor as it seems
somewhat out of place in this wild landscape. It is
indeed elegant and has such proportions that it has
been described as a perfect doll's house. Indeed it
looks as if some giant's hand has dropped this doll's
house into the park. It stands with its west facade
looking onto the river while the east faces the village.
The visitor can continue on this path, passing on his left
the curious Black Mouse stone, and then down into
the village emerging between cottages in the village
street. Refreshments can be had at the local inn, the
Black Lion, a delightful black and white Elizabethan
building dated 1590.

Return to Ashton car park by the main road or
retrace your footsteps along the path.

2) Unit 2 A Treasure Hunt

Harry Evans buried the Hadley Jewel somewhere in the Emm Valley area. Here are some of the clues he left:

> Whether it rains or whether it shines
> This is the middle of the precious lines.
>
> If you come early or if you come late,
> Go under the three birds that sit on the gate.

Here is an extract from *A Visitor's Guide to the Emm Valley:*

If you want to see a really beautiful village you must not miss Harbury. As you enter the village on the B3300 road you see first the village pond which lies beside the old church of St Mary. Shaded with willow trees, the quiet water reflects the church tower as ducks and moorhens swim at their leisure. Opposite the church is one of the finest Elizabethan inns in the country where the tired traveller will find good company as well as refreshment. The inn is built on a far older site as there was originally a hospice there, run by monks and offering food and shelter to pilgrims on their way to Canterbury. Don't miss the remains of the monastic garden which reaches down to the river. This walled garden is now preserved by the villagers as part of the national heritage and is a pleasant place to sit a while. If the sun is shining you can check your watch with the time shown by the old sundial in the centre of the garden. Made in local stone in 1760 the top of the sundial has a fine brass plate where the hours are clearly written and the surrounding metal is decorated with grapes and vine leaves. Delightful though this tranquil scene is, you should press on to see what is perhaps the highlight of the village, the Earl of Swinley's stately home.

Unit 2 A Treasure Hunt

Harry Evans buried the Hadley Jewel somewhere in or near the village of Harbury.
Here are some of the clues he left:

```
Whether it rains or whether it shines
These are the first of the precious lines.

If you are short or if you are tall
From Alfred's hill you can see it all.

Walk quickly south past the old doll's house,
Seek a black lion, not a black mouse.
```

Here is an extract from *The Country Lover's Guide to Villages:*

The River Emm winds its way through the charming village of Harbury, which is well worth a visit. Harbury has more than its fair share of places of historical interest: a stately home, a fine church and a village pub which would look well in any photograph. However, perhaps the oldest building in the village is in some ways the most interesting. As you come into Harbury from the south, the village pond is on your right and a little further on to your left you will see some high walls and a splendid old gateway built straight onto the village street. This is all that remains of the old abbey and the walls enclose a beautiful walled flower garden. The garden and the walls adjoin the old village inn and the walls run round the corner down a narrow land and north-west to the river. The gateway itself has been dated at about 1295 although the walls may be earlier. The visitor who looks up will see an interesting stone carving of a shield above the arch of the gate. On the shield can be seen three birds beautifully carved in white stone. Nothing is left of the abbey itself.

Source: M. Geddes and G. Sturtridge, *Reading Links*, Unit 2, copyright Heinemann, 1982.

3)

SORRY DARLING BUT I DO THINK IT'S SAFER

by Catherine Bennett

Nightmares that end up in death

Fortunately, an occurrence strong enough to lead to an attack is very rare. Oswald considers it would be irresponsible either to over publicise the phenomenon – "in case people get ideas" – or to suggest that spouses should live in fear of their partners.

However, Professor Ian Oswald, a psychiatrist at Edinburgh university who recently wrote a paper about night terror – in which a nightmare moves into physical action – cites it as a form of behaviour "as old as mankind".

Women's groups yesterday described it as a "charter to kill".

"Acquittals like this have been going on for hundreds of years,", he said yesterday. The first recorded in Britain was in the 1600s when a soldier in the grip of night terror killed his colonel. He was cleared on the grounds that when a man is asleep he cannot form the intent essential to a conviction.

THE acquittal last week of Colin Kemp, a 34-year-old salesman, for the murder of his wife, on the grounds that he strangled her during a nightmare, has caused a sensation after being described by Judge Thomas Pigot as "an extraordinary and difficult case".

"It's not the same thing as a nightmare," explained Oswald. "Night terrors are generally phenomena of the early night, arising during very deep, slow-wave sleep. Nightmares occur much later in the night and are phenomena of rapid eye movements when the body is paralysed."

Despite this precedent, Kemp's case is uncommon as he claims to have remembered his dream, in which he was being attacked by two Japanese soldiers. Sufferers from night terror do not normally recall the thoughts which led to physical action.

The reasons for night terror remain a mystery. But certain patterns have been discovered. The propensity often runs in families: It can be related to drugs which act on the central nervous system and is often followed by sleep-walking.

Source: Nightmares that end up in death, copyright Times Newspapers Ltd

Feedback to Learners

Earlier in the chapter we mentioned that reading is essentially a private activity. However, it remains a fact that as we 'teach' reading skills in the classroom this often requires us to have some sort of observable (testable) outcome. In its most extreme form this may actually be embodied in the materials themselves, which sometimes do little more than test the students rather than helping them to develop different, relevant reading skills.

Questions to learners can be either in written or spoken form and it is generally thought that a balance of the two is appropriate for most learning situations.

One way of thinking about reading comprehension questions is to consider the *form* of the question; for example, yes/no; true or false; multiple choice; non-verbal matrix to be completed; open ended question and the type of question; what the question is actually trying to get out of the reader.

Nuttall (1982) identifies five basic question types which are commonly used for reading. The first of these is literal comprehension. By this she means that if readers do not understand the literal meaning of a particular text, then they are probably not going to get very much else out of that text. The second is reorganizing or putting the information in the text into a different order. Then come questions of inferring or 'reading between the lines'. Writers do not always state explicitly what they mean. An efficient reader can infer meaning which is not explicitly stated in the passage. This may be seen as an intellectual skill as opposed to a reading skill by some, although there is clearly a measure of overlap. Question types requiring a measure of personal response are often to be found in literary passages where the reader has to argue for a particular personal response supported by reference to the text. The last type of question is quite sophisticated and not all students would need it. Questions of evaluation would require the reader to assess how effectively the writer has conveyed her intention. If the writing is intended to convince or to persuade, how convincing or persuasive is it?

When evaluating questions for use with particular learners there may not be enough of the right type or form to match their purpose or what the teacher knows about their personal background. Generally speaking, a variety of different question forms and types which enable learners to use their different reading skills in appropriate ways is of most use.

Look at the following question which accompanies the passage entitled 'Paying to learn' on p. 110. What form and type of question is it according to Nuttall's classification outlined above?

'Complete the following chart with reasons why parents send their children to private schools and state whether the author considers each reason valid or not.'

Reason   *Valid? Yes/No*

1. _____

2. _____

3. _____

4. _____

Asking questions of the learner is not the only way to check comprehension. It is increasingly common to find materials which require the learner to extract meaning from them and then to use that information in order to do something else – such as jigsaw reading or assembling an object from a set of instructions. Successful reading thus enables a certain task to be completed. In many respects this is more akin to what most people do in their L_1 or in the 'real' world; it is rare for people to have to answer questions on what they have read.

Conclusion

We began this chapter by examining some of the reasons why we read as well as the types of material that we might typically read in our daily lives. We then considered how our understanding of the reading process and how changes in the concept of reading skills have affected approaches to the design of materials for the teaching of reading, particularly the insights offered by Schema theory. We then looked at these implications for classroom practice and procedure and discussed a range of approaches and materials which currently feature in reading classrooms. Finally, we looked at some of the different ways available to teachers for providing feedback to learners on their reading.

In what ways might your approaches to the teaching of reading be modified as a result of this chapter?

Further reading

The following books provide a useful insight into the area:

1   Carrell, F., et al. (eds.) (1988): *Interactive Approaches to Second Language Reading* gives a more theoretical overview, whereas the other titles listed here offer background discussion with a practical perspective.

2   Grellet, F. (1981): *Developing Reading Skills.*

3   Nuttall, C. (1982): *Teaching Reading Skills in a Foreign Language.*

4   Williams, E. (1984): *Reading in the Language Classroom.*

7   Listening skills

Introduction

The previous chapter has pointed us in the direction of several themes, both of principle and practice, that will be relevant for the consideration of listening skills to which we now turn. Most obviously, we are dealing with the other key skill under the heading of 'comprehension', and it is simple commonsense to assume that reading and listening will share a number of underlying characteristics. The language teaching world turned its attention to listening rather later than it did to reading comprehension. This was due in part to the relevance of quite a large body of research on reading: more importantly, the 'library language' perspective was significant in English language classrooms long before a shrinking world and increased international inter-dependence led to a greater focus on face-to-face language skills. Even now, however, many learners do not have much opportunity to interact with native speakers, let alone travel to English-speaking countries, so this time-lag in the attention given to the different skills is readily understandable.

This chapter will first briefly consider the similarities between reading and listening comprehension, and the ways in which they differ. We shall then examine the nature of listening as a skill and the features of the spoken language to which the skill is applied. Implications for the classroom will be looked at in detail, together with an exploration of how teaching materials reflect the current state of knowledge. As with reading, we shall concentrate somewhat artificially on listening as an individual, discrete skill (although it should be evident that the chapter both looks back to reading and ahead to speaking skills). It is important to be able to pick out the key characteristics of a particular skill, and the integration of skills is to be given explicit treatment in the final chapter of this part of the book.

Reasons for Listening

Pause for a moment and jot down the kinds of things you have listened to in the last few days, both in English and in your own L_1 if it is different.

The authors' own list is set out here in the order in which the items came to mind:

- Listening to the radio: news, a play, Parliament, a comedy programme (sometimes on a car radio)
- Conversations with neighbours, colleagues, friends
- Answering the telephone at home and at work
- Overhearing other people talking to each other: on a bus, in the office
- Attending a lecture
- Listening to arrival and departure announcements at the railway station
- Watching TV
- Listening to a list of names being read out at a prize-giving
- While working in the library, trying *not* to listen to other people talking.

(You might like to compare your list and ours with the ones offered by Underwood (1989: ch. 1) or Ur (1984: ch. 1) for example.)

There are several points that we might notice here and that will recur in the course of this chapter. Firstly, there is great range and variety in the type of 'input' – in length or topic, for example. Secondly, in some situations we are listeners only, in others our listening skills form just a part of a whole interaction, and an ability to respond appropriately is equally important. Thirdly, there are different purposes involved (to get information, to socialize, to be entertained and so on), so the degree of attention given and possibly the strategies used will differ. A related point is whether we are listening in a face-to-face situation, or through another medium such as the radio or a station intercom system: in some cases, there will be a certain amount of interference or background noise that may affect our ability to process what is being said. A fifth factor is to consider the people involved in any particular listening context – how many of them, their roles, and our relationship with them. Finally, we should note that in many situations there is a visual element which gives important clues beyond the words actually used.

The Relationship Between Listening and Reading

It is useful now to highlight some of the ways in which reading and listening comprehension are both related and different. This short section will therefore act as a bridge, linking our earlier consideration of reading with a framework for thinking about listening skills.

What do reading and listening have in common?

We have seen that the traditional labelling of reading as a 'passive' skill is both misleading and incorrect: this is now well recognized as being equally so for listening. Like the reader, the listener is involved, for instance, in guessing, anticipating, checking, interpreting, interacting and organizing. Rost (1990) even sees the listener in certain circumstances as 'co-authoring' the discourse, not just waiting to be talked to and respond, but actually by his responses helping to construct it. These are all active verb forms, indicating what people do and not what is done to them. An exception, of course, is when we choose to 'switch off' and pay no attention to what is being said to us, in which case we have decided not to engage our capacity. In other words, we can make the following distinctions, with their reading skill parallels:

Attention	*Recognition*
Listening	Hearing
Reading	Seeing

So just as we might see an object but either not recognize it or regard it as significant, so we can distinguish 'Can you *hear* that man?' from '*Listen* to what he's saying'.

What human beings seem to have, then, is a general processing capacity which enables them to deal with written and spoken input using comparable cognitive strategies. (See, for example, Anderson and Lynch, 1988, for further discussion of this point.) The nature of the processing mechanism for listening comprehension, and how it interacts with what is being listened to, will be discussed a little later. We shall also examine some of the potential difficulties for learners of English: just because a general capacity can be identified does not necessarily mean that the two skills can be activated and 'learnt' equally easily. First of all, we shall look at the most obvious differences between reading and listening.

How do they differ?

The clearest way of distinguishing between listening and reading is to think of the medium itself, and the nature of the language used. The next chapter will be concerned in detail with features of the spoken language, but we can introduce some of them here because they affect the listener's – and especially the learner's – ability to understand:

- The medium is sound, and not print. This self-evident statement has a number of implications. We are dealing, for example, with a transient and 'ephemeral' phenomenon which cannot be recaptured once it has passed (unless it is recorded, or we ask for repetition).

- A listening context often contains visual clues, such as gesture, which generally support the spoken words. More negatively, there can also be extraneous noise, such as traffic, or other people talking, which interferes with message reception.

- Information presented in speech tends to be less densely packed than it is on the page, and it may also be more repetitive.

- There is evidence to show that the spoken language is often less complex in its grammatical and discourse structure. At the same time, however, much speech gives a 'broken' impression, with new starts in mid-sentence, changes of direction or topic, hesitation and half-finished statements. This is obviously more true of informal than of formal speech. (Brown and Yule (1983a) contains a full discussion of the features of spoken English, and is referred to at greater length in the next chapter, on speaking skills.)

These are significant distinctions, which were often blurred in traditional language teaching materials that took the written medium to be necessarily dominant. More recent materials claim to be sensitive both to the skill itself and to the spoken medium. Here are some typical instructions for types of activities and exercises taken from two Listening Comprehension courses that are fairly widely used (*Listeners* and *Intermediate Listening*):

Listening for Gist
You will hear 10 people talking. Listen and write down what you think their jobs are, and one word which helped you decide.

Predicting What People Will Say Next
Listen to the people talking ... and say if the statements written below are suitable ways of continuing what was said ...

Guessing About the Speaker
... try to identify the situation which is taking place, and who is speaking (this requires the completion of a table).

Listening for Specific Information

Fill In a Column with Your Own Ideas (about what 'an Englishman' looks like) *THEN COMPARE YOUR IDEAS WITH WHAT YOU HEAR ON THE TAPE.*

Tick the Words that you Hear

Fill In the Gaps for the Missing Words

Make Notes on What the 2 People on the Tape Say ...

Notice in particular that many of the tasks are based on what people do when they listen – on the active processing of meaning that we commented on a little earlier in relation to both reading and listening comprehension. This may be listening to get the general idea, listening to catch something specific, or anticipating what comes next. Again, although actual content is clearly important, several of the tasks use tables and other ways of recording information, rather than just requiring a (written) full-sentence answer.

We shall now turn to a more detailed consideration of the skill of listening, and to its pedagogic implications.

The Nature of Listening Comprehension

Product and process

Implicit in what has been said so far is the distinction, already made in chapter 6, between the twin concepts of 'product' and 'process'. This distinction has become an important one for all language skills, particularly those labelled 'receptive', and it signals an increasing recognition that language as a fixed system, a 'finished product', is just one part of the picture. It has been a major characteristic of language teaching methodology in the 1980s and early 1990s that much more attention is paid to human beings as language processors than was previously the case, when 'texts' (whether written or spoken) were presented as objects to be understood. It is arguably with the skill of listening that a 'processing' focus is most crucial, given the transient nature of the language material compared with the relative stability of written texts. Later in this chapter we shall look at how process considerations might come together in different ways for different kinds of learners. For the moment, let us review the nature of the product, and then ask ourselves what proficient listeners actually do.

We have already noted some of the features of authentic spoken language. It varies, for example, in degrees of formality, in length, in the speed of delivery, in the accent of the speaker, in the role of the listener, and according to whether it is face-to-face or mediated in some way. A number of writers (for instance Brown and Yule, 1983a) make a basic distinction between 'transactional' speech, with one-way information flow from one speaker to another, as in a lecture or a news broadcast, and two-way 'interactional' speech. Rost (1990) makes an important point in relation to the latter: he refers to it as 'collaborative' and argues that, in such a setting, where we are both listener and speaker, the 'product' cannot be entirely fixed, because we have a part to play in shaping and controlling the direction in which it moves.

1 If you overheard the following while you were out shopping, how would you interpret it, and what else would you want to hear in order to be able to interpret these words?
 'Really? I didn't know that. How long has she been there?'
And what would be happening if the shop assistant said to you:
 'Five?'

2 Look back at the list you made earlier of the kinds of things you have listened to recently. Take any one of them, and ask yourself how you came to understand what was being said. For example, what aspects do you think you concentrated on? It might have been on the vocabulary, or the speaker's intonation, or some visual element, for instance. Did you understand everything and, if not, what interfered with 'perfect' comprehension?

How do you think your own learners would have managed listening to the same thing in English?

Listening skills

As a proficient listener, you will obviously not have achieved understanding in any of these illustrative situations by simply 'hearing' the sound: you will have been actively processing this stream of noise on a number of levels which, taken together, make up the concept of 'comprehension'. Let us now look at each of these levels in turn. The first two see the listener as a processor of language, and require a consideration of the micro-skills – the various components of this processing mechanism.

a) Processing sound   Full understanding, we have noted, cannot come from the sound source alone, but equally obviously, it cannot take place without some processing of what one student of our acquaintance has called a 'word soup'. At its most basic, a language which is completely unknown to us will sound to our ears like a stream of sound.

Assuming, however, that listeners can identify which language is actually being spoken, then they must have the capacity to do at least the following:

- Segment the stream of sound and recognize word boundaries. This is complicated in English because of the phenomenon whereby, in connected speech, one sound runs into the next. For example, 'I like it' actually sounds like /ai'laikit/ ('I li kit'), 'my name's Ann' like /maineimzæn/ ('My name zan') and so on.

- Recognize contracted forms. 'I'd have gone to London if I'd known about it' sounds very different from its 'full' printed form in many grammar book examples.

- Recognize the vocabulary actually being used.

- Recognize sentence and clause boundaries in speech.

- Recognize stress patterns and speech rhythm. English sentence stress is fairly regular, and tends to fall on the main information-carrying items (nouns, main verbs, adjectives and adverbs) rather than on articles, pronouns, conjunctions, auxiliaries and so on. Thus 'I went to the town and had lunch with a friend' gives a standard mix of 'strong' forms (marked with stress) and 'weak' forms (and, a) where the sound is often reduced to /ə/. We shall comment later on the language learning difficulties that this can cause. Stress patterns can also be systematically varied, to accommodate a particular, intended meaning by the speaker. For example, 'I waś there' (no weak form) carries a tone of insistence; 'Whát did he say?' perhaps suggests surprise or disbelief.

- Recognize stress on longer words, and the effect on the rest of the word. Think of the sound of 'comfortable' or 'interesting', for instance.

- Recognize the significance of language-related ('paralinguistic') features, most obviously intonation. Falling intonation, for example, may indicate the end of a statement; a rise, that an utterance has not yet been completed and the speaker intends to carry on.

● Recognize changes in pitch, tone and speed of delivery.

None of the micro-skills of listening are used in isolation, of course, and those listed so far merge into the second major processing category, the processing of meaning.

b) Processing meaning   If you think back to something you listened to earlier today, perhaps a news item that you found particularly interesting, it is extremely unlikely that you will be able to remember any of the sentence patterns, or much more than the vocabulary generally associated with the subject-matter. You will, however, be able to recall in some sense what it was 'about'. (We are not referring here to a stretch of language learned 'by heart', such as a poem.) Research on listening has shown that syntax is lost to memory within a very short time, even a few seconds, whereas meaning is retained for much longer. Richards (1985: 191) comments that 'memory works with propositions, not with sentences', and Underwood (1989) draws a familiar distinction between 'echoic' memory (about one second), 'short-term' memory (a few seconds) and 'long-term' memory. What listeners appear to be able to do here is:

● Organize the incoming speech into meaningful sections. This involves the ability to use linguistic clues to identify discourse boundaries. For example, a person giving a talk may signal a new point by explicit markers such as 'Next' or 'My 3rd point' or 'However'; alternatively, a change in direction or topic may be indicated by intonation, or pauses. Related to this is the use of cohesive clues to establish links between different parts of a spoken 'text'. Brown and Yule (1983a) refer to this linguistic context as the 'co-text'.

● Identify redundant material. Speakers often repeat what they say, either directly or by making the same point in different words. Efficient listeners know how to turn this into a strategy to gain extra processing time to help organize what they hear.

● Think ahead, and use language data to anticipate what a speaker may be going on to say. For instance, a lecturer who says 'So much for the advantages' is obviously going on to talk about disadvantages; a change in intonation may mark a functional shift in a conversation, perhaps from an explanation to an enquiry.

- Store information in the memory and know how to retrieve it later, by organizing meaning as efficiently as possible and avoiding too much attention to immediate detail.

We can now summarize the discussion so far. The strategies used for processing meaning are not themselves merely skills of recognition. Although they depend on an ability to recognize key aspects of the sound system, they require the listener to combine, interpret and make sense of the incoming language data.

Finally, processing skills are often discussed under two related headings, which are tabulated below (the equivalences are not exact, but they capture the points made in this section):

Processing sound	Processing meaning
Phonological	Semantic
Lower-order/automatic skills	Higher-order skills of organizing and interpreting
Recognition of sounds, words	Comprehension
Localized: the immediate text	Global: the meaning of the whole
Decoding what was said	Re-construction after processing meaning
Perception	Cognition

In the spirit of the introductory remarks in this chapter and the previous one, the two sets of micro-skills just discussed certainly view the listener as 'active'. However, taken alone they might imply that listening is an internal processing mechanism, a cognitive device disembodied from everyday life. This is clearly not the case, and as social beings we are equipped with other kinds of capacities, which can be thought of as (i) sensitivity to context and (ii) knowledge. Both are to do with the way in which expectations are set up by the non-linguistic environment. For convenience we shall take them together.

c) Context and knowledge Most statements, taken out of context, are open to a number of interpretations (and incidentally offer a rich source of humour). A simple 'I spoke to him yesterday' may indicate a justification, doubt, a proof that the other person was where he was supposed to be, straightforward information, a statement on which further action will be based, and so on. Its meaning will usually be clear and unambiguous from the context in which it was said. 'Context' here is taken to cover: physical setting (home, office, school, etc.), the number of listeners/speakers, their roles, and their relationship to each other. Rost refers to this as 'pragmatic context', distinguishing it from syntactic and semantic. He is critical of the information-processing model of comprehension where the listener is seen as 'a language processor who performs actions in a fixed order, independently of contextual constraints' (1990: 7). He pushes the significance of the social context further in an interesting discussion of 'collaborative' or 'interactional' speech (see also chapter 8 of this book). His point, essentially, is that the listener interprets what is being said, constructs a meaning, and responds on the basis of that interpretation. The listener is therefore a key figure in the shaping of the whole interaction: in this view, the listening context is open-ended, likely to change direction, and not fixed in advance. (Readers who wish to pursue this further are directed to chapter 3 of Rost's book.)

   Finally we turn to the knowledge that listeners bring to a listening experience. This may be knowledge of a topic, or a set of facts. A student following a course in (say) computing, will gradually accumulate a body of information and technical vocabulary to which he can 'refer' in each new class or lecture; if my neighbour has a new grandchild and comes to tell me about it, then I have some idea of the direction the conversation will take. Previous knowledge is not necessarily as detailed as in these examples. Schema theory, as we saw in chapter 6, has shown that we are equipped with pre-organized knowledge of many kinds. It may be that we simply have a set of general expectations when entering a listening situation. If we switch on the TV news, we can probably anticipate both its format and the kind of topic that will occur; if we go to a children's tea party, we expect certain behaviour patterns, and are unlikely to hear a discussion on nuclear physics. These frames of reference are also social and cultural. As members of a particular culture, we have learned the rules of conversational behaviour, and specific topics 'trigger' specific ideas and images.

   Listening comprehension, then, is not only a function of the interplay between language on the one hand and what the brain does with it on the other: it also requires the activation of contextual information and previous knowledge. At this point you might like to think back to the tasks early in this section, and look at your comments in the light of the present discussion. There is no 'right answer', except to tell you that when the shop assistant said 'Five?', she knew that I always bought a certain kind of bread roll and a certain number. Her one-word query was enough to trigger the frame of reference for both of us, and a simple 'Yes please' was all that was required.

Many of these points are explicitly acknowledged in materials for the teaching of listening. In the Introduction to *Intermediate Listening*, for example, which we quoted earlier, the writer makes the following points:

- We sometimes have an idea of what we are going to hear

- We listen for a variety of reasons

- Important information-carrying words are normally pronounced with more stress

- In face-to-face interaction, gestures and expression are important, as well as the actual words used

- Natural speech is characterized by hesitation, repetition, rephrasing and self-correction (Brewster, 1991: 2)

Listening Comprehension: Teaching and Learning

Before reading on, consider your own situation. To what extent do any of the materials you use to teach listening take into account the components we have been discussing? How might the various components of listening comprehension help your learners to listen more effectively?

In a competent listener, the micro-skills we have been surveying are engaged automatically. Language learners, however articulate in their L_1, are confronted with a rich and complex medium, a daunting array of skills, and a foreign language. We shall first comment briefly on the kinds of difficulties that learners typically experience in relation to what proficient listeners appear to do. We shall then raise some issues about the application of the discussion so far to the classroom environment. Finally in this section, we shall explore the ways in which teaching materials have developed in line with an increased understanding of the nature of the skill.

Learners

There is, of course, no such person as the 'typical learner'. Learners are at various stages of proficiency, and they differ across a range of characteristics – age, interests, learning styles, aptitude, motivation and so on. The only claim that can be made is that learners, by definition, are not fully competent listeners in the target language. We can suggest, in other words, that they will be operating somewhere on a scale of approximation to full proficiency. With this in mind, several general observations can be made which at the same time are not true of all learners everywhere.

Firstly, it seems that there is a tendency to focus on features of sound at the expense of 'co-text' – the surrounding linguistic environment. For example, in 'The East German government has resigned. Leaders are meeting to discuss the growing unrest in the country', the learner heard 'rest' and did not notice the prefix, despite the clear implication of national instability coming from the passage. A second, related point is that previous knowledge and/or context may be largely ignored in the interests of a mishearing. One student, rather improbably, claimed to have heard 'fish and chips' in a talk on telecommunications. This kind of listening error can be difficult to separate, thirdly, from mishearings caused by using an inappropriate frame of reference: another student, possibly thinking of a sadly familiar problem in her own country, heard 'plastic bullets' for 'postal ballots' in a text that was explicitly about electoral procedure. Fourthly, there is sometimes a reluctance to engage other levels of the listening skill to compensate for not understanding a particular stretch of language. For example, a learner may be unwilling to take risks by guessing, or anticipating, or establishing a framework for understanding without worrying about details, perhaps by using, in Rost's terms, 'points of transition relevance' (1990: 100). The most frequently quoted example here is that of a teacher beginning a lesson by saying 'First of all . . .'. If this is not processed phonologically, learners often do not understand at all, or sometimes suppose that a holiday is being announced, having heard 'festival'. Either way, the lesson cannot proceed until the misunderstanding is cleared up.

Underwood (1989) looks at the same points from another angle, and suggests that potential problems arise for seven main reasons:

1   The learner–listener cannot control speed of delivery
2   He/she cannot always get things repeated
3   He/she has a limited vocabulary
4   He/she may fail to recognize 'signals'
5   He/she may lack contextual knowledge
6   It can be difficult to concentrate in a foreign language
7   The learner may have established certain learning habits, such as a wish to understand every word

What all this amounts to is that learners sometimes 'hear' rather than 'listen'. They appear to suspend their own mother tongue skills which would allow them to approach a listening task as a multi-level process. Instead there is a marked tendency to depend too much on the lower-order skills, leading to attempts at phonological decoding rather than attention to the wider message.

Classroom applications: some issues

How, then, can the points that have been made in this chapter be reflected, directly or indirectly, in the classroom? Every classroom has its own set of objectives and its own 'climate' and patterns of relationships, all within a specific educational environment. It is therefore not surprising if the principles of language and language processing are taken only variably into account. We might imagine the classroom as a filter for some of the following issues, which are set out as questions to consider for your own situation rather than as a 'recipe book' of ready answers. The section on materials will refer to these points again.

• Research into listening comprehension has shown that we are dealing with a complex skill. At the same time, our job is to teach *language*. What is a suitable balance for the classroom between 'tasks' (the skill) and 'text' (the language material)?

- How closely should the classroom attempt to replicate authentic language and authentic listening tasks? As we have seen, a real-life listening experience is very complex and is unlikely to transfer easily to the classroom, except perhaps with very advanced learners. Rixon (1986) makes a useful distinction between the difficulties associated with full authenticity, and the need to preserve the 'naturalness' of the spoken language – see our earlier discussion on sentence stress and strong/weak forms, for example.

- To what extent should spoken material be modified for presentation in the classroom?

- Is it more appropriate to grade tasks (using the micro-skills of listening as a starting-point) from 'lower-' to 'higher-order', or is it preferable to make sure that global understanding has been achieved before focusing on detail? In other words, should we first make sure that learners can listen 'for gist'?

- What resources do we need to teach listening comprehension effectively? Is audio equipment sufficient, or does it leave out the non-linguistic information that video or TV might capture? Is it possible that sometimes the teacher may be more effective in creating a listening environment than the availability of a piece of electronic equipment?

- We can think of the listener's role on a scale of decreasing involvement from participant to addressee to overhearer (adapted from Rost, 1990). Is it possible that the classroom stresses the last of these at the expense of the others? We typically expect our students to listen to (perhaps taped) conversations between other people.

Materials for Teaching Listening Comprehension

What materials, if any, do you have available for teaching listening? Do you have special supplementary materials, or is listening practice incorporated into a main coursebook? Is it necessary for you to devise your own listening exercises?

Traditionally, much classroom practice consisted of the teacher reading aloud a written text, one or more times, slowly and clearly, and then asking a number of comprehension questions about it. The skill itself was not given much attention, nor were the characteristics of natural spoken English. The objective was to provide an alternative way of presenting language and testing that it had been understood, such as the text about the Smith family printed in chapter 6.

There is nothing wrong with this approach in itself, but it could not claim to be teaching listening comprehension. Many current materials, on the other hand, manipulate both language and tasks, and take into account a range of micro-skills, listener roles, topics and text types. There is space here only to illustrate the main trends. Many more examples will be found in the further reading listed at the end of the chapter (see particularly Ur, 1987).

The first thing to say is that the components of listening – processing sound, organizing meaning, and using knowledge and context – provide a convenient way of laying out the issues, but they are not there to be transferred directly to a teaching sequence. The way they are used depends on the objectives and levels of particular courses, although certain kinds of task draw more heavily on some micro-skills than on others.

a) Pre-listening activities   The principal function of these activities, which are now common in teaching materials, is to establish a framework for listening so that learners do not approach the listening practice with no points of reference. This perspective is clearly in line with the use of 'knowledge schema' and the establishing of a context. Activities include:

A short reading passage on a similar topic
Predicting content from the title
Commenting on a picture or photograph
Reading through comprehension questions in advance
Working out your own opinion on a topic

Any such activity is bound to generate language. However, in some cases more explicit attention is given to language practice, particularly to the activation and learning of topic-related vocabulary. Clearly a reading activity can serve both functions of framework-setting and language practice quite well, provided that it does not become too important a focus in its own right.

b) Listening activities   By this we mean tasks carried out during or after listening that directly require comprehension of the spoken material. We find here a basic and quite standard distinction between 'extensive' and 'intensive' listening.

Extensive listening practice, or whatever term is used, is mainly concerned to promote overall global comprehension, and encourages learners not to worry if they do not grasp every word. The range of possible activities is enormous, and which ones are selected will depend largely on proficiency. At lower levels, learners cannot be expected to mentally 'organize' what they hear without considerable support. In the early stages, this support may be in a non-verbal form:

> Putting pictures in a correct sequence
> Following directions on a map
> Checking off items in a photograph
> Completing a grid, timetable, or chart of information

As proficiency develops, tasks will gradually become more language-based, eventually requiring students to construct a framework of meaning for themselves, and to make inferences and interpret attitudes as well as understand explicitly stated facts. (Rost (1990) offers a scale from 'closed' to 'open' tasks.) For example:

> Answering true/false or multiple-choice questions
> Predicting what comes next (preceded by a pause)
> Constructing a coherent set of notes
> Inferring opinions across a whole text

Intensive listening, as the name implies, deals with specific items of language, sound or factual detail within the meaning framework already established:

> Filling gaps with missing words
> Identifying numbers and letters
> Picking out particular facts
> Recognizing exactly what someone said

Note that sequencing and grading can be carried out using both linguistic and psychological criteria: in other words, grading only according to some notion of syntactic complexity is no longer regarded as satisfactory. Further possibilities for grading include (i) task complexity, whether global → specific or vice versa, or indeed global → specific → global (this last technique is evident in the second sample Unit printed at the end of this chapter); (ii) varying the amount of language to be processed, for example, from shorter stretches to longer ones; and (iii) using a range of authentic and specially written material.

c) Language material   Two of our earlier observations are relevant here. Firstly, we distinguished 'interactional' and 'transactional' listening. Secondly, we saw that listeners can have a number of roles, on a scale from participant to addressee to overhearer. Both these elements are represented in listening materials. The most straightforward case is where the learner is an addressee or overhearer in a transactional context, such as:

Attending a lecture
Following instructions or directions
Listening to an interview, or a story, or to people describing their jobs

At the same time, it is clearly important that learners are exposed to the interactional nature of everyday conversation (quite distinct from fixed 'dialogues' to be read aloud). This is rather more difficult to construct in the classroom environment, except artificially. In a way it is a paradox that students may overhear on tape what others say when it would be more 'natural' for them to participate. (This is not always negative, however: learners have the opportunity to listen to the spoken language in an unthreatening situation.)

d) Post-listening activities   We shall only comment briefly here on these activities, because they are usually not listening exercises as such. The category is very open-ended, and looks ahead to our discussion on the integration of skills at the end of this part of the book. Essentially, the post-listening stage is an opportunity for many kinds of follow-up work – thematic, lexical, grammatical, skills developmental and so on. Here are just a few examples:

Using notes made while listening to write a summary
Reading a related text
Doing a role-play
Writing on the same theme
Studying new grammatical structures
Practising pronunciation

Conclusion

Listening comprehension has a number of roles to play within a language course, and its importance clearly depends on the aims of the programme as a whole. It may only be a minor feature, just to give learners some exposure to what English actually sounds like: alternatively, it may have a major function for someone planning to study in an English-speaking country or to interact extensively in the language. Whatever its purpose, we have tried to show in this chapter how current views on the learning and teaching of listening have developed from a growing understanding both of the nature of the skill itself, and of the variety and range of language on which it can be practised.

1) Two Units are printed on the following pages. How closely do you feel that the listening process is mirrored in these materials (at least insofar as you can judge without having the tapes available)? How suitable would they be for your own class?

2) Look back to the text entitled 'Paying to learn: is it snobbery?' in chapter 6 on p. 110. If you had no recorded listening material available, how could you convert this from a reading into a listening exercise? Alternatively, choose another text that was originally intended for reading.

UNIT ELEVEN

The News

This is not a recent news broadcast but you can hear very similar events reported today.

ULSTER

TAIWAN

Pre-listening

1 Predicting vocabulary

a) Look at the photographs above.
What do you think has happened in each case?

b) For each photograph, make a list of the vocabulary you might expect to hear in a report describing such an event.

Extensive listening

1 Understanding organisation

Number the four sections of the news in the order you hear them.

UK news		traffic report	
world news		foreign correspondent's report	

2 Listening for the main points

a) Which of the topics below is in the news?

b) Which one is the main news item?

an earthquake		a hi-jack	
drugs		political violence	
a fight in a pub		a typhoon	
an international agreement		a plane crash	
a road acccident		a strike	

3 Understanding implications

How do you think these people were feeling after listening to the news? Choose the appropriate word from the box.

pleased	worried	disappointed	frustrated

a) **Mrs Beale**
Her husband is a member of the RUC in County Antrim and he has not come home from work yet. She expected him back two hours ago.
b) **Joseph Doyle**
He is a drugs squad officer in the New York police department.
c) **Mr Gilpin**
His British firm has been negotiating for oil prospecting rights in India.
d) **Mary Hanlon**
She is a sales representative planning to drive south from Preston in Lancashire to Birmingham.

Intensive listening

1 Guessing vocabulary from context

Choose the correct meaning of these words.

a) *'casualty'* means
   i) damage to property
   ii) a person who is hurt accidentally
   iii) a person who helps injured people

b) *'hampered'* means
   i) made easier
   ii) made impossible
   iii) made more difficult

c) *'guarantees'* means
   i) suggests
   ii) promises
   iii) insists

d) *'factions'* means
   i) armies
   ii) leaders
   iii) groups

■ VOCABULARY ■

correspondent a newspaper, TV or radio reporter who reports from a distant place
seize to take by force or by official order
Ulster Northern Ireland (Note: the United Kingdom of Great Britain and Northern Ireland)
RUC Royal Ulster Constabulary (the police force)
loyalist a person who wants Northern Ireland to remain part of the United Kingdom
republican a person who wants Northern Ireland to become part of the Republic of Ireland (Eire)
parade a procession or march
civilian a person not in the armed forces or police
stable not changing or moving
in custody held by police
witness a person who sees something happening
congestion an overcrowded or blocked condition

2 Checking comprehension

Choose the correct item to complete the sentences.
a) The part-time policeman in Northern Ireland
   i) was hit in a car.
   ii) was shot at from a car.
   iii) shot at a car.

b) In Stoke
   i) one man was hurt and one killed.
   ii) two men were seen with knives.
   iii) two men are being held by police.

c) Mr Williams
   i) knew he was growing a drug, but thought the plants looked nice.
   ii) didn't know that cannabis is a drug.
   iii) didn't realise he was growing cannabis.

d) Drivers were told
   i) the warning signals were not working.
   ii) to take extra care when they saw the warning signals.
   iii) to approach junction 32 with extra care.

Follow-up

1 Oral summary

a) In groups, make a list of events which have been in the news recently and discuss what you know about them.
b) Each student should choose one news item from the list and make notes of the most important facts. i.e. who/what/when/where.
c) Use your notes to give a brief oral summary of the news item.
d) Decide on the best order for your group's news.
e) Now listen to another group giving their reports.

Study point

1 The passive

a) The passive is often used in news broadcasts. What reasons can you suggest for this?

b) Make sentences in the passive using the tense indicated in brackets, like this:
Five hundred houses/wash away/by floods (Past)
Five hundred houses were washed away by floods.

All the sentences are taken from the news you heard in this Unit.
i)   Two passenger ferries/sink   (Past Perfect)
ii) A part-time policeman/injure   (Present Perfect)
iii) He/hit/by shots fired from a car   (Past)
iv) Two motor bikes/set/on fire   (Past)
v)   Drivers/ask/to take extra care   (Present)

2 Style and vocabulary

News reports often use vocabulary which gives a strong or dramatic effect. Look at the differences between these sentences.

i)   Typhoon Wayne came to the west coast yesterday.
ii) Typhoon Wayne reached the west coast.
iii) Typhoon Wayne hit the west coast.
iv) Typhoon Wayne struck the west coast.

Sentences i) and ii) are neutral while iii) and iv) are more dramatic. Sentence iv) was used in the news you heard in this Unit.

a) Put these verbs into pairs with similar meanings and make a list, like this:

erupt   tear   smash   break   disrupt   rip   cripple   break out

You may need to use a dictionary.

Neutral	Strong/dramatic
reach	strike

b) Now use the more dramatic verbs to complete these sentences. Make sure the verbs are in the correct form. All the sentences are taken from the news you heard in this Unit.
i)   The typhoon _____ across central Taiwan yesterday.
ii) Communications in many areas were _____.
iii) Violence _____ in Ulster last night.
iv) The windows of two pubs and three houses were _____.

Writing News reports

a) Write a short report of another disaster you have heard about. It can be a natural disaster or one caused by human error. Your report should be in a neutral style.

b) Now write another report of the same disaster. This time use a more dramatic style.

Source: S. Axbey, *Soundtracks*, Unit 11, pp. 50–3, copyright Longman, 1989.

18. NEWSPAPER REPORTERS

The British press presents all political views to people with different standards of education and varying interests. There is no censorship of the press. In addition to well over a hundred daily and Sunday papers, there are just over 1,200 weekly local papers, which are, on the whole, non-political and deal mainly with news of interest to people in the area in which they are sold.

Local papers are a valuable medium for local advertising which helps to keep down the cost of the papers by producing a considerable income. Most local papers have circulations of between 8,000 and 35,000, whereas some of the dailies have circulations counted in millions.

Please listen to two reporters discussing their work and their newspaper.

I   *Now that you have listened to the whole discussion, look at the questions below. Listen carefully again and answer the questions by choosing the right answer from A B C or D.*
1.   The town's biggest fire started
     A in a factory with celluloid in it
     B in a factory opposite the celluloid factory
     C in two factories at the same time
     D in a house near to a factory
2.   Some people were burnt in their beds because
     A the fire started in a bedroom
     B they refused to move
     C they were asleep when the fire started and so were too slow to get away
     D there was an explosion
3.   The newspaper reporter heard about the fire
     A on his way home
     B when he went down to the factory
     C when he got up in the morning
     D when he went to work next morning

4. All the local paper's reporters worked on the story of the fire because
   A there were so many aspects of the fire to write about
   B the paper had only two reporters
   C there was no other news at all
   D the victims of the fire had been rehoused in different parts of the town
5. Some people were put into welfare homes for the night after the fire because
   A they were injured
   B they had been in the burning factory
   C they had had to leave their houses
   D they wanted to avoid talking to journalists
6. The reporter says that accusations and counter-accusations followed the investigation of
   A why the reporting went on for six months
   B whether or not it was the biggest fire ever in the town
   C the signal-man's story
   D how long it had taken the fire brigade to get to the fire
7. Newspaper advertising
   A increased after the war and has been increasing ever since
   B increased after the war but decreased when television started
   C decreased after the war but increased when television started
   D decreased after the war and has been decreasing ever since
8. Newspapers are bigger around Christmas because
   A people have more time to read them
   B they carry more advertisements
   C there's more news around Christmas
   D reporters are not on holiday in the winter
9. In summer, newspapers include
   A lots of advertising   C more news
   B lots of holiday advertisements D less ordinary news

II *Now write answers to the following questions.*
1. How many people were killed in the town's biggest fire?
2. At what time did the fire start?
3. What was the reporter's normal time for arriving at the office?
4. Who gave the first alarm of the fire?

5. Why did the reporter have to go back at ten o'clock to interview the signal-man?
6. How much space in the local paper was given to the story of the fire?
7. Have the circulations of local papers grown much since the War?
8.. What effect did the boom in advertising in the post-war years have on local papers?
9. What does the size of local papers depend on?
10. In what months are the smallest papers produced?

Source: M. Underwood, *Listen to this,* Unit 18, pp. 70, 72, 73, copyright Oxford University Press, 1975.

Further reading

1   Underwood, M. (1989): *Teaching Listening.*

2   Ur, P. (1987): *Teaching Listening Comprehension.*

Both these books offer a wide range of examples of listening comprehension tasks and exercises in the context of a clear discussion of the principles of the listening skill.

8   Speaking Skills

Introduction

As a language skill, speaking is sometimes undervalued or, in some circles, taken for granted. There is a popular impression that writing, particularly literature, is meant to be read and as such is prestigious, whereas speaking is often thought of as 'colloquial', which helps to account for its lower priority in some teaching contexts.

However, as we shall see in this chapter, speaking is not the oral production of written language, but involves learners in the mastery of a wide range of sub-skills which, added together, constitute an overall competence in the spoken language.

With the recent growth of English as an international language of communication, there is clearly a need for many learners to speak and interact in a multiplicity of situations through the language, be it for foreign travel, business or other professional reasons. In many contexts, speaking is often *the* skill upon which a person is judged 'at face value'. In other words, people may often form judgements about our language competence from our speaking rather than from any of the other language skills.

In this chapter we shall look at some of the reasons that we might have for speaking in a variety of contexts. Then we shall examine how our concept of speaking has evolved over the last two decades. Next, we investigate the characteristics of spoken language in order to see what their implications might be for language classrooms, and, finally, we consider various types of activity that we can use to promote speaking skills in the classroom.

What are your learners' speaking needs? Do you feel that your materials currently fulfil them?

Reasons for Speaking

As a skill which enables us to produce utterances, when genuinely communicative, speaking is desire and purpose-driven, in other words we genuinely want to communicate something to achieve a particular end. This may involve expressing ideas and opinions; expressing a wish or a desire to do something; negotiating and/or solving a particular problem; or establishing and maintaining social relationships and friendships. To achieve these speaking purposes we need to activate a range of appropriate expressions which will fulfil these particular purposes.

List the different kinds of things that you have talked about in the last few days both in English and in your own L_1 if it is different.

Our own list came out as follows, not in any particular order of priority:

Asking for assistance and advice in a shop
Asking for directions in a different town
Making an appointment by telephone
Discussing and negotiating arrangements
Talking socially to a variety of people
Sorting out arrangements for a car to be serviced

These are just a few of the reasons why people may wish to speak in any language. If we are hoping to make our learners communicatively competent in English as a foreign or second language, then it seems fair to assume that speaking skills will play a large part in this overall competence, although we should point out at this stage that in the early years of communicative language teaching, 'communicative' was interpreted by and large as oral production with the other three skills lagging somewhat behind. However, in recent years there has been a tendency to redress the balance. Speaking is an active process and one which is difficult to dissociate from listening in many ways. Nunan (1989) points out how successful oral communicators have developed what he terms 'conversational listening skills'. We saw in the last chapter how Rost (1990) developed the idea of 'collaborative listening', whereby the listener can also 'shape' the discourse with the speaker. These two skills often enjoy a dependency in that speaking is only very rarely carried out in isolation; it is generally an *interactive* skill unless an uninterrupted oral presentation is being given. This notion of interaction is often developed in more recent EFL teaching materials. As Widdowson (1978: 58) comments: 'what is said is dependent on an understanding of what else has been said in the interaction', and it is this reciprocal exchange pattern which becomes important for learners to be exposed to and to practise at various stages of their foreign language career.

There is clearly an overlap in the interaction which takes place between the speaker/listener and the writer/reader, for the listener has to interpret the speaker just as the reader has to interpret the writer. The essential difference, though, is that speaker/listener interaction takes place in real time, thereby allowing very little time for the speaker to respond to the listener if the rules of a conversation are to be maintained. In the writer/reader relationship, however, the reader usually has the opportunity of re-reading what has been written, time and time again if necessary. This obviously has important classroom implications which will be explored later. Let us now turn our attention to how advances in our understanding of speaking have evolved over the last two decades.

Speaking Skills and Communicative Language Theory

In their analysis of the theoretical base of communicative language teaching, Richards and Rodgers (1986: 71) offer the following four characteristics of a communicative view of language:

1 Language is a system for the expression of meaning
2 The primary function of language is for interaction and communication

3 The structure of language reflects its functional and communicative uses

4 The primary units of language are not merely its grammatical and structural features, but categories of functional and communicative meaning as exemplified in discourse

This analysis shows how easily speaking skills can be accommodated within this particular view of language. When we ask our students to actively use the spoken language in the classroom, we require them to take part in a process which not only involves a knowledge of target forms and functions, but also a general knowledge of the interaction between the speaker and listener in order that meanings and negotiation of meanings are made clear. For example, listeners may give the speaker feedback as to whether or not the listener has understood what the speaker has just said. The speaker will then need to reformulate what was just said in order to get the meaning across in a different way.

We shall shortly see how some recent materials that have been produced for speaking skills often try to encapsulate these views by trying to promote the expression of meaning, interaction and general communicative use on the part of the speaker.

Characteristics of Spoken Language

It is useful for the teacher of speaking skills in the classroom to look at the characteristics of the spoken language in order to ascertain what native speakers actually do when they participate in oral interactions. On the one hand, EFL learners require what Bygate (1987) calls the 'motor-perceptive' skills, by which he means what may be broadly termed the correct use of the sounds and structures of the L_2. In the classroom this would involve the learner in such activities as pattern practices, pronunciation development work and so on. On the other hand, with the growth in recent years of fields of enquiry such as discourse and conversational analysis, we now have a much clearer picture of how conversations are structured. Although the former skills are obviously important, it is the area of communicative interaction in particular which has nourished an approach to the teaching of speaking skills in a communicative way.

Brown and Yule (1983a) have shown that, broadly speaking, spoken communications are essentially 'transactional' or 'interactional'. 'Transactional' language is said to be that which contains factual or propositional information. The language used by the participants is primarily 'message' based. Typically, written language is transactional. Examples of transactional language would be a policeman giving directions to a driver or of someone filing an insurance claim. In each case the message has to be very clearly communicated. Spoken language, however, is also used to establish and maintain social roles, and this is termed interactional communication. In certain cases, we may say that the actual *content* of the conversation may be relatively unimportant; what is of importance, however, is the ability of the speakers to establish and maintain a relationship. It is often when transactional and interactional language need to be used at the same time that difficulties can occur – even for native speakers. It is consequently a skill which non-native speakers may need to learn and practise at length. An example of this would be someone trying to ask a bank manager for a loan where the speaker is trying to conflate serious message oriented language with the language needed to maintain the social roles of the participants.

Brown and Yule (1983a) also examine the various forms of language which are most frequently used by speakers of the language. These are:

- incomplete sentences

- very little subordination (subordinate clauses etc.)

- very few passives

- not many explicit logical connectors (moreover, however)

- topic comment structure (as in 'the sun – oh look it's going down'). The syntax of the written language would probably have a subject-verb-predicate structure

- replacing/refining expressions (e.g. 'this fellow/this chap she was supposed to meet')

- frequent reference to things outside the 'text', such as the weather for example. This kind of referencing is called 'exophoric'

- the use of generalized vocabulary (thing, nice stuff, place, a lot of)

- repetition of the same syntactic form

- the use of pauses and 'fillers' ('erm', 'well', 'uhuh', 'if you see what I mean', and so on.)

If your L₁ is not English, what similarities and differences would there be to the forms outlined above?

We may also say that spoken language follows certain distinct patterns or 'conversational routines' and rules which must be observed if a satisfactory outcome for each participant is to be achieved, and clearly there has to be something worth talking about in the first place for participants to want to continue a conversation to the end.

Next, within the 'framework' of the conversation, 'turns' have to take place if the conversation is not to be totally one-sided. Certain strategies have to be put into operation by the speaker. In practice, this may mean trying to 'hold the floor' for a while in the interaction which will also involve knowledge of how 'long' or 'short' the turn can be; interrupting the other speaker(s); anticipating and inferring what is about to happen next; changing the 'topic' if necessary; and providing appropriate pauses and 'fillers' while processing the language.

The essential thing to note from the foreign language teaching perspective is that what may appear to be casual and unplanned in a conversation may be said nonetheless to follow a deeper organized pattern which the learner has to be made aware of.

Do you think that it is useful to apply native speaker strategies *directly* to classroom use?

Classroom Implications

If what we have seen above shows native speaker behaviour in conversations, research indicates that the non-native speaker is often reluctant to use some of these strategies when speaking. One such area is the use of pauses and fillers which, as we have seen, enable the speaker to hold the floor by filling in the silence at that particular moment.

This can often be a cultural phenomenon: some otherwise proficient L_2 speakers find this 'switch' a difficult one to accomplish if they come from an L_1 culture where silences in conversations are more acceptable. Another area that some non-native speakers tend to neglect is that of making encouraging noises to the speaker such as 'really', 'I see', 'aha' during the conversation which enables the other speaker(s) to see that the conversation is being followed and processed.

One implication that these routines have is that there is a need for speaking skills classes to place more emphasis on the 'frames' of oral interactions. We know that conversations have to be started, maintained and finished. The phrases that we use to accomplish this are called 'gambits'. An example of an opening gambit could be: 'Excuse me, do you happen to know if . . .' Within the framework of the conversation the speakers also take 'turns' and, where pertinent, change the topic under discussion. This is not always an easy task to accomplish successfully. However, if sensitivity to how these conversation 'frames' work can be encouraged from the early stages of language learning by exposing near beginners to samples of natural speech to develop their awareness of conversational features and strategies, then learners will find themselves much more able to cope later on when they need or want to take part in real conversations outside the classroom.

Look at the extract on pp. 158–9 from materials designed to introduce learners to conversation 'gambits'. How effective might it be for your own learners?

What has happened in materials and classrooms in recent years has clearly been influenced by a number of the findings that we have outlined above. In what might rather loosely be termed 'pre-communicative' language teaching, dialogues were often used in class, but the purpose was not to teach the rules of communication, appropriacy and use: the focus was nearly always a structural one and

9. The Main Problem

The trouble is . . .

The problem is . . .

The real problem is . . .

The point is . . .

The 'awful thing is . . .

Don't forget that . . .

Divide into two teams. The students in one team pick one of the topics from Column A.

A member of the other team has to say a related sentence from Column B, starting with a phrase from the list — within 15 seconds.

Some of the sentences in column B fit more than one topic — or none at all! If in doubt, ask the players to explain any choices you don't understand.

Example

Highjackers **The trouble is, nobody knows
how to handle them.**

Round 1

A	B
Raising children	It makes saving a waste of time.
The rising cost of living	Nobody knows how to handle it.
Learning a language on your own	It's an uphill struggle.
Living together	The further away you are, the worse it is.

Round 2

A	B
Television	It wears you out before the day is over.
Mother-in-law for the weekend	Nobody knows how to handle it.
	It makes you feel so depressed.
Jogging	It bores you to tears.
Smoking	Everybody gets on everybody's nerves.
	You need will-power to stop.

Round 3

1. Alternatives to *awful* are *terrible, worst.*

Try again. This time the topics are given, the other team has to make up a suitable response using one of the phrases.

Topics. Drugs, football hooligans, unemployment, famine, forgetting to do your homework, flying, computers, politics, learning English.

10. A Surprising Fact

Speaking

Sometimes the best way to support an argument is to come up with an unexpected fact.

The following paragraph contains some surprising facts (given in *italics*).

Read the paragraph aloud and introduce each of these facts with one of the phrases from the top list, and add a qualifier from the bottom list.

Example

TV plays a very large part in British life. (There were 2.3 TV's per household in Britain in 1987.)

— Do you realize that there were, on average, 2.3 TV's per household in Britain in 1987? Normally TV is an important part of British life.

TV has a tremendous effect on children. (*Children spend more time watching TV than doing anything else in their waking hours.*) Early in life, children learn from TV to influence their parents about what to buy — not just in the area of toys, but also at the supermarket. (*Women buy more snack foods when accompanied by children.*) Also, when parents don't limit their children's TV watching, they become so dependent on television for their entertainment that they begin to lose their potential for creativity. (*A study has shown that children without TV who are left to themselves develop their own creative powers.*) Many people are also worried about the high percentage of programmes that highlight violence. (*Children have been shown to learn violence from TV.*) In short, the negative effects of TV probably outweigh its possible positive influence in presenting the world to the growing child.

Writing

Write out the sentences in italics — each with its opening phrase and its qualifier.

Discussion

Do you agree with the text you read?
If not, give your arguments and try to include some surprising facts which you know.

Start:

Do you realise that . . .

Believe it or not,

You may not believe it, but . . .

It may sound strange, but . . .

¹The surprising thing is . . .

¹Surprisingly,

²Oddly enough,

²Funnily enough,

End with:

Generally

By and large

As a rule

Normally

Usually

On the whole,

1. These relate to a point you have already made — they come in the middle of what you are saying.

2. These connect what you say to what has just been said — usually they introduce a *coincidence*. All of these expressions are rather informal, and will sound natural used to somebody you know rather well.

Source: E. Keller and S. Warner, *Conversation Gambits*, pp. 16–17, copyright Language Teaching Publications, 1988.

learners were rarely given an information gap task which would have enabled them to engage in some real communication. No account was offered as to how a sentence takes on meaning from its relation to surrounding utterances and to non-linguistic factors. It was also rare for attention to be drawn to who was actually speaking to whom and the consequences of this are obvious. Pattison (1987) comments on how students lacked the 'transfer skills' to actually then say anything meaningful *outside* the classroom.

In the light of what we have mentioned above, look at the following examples. How would you characterize each one as *spoken* language? How do they differ?

Example 1:

A: Well, in this job we do er a lot of cradle work you see, and, er on different tower blocks in Birmingham.
B: A lot of what did you say?
A: Cradle work. That's ou, outside work, on the er blocks of flats, where you can see the outside cradles up the outside of the tower blocks.
B: Oh, I'm with you now, you sort of sta, hang in a basket to clean the windows then?
A: Yeah, that's right, I do, yeah! Good job we're well insured isn't it!

Example 2:

JOHN: Hello, how are you?
TOM: I'm fine thank you. How are you?
JOHN: I'm also fine thank you.
TOM: How's your wife?
JOHN: She's very well thank you. How is your wife?
TOM: She's also very well thank you.

The first example shows two people who clearly have a desire to communicate; they have a purpose; there is an information gap to fill in because B does not understand at first what A is talking about. They are also selecting appropriate language for their needs. The second one is rather artificial as conversation and it sounds more like a script than a piece of spontaneous language.

In the pre-communicative speaking skills classroom, therefore, learners were expected to respond to teacher prompts by using instances of language which were usually predictable. In the communicative classroom however, interaction is far less teacher-centred and focuses on learners speaking to each other for a specific reason in order to achieve a specific outcome.

From the materials point of view, within the pre-communicative framework, there is far more control of the form of the language. Sometimes only one item will be the focus of a particular lesson; it might be practice in the use of the pronouns 'it' and 'one', or conversations which are specially written to drill comparative forms. Brumfit (1984) writes about language activities which are designed to foster accuracy and those which are designed to foster fluency. When applied to language tasks these do not necessarily have to be seen as 'opposites', but can be complementary depending on the actual aims and purpose of the speaking skills class in question. Within the pre-communicative framework it is evident that the speaking skills were accuracy-focused to a large extent. Within the more communicative framework, however, the emphasis is far more open-ended with the whole target language being a potential vehicle for communication and not just a restricted object of study: hence activities are designed to develop fluency in the learner.

Consider your own speaking skills classes with respect to the information above. Does this tell you anything about *your* approach to teaching speaking skills or the approach favoured by the materials?

The titles, with dates of several popular speaking skills courses, are listed here. Pause for a moment to look at them and ask yourself what significance the titles might have. How do the dates of publication approximately parallel what you know of changing perspectives on language and language learning?

OPEAC Oral Drills Workbook (1970)
Between You and Me: Guided Dialogues for Conversation Practice (1974)
It's Your Choice: Six Role Playing Exercises (1977)

Communicate (1979)
Discussions That Work (1981)
Interact: An Interaction Workbook (1982)
Eight Simulations (1983)
Speaking Personally (1983)
Conversation Gambits: Real English Conversation Practice (1988)
Speaking Out (1988)

These are *speculative* questions in a sense and we do not want to suggest that there is a rigid relationship between titles, dates and a 'movement' in language teaching.

Types of Activity to Promote Speaking Skills

In this section of the chapter we examine some activities which are used in the classroom to promote the development of speaking skills in our learners. For focusing purposes, we shall begin by looking at an example of some 'pre-communicative' materials and then move on to consider what might broadly be termed communicative activities or games. After this we shall examine some oral problem solving activities, role play and simulation materials for decision making, and materials requiring personal responses from the learners. We finish this section by discussing materials which are designed to teach the rules and patterns of conversation.

In recent teaching materials a lot of attention has been paid to designing activities which focus on tasks that are mediated through language or involve the negotiation and sharing of information by the participants. The idea behind this thinking is that learners should be provided with the opportunity to actively use the language that they know in meaningful activities that they feel motivated to talk about. There are obviously going to be different levels of 'authenticity' in the materials, depending on whether they are concerned with what Rivers and Temperley (1978) call 'skill getting' or 'skill using'. In the former, activities can be designed which are more controlled or what we might call 'pseudo-communication'. In the latter, the idea is to stimulate genuine interaction. By way of contrast, before looking at some different types of activity to further illustrate the genuine interaction principle, we shall have a brief look at an example of pre-communicative speaking skills.

Many of the pre-communicative materials used guided dialogues as a way of trying to develop oral practice with learners. Conversations were frequently structurally graded. Let us look at an imagined example designed to practice the 'not enough' structure:

A: Can John paint the ceiling?
B: No. He can't reach. He isn't tall enough.
A: What about if he uses a ladder? Will he be able to do it then?
B: I should think so.

The pattern practice that learners have to follow and which can then be applied to other conversations is as follows:

A: Can X do Y?
B: No. He/she isn't tall enough.
A: What about if he/she uses a Z? Will he/she be able to do it then?
B: I should think/imagine so.

In contrast to this we now turn our attention to materials for the teaching of speaking skills which form part of the communicative approach beginning with communication games.

Communication games

Speaking activities based on games are often a useful way of giving students valuable practice, especially, although by no means exclusively, where younger learners are involved. Game-based activities can involve practice of oral strategies such as describing, predicting, simplifying, asking for feedback, through activities such as filling in questionnaires and guessing unknown information. Even though these activities are called games, thereby implying fun, they are also communication based and require the learners to use the information they find out in a collaborative way for successful completion of a particular task.

One such activity based on questionnaires can be found in *Interact: An Interaction Workbook* (Aston, 1982) where learners have to decide what constitutes job satisfaction. They have to decide first of all what criteria would lead to job satisfaction and then the class is divided into 4 or 8 equal groups, A to D or A to I for example. Each group then decides which job/s are going to be discussed (own parents', husband's, wife's and so on). Each group has to interview members of another group and then learners have to discuss who of the group they interviewed has the best job. The questionnaire can include details of job, the approximate salary, the hours worked, distance to work, holiday entitlement, what fringe benefits are included and so on.

At the end of the activity each group can tell the rest of the class about the best job that they found. They then compare these and decide which is the best in the whole class and why. Successful completion of this type of activity clearly depends on the effective communicative use of the language and of the sharing of information amongst the participants.

The 'Describe and Draw' principle is based on a series of plans and diagrams which one student has to describe to another so that the latter can complete the task. The idea behind this 'describe and draw' communication activity is to give learners practice in handling, by means of oral description and drawing in pairs, a core of material of non-verbal data, i.e. maps, plans, shapes, graphs. The activities are motivated by the fact that many EFL learners have difficulty when trying to handle this sort of data in the spoken form. This activity is also a useful way of developing Nunan's (1991) notion of conversational listening skills in that the 'listener/drawer' can ask for further clarification if something has not been understood. A typical example would be:

Learner A has a plan of a town centre containing the High Street, churches, school, library, shops, houses or the floor plan of a building such as a school or a company. Learner B then has to draw the plan as accurately as possible from the description given by learner A. For further examples of these activities see Jordan, (1982).

Problem solving

Many speaking skills materials start from the premise that a communicative purpose can be established in the classroom by means of the information gap that we mentioned earlier in the chapter. An example of an information gap principle using the 'jigsaw' materials can be seen at work in materials developed by Geddes and Sturtridge (1980). The materials, primarily for listening in this case, nevertheless include purposeful speaking activities. By getting students to listen to different chunks of information on a tape, the authors set up an information gap whereby the students have to share the information that their group has acquired with other groups in order to build up a complete picture of that particular situation. In the example on pp. 166–7 learners hear tapes containing different information on them as to how this young couple could economize. The ensuing discussion is therefore meaningful to the students in that they have to communicate with each other in order to fill the information gap. The discussion stage in this particular extract involves students in sharing information about cutting down on expenses:

Think of how you might set up speaking skills activities with an information gap in your own classroom.

Simulation/role play materials

One way of getting students to speak in different social contexts and to assume varied social roles is to use role-play activities in the classroom. Materials are generally aimed at the more proficient EFL learner, although this is not always the case, as they can be set up in a highly structured way with a lot of teacher control. At the other end of the spectrum, however, a considerable amount of choice may be exercised by allowing the students more freedom in what they will say. Role play activities are also a pertinent way of integrating skills in the language classroom and therefore we examine them from this perspective in more detail in chapter 10.

Role play materials are often written specifically to get learners to express opinions, to present and defend points of view and to evaluate arguments based on the notion of what Prabhu (1987) calls an opinion gap, in that the activity involves the learner in formulating an argument to justify an opinion for which there is no one objective way of demonstrating the outcome as right or wrong. For example, learners may be asked to consider the planning of a new motorway which would have to go through farmland, some countryside of

UNIT 14 How Can We Cut Down?

Vocabulary

a salary	to earn
a bill	to economize
the rent	to cut down on (doing) sth.
fares (a fare)	to spend £x a week/a month/a quarter (on sth.)
p (pence)	to include
a playschool	
a babysitter	

Listening Stage

Joyce and Patrick are a young couple with a small son, Mark. They want to start saving about £50 a month. You will hear them talking about what they spend their money on and suggesting to each other how they could economize. As you listen, fill in as many details as you can in the tables below.

TABLE 1

INCOME

Patrick earns £_____ a month.   Joyce earns £_____ a week.

REGULAR EXPENSES	Cost per week		Cost per month		Cost per quarter	
ITEMS	£	p	£	p	£	p
rent						
electricity						
telephone						
car						
TV						
supermarket						
meat						
milk						
dog food						
hairdresser						
cigarettes						
fares						
Mark's playschool						
babysitter						

ADDITIONAL EXPENSES THIS MONTH	COST	
ITEMS	£	p
Coat for Mark		
Shoes for Mark		

TOTAL EXPENSES THIS MONTH
This month Joyce and Patrick spent   £_____.

TABLE 2 Under **SUGGESTIONS** write down, in note form, Joyce and Patrick's suggestions for economizing. Under **REACTIONS** write down what they feel about the suggestions.

SUGGESTIONS	REACTIONS

Discussion Stage

1. Complete Table 1 with the help of the other 2 groups.
2. Calculate how much Joyce and Patrick saved this month.
3. Find out from the other 2 groups what suggestions for economizing they heard Joyce and Patrick making.
4. Decide how Joyce and Patrick could best save about £50 each month.

Source: M. Geddes and G. Sturtridge, *Listening Links*, pp. 34–5, copyright Heinemann, 1980.

outstanding beauty, as well as through the outskirts of a large town, as in Lynch, (1977). The learners' role cards would be written from the various points of view of all the parties concerned in the planning project and each learner (or pair or group, depending on the number of people in the class) would be asked to prepare notes to speak from in a meeting. As we suggested above, there is not one answer to this type of negotiated activity, and in this sense the outcome of the discussion is very much up to the learners themselves. There are many subject topics available for role play purposes, including the re-enacting of the trial of an accused person in a courtroom, or compiling and presenting a news magazine programme for radio or television.

With reference to the types of material we have examined thus far, Littlewood (1981) makes a distinction between what he calls 'functional communication activities' (which could include problem solving; questionnaires and describe and draw activities) and 'social interaction activities' (such as role-play and simulation). This distinction could be seen as reflecting the transactional/interactional distinction that we examined earlier in the chapter, because the functional language activities require learners to use the language that they know to get the meaning across as effectively as possible. The social interaction activities, on the other hand, also require the learner to pay more attention to the establishment and maintenance of social relationships.

Materials requiring personal responses

Some speaking materials have been designed in order for learners to become more closely involved with the materials so that they can have more meaningful things to talk about and thereby learn more readily and efficiently. A logical extension of this would then be to actually get outside the materials themselves and to use the learners' own backgrounds and personalities in speaking classes so as to give them more genuine reasons for wanting to communicate with each other. One example of materials is *Speaking Personally* by Porter-Ladousse (1983), which contains twelve units of fluency practice which have been devised along these lines. The aim of these materials is to encourage learners to react individually to questions concerning many aspects of their daily lives on such topics as: their image as seen by others; their futures; views on honesty and truthfulness; and so on. The extract on pp. 170–71 is taken from the unit on 'Life's Tensions'.

Read the extract and consider how you might organize the learners and the classroom in order to use the material effectively.

This is how the author of the book (Porter-Ladousse) sees the materials as being used:

> The material in this book is to a great extent designed to be used by students working in pairs or in small groups. Consequently, the role of the teacher is not so much to give a model of fluency in the target language as to encourage fluency in the learner. It is less to explain words and grammatical structures than to act as a facilitator, enabling the learners to work these things out for themselves. The teacher will present the material, organize the classroom, keep the students working and smooth out the difficulties they meet. The kind of classroom in which there is an empty space or in which the furniture can be moved is particularly suitable for the material in this book. In a traditional classroom, students will work with their immediate neighbours, on both sides as well as in front and behind. (1983: 106)

Thinking of this material, are there other ways in which you can use the background of your own learners to get them to genuinely communicate with each other?

Materials illustrating rules/patterns of conversation

At the present moment of writing, very few of the speaking skills materials available on the market actually emphasize the patterns and rules of conversation that we mentioned and illustrated earlier in the chapter. *Conversation Gambits* by Keller and Warner (1988) is one of the exceptions, however. Their book aims to introduce learners to the effective use of gambits in conversations. The materials are divided up into opening gambits (starting and introducing ideas into a

5   Life's tensions

5.1   How stress-proof are you?   ☆

Study the following situations and consider what your reaction would be in each of them. If you think you would have any of the reactions listed beneath each situation, place a tick in the box beside it.

Example
You have been invited to dinner with your boss to meet some very important business contacts. During the meal you knock over an almost full bottle of wine. Would you blush? Would you stammer? If so, fill in the boxes as in the example. Would you:

feel embarrassed?	☐	feel calm?	☐
blush?	☑	feel amused?	☐
stammer?	☑	be indifferent?	☐

You may sometimes find yourself ticking columns on the left and the right. For example, you might feel embarrassed but calm in the situation above.

---

1 You have driven through some traffic lights as they were turning red. You are stopped by a policeman who senses that you are in a hurry and seems to be taking his time deliberately. Do you:

feel uneasy?	☐	behave in a friendly manner?	☐
start perspiring?	☐	act coolly?	☐
behave aggressively?	☐	look detached?	☐

2 At a friend's wedding you are unexpectedly asked to make a speech. Do you:

blush?	☐	feel amused?	☐
feel your hands trembling?	☐	feel composed?	☐
begin to stutter nervously?	☐	feel pleased and flattered?	☐

3 You have just finished dining in a restaurant and have asked the waiter for the bill. You suddenly discover that you have left both your wallet and your cheque book at home. Do you:

feel embarrassed?	☐	remain calm?	☐
start stammering?	☐	simply tell the waiter what has happened?	☐
have a nervous laugh?	☐	have a natural laugh?	☐

4 You are caught travelling on a bus without a ticket. Your reaction is:

a feeling of shame?	☐	a feeling of indifference?	☐
a forced smile?	☐	an amused smile?	☐
a shortness of breath?	☐	a look of imperturbability?	☐

5 Travelling down the motorway at 70 m.p.h. (approx. 113 km.p.h.) you have a flat tyre. You manage to stop on the hard shoulder. Do you:

feel rage?	☐	remain unflappable?	☐
feel at a complete loss?	☐	feel quite able to cope with the	
become exasperated?	☐	situation?	☐
		reflect calmly on what to do	
		next?	☐

6 You are caught between floors in a lift. You are alone. Do you:

get damp palms?	☐	keep your composure?	☐
grow pale?	☐	feel not particularly worried?	☐
panic?	☐	wait patiently to be rescued?	☐

7 You are returning from a holiday abroad and have more cigarettes and spirits in your suitcase than are permitted by the regulations. A customs officer asks you to open your suitcase. Do you:

get worked up and agitated?	☐	keep your self-control?	☐
feel afraid?	☐	behave with resignation?	☐
find your hands trembling?	☐	consider that you have lost this	
		round in a fair game?	☐

8 At a party you meet someone who greets you very warmly as an old friend, but you cannot remember his name, or even where you have met him before. Do you react:

with embarrassed		by bluffing your way out of the	
self-consciousness?	☐	situation?	☐
with anxiety?	☐	by honestly avowing the	
with a sinking feeling in your		inadequacy of your memory?	☐
stomach?	☐	by laughing the matter off?	☐

9 You are walking out of a department store when you suddenly realise you are clutching an article that you have forgotten to pay for. You see someone who looks as if he might be the store detective looming up. Do you:

lose your sang-froid?	☐	behave in a friendly manner?	☐
wish the ground would open up		remain completely unruffled?	☐
and swallow you?	☐	act nonchalantly?	☐
have palpitations?	☐		

➤➤

Source: G. Porter-Ladousse, *Speaking Personally*, Unit 5.1, copyright Cambridge University Press, 1983.

conversation), linking gambits (linking your ideas to what someone else has just said), and finally responding gambits (agreeing/ disagreeing at different levels).

The authors stress throughout that a lot of the misunderstanding between people comes from *how* they speak, not necessarily *what* they say. The overriding principle behind this type of material is to try and make learners sound more natural when participating in conversations and discussions. People who never use gambits when they are speaking may be interpreted by the other participant/s as being abrupt, direct or even rude in some cases. For example, we do not generally go into a shop and ask 'How much is this?', but would probably say, 'Could you tell me how much this is please?' Similarly, we may want to introduce a piece of surprising news with, 'You may not believe this, but . . .'. If we are in a shop and wish to leave without purchasing something we may say: 'I'm afraid I can't make up my mind at the moment', or, 'I'll have to give it some thought'. The materials contain mini-conversations which allow learners to practise the gambits as they speak.

Have another brief look at the activity types in this section. What are the organization principle/s behind each of them?

Conclusion

We began this chapter by examining the needs that learners may have to speak in a foreign language in the first place. Then we discussed some of the background to speaking skills by emphasizing speaking as an active skill. Subsequently we looked at the ways in which speaking and listening interact and how research into communicative language theory and the characteristics of spoken language has had important classroom implications over the last two decades. Finally, we offered a brief overview of the design principles underlying some of the speaking skills materials which have been produced over the last decade.

Further reading

1 Bygate, Martin (1987): *Speaking*, gives a very useful insight into the nature of the speaking skills within a broad pedagogical framework.
2 Brown, Gillian and G. Yule (1983a and 1983b): *Discourse Analysis* and *Teaching the Spoken Language* offer very clear accounts of speaking in an extensive range of contexts.

9 Writing Skills

Introduction

Writing in the language class – the last of the skills that we discuss here as 'discrete' – reflects many of the recurrent themes of this book so far. We shall need, for instance, to call on various communicative criteria; on the concepts of 'product' and 'process'; and on the role of formal language practice, to see how, along with other skills, writing too has developed and has accumulated many insights into the nature of language and learning. However, as well as having much in common with other skills, we shall see that writing differs in some significant ways to do with the purpose of writing in class and in everyday life, and the relationship between these two settings.

This chapter will first survey the reasons for writing and the different types of writing associated with them. The central section will focus on a number of approaches to teaching writing, particularly as expressed in teaching materials, and will try to show how perspectives have gradually changed. We shall then move on to the classroom environment itself, including some possibilities for writing-related activities, the issue of error correction and the role of the teacher.

Reasons for Writing

At this point it would be helpful to note down your reasons for needing – or wishing – to write in the course of a typical week, and the form that your writing takes. Try to think of all possible contexts. Can the kinds of writing you do be grouped together in any way?

How do you think your own list might compare with that of other people you know: perhaps a friend who isn't a teacher, or your students?

Our own list included the following, not in any particular order:

Shopping list	Notes from a book	Official forms
This chapter	Parts of a prospec-	Letter requesting
	tus	tourist information
Telephone messages	'Reminder' lists	An essay
Letter to a friend	A meeting agenda	Business letters
Comments on stu-	Invitations	Diary (narrative and
dent work		appointments)
Birthday card	Office memoranda	Map showing how
		to get to our house

We can now make a few initial observations arising directly or indirectly from thinking about the kinds of writing we do. The implications of these points for the teaching of writing will be taken up in subsequent sections:

1 A typical 'writing profile' covers a great range of styles. We may just write a list of nouns, or a number, or even simply a visual representation (a list, taking a phone message, drawing a map). Alternatively, taking notes from a book or a verbal message will require some facility with reducing language structure into note form in the interests of speed and efficiency. Discursive writing has many different functions (narrative, persuasion, setting out an argument and so on) and makes considerable demands on our ability to carefully structure an extended piece of writing. Moreover, in some cases we ourselves initiate the need to write – different kinds of letters, a shopping list, or a short story, perhaps – whereas in other cases the writing is a response to someone else's initiation, as when we respond to an invitation or a letter. The final point to make here is that our writing has different addressees: family, colleagues, friends, ourselves, officials, students and many more.

Reasons for writing, then, differ along several dimensions, especially those of language, topic and audience.

2 In straightforward terms of frequency, the great majority of people write very much less than they talk and listen. Many adults, in fact, do not need to write much in their everyday lives: and if there are

Types of writing

Personal writing	Public writing	Creative writing

diaries
journals
shopping lists
reminders for oneself
packing lists
addresses
recipes
	letters of – enquiry
	        – complaint
	        – request
	form filling
	applications (for memberships)
		poems
		stories
		rhymes
		drama
		songs
		autobiography

Social writing	Study writing	Institutional writing	

letters
invitations
notes – of condolence
     – of thanks
     – of congratulations
cablegrams
telephone messages
instructions – to friends
     – to family
	making notes while reading
	taking notes from lectures
	making a card index
	summaries
	synopses
	reviews
	reports of – experiments
	     – workshops
	     – visits
	essays
	bibliographies
		agendas
		minutes
		memoranda
		reports
		reviews
		contracts
		business letters
		public notices
		advertisements
			posters
			instructions
			speeches
			applications
			curriculum vitae
			specifications
			note-making
			(doctors and other
			professionals)

Source: T. Hedge, *Writing*, p. 96, copyright Oxford University Press, 1988.

few 'real-world' reasons for writing in our L_1, there are even fewer for doing so in a foreign language. Writing for most of us only happens to any significant extent as part of formal education. This dominance of oral/aural over literacy skills holds even for those of us for whom writing is an integral part of our professional lives.

3   Some ways of classifying types of writing can be suggested. White (1980: 14–15), for example, proposes a simple and useful two-way distinction between *institutional* and *personal* writing, each of which he sub-divides further. 'Institutional' includes business correspondence, textbooks, regulations, reports; 'personal', for White, covers the two main areas of personal letters and creative writing. Hedge (1988) offers a more detailed breakdown under the six headings of *personal*, *study*, *public*, *creative*, *social* and *institutional*. Her checklist is self-explanatory, and its reproduced above in full. We shall refer back to it when discussing the 'products' of writing appropriate to the language classroom. In the meantime, you will certainly recognize some elements of your own list here. You might like to see whether your writing fits into the categories that Hedge uses.

Writing Materials in the Language Class

It is now time to ask what part writing can and does play in the language class, given its more limited role for most people outside an educational setting. We have seen in previous chapters that some attention to 'real-world' language and behaviour is regarded as increasingly important in the current English language teaching climate. It would be difficult to argue the case that writing in the language class should only mirror the educational function (writing essays and examination answers, taking notes from textbooks and so on) except perhaps in certain 'specific-purpose' programmes. At the same time, it is not immediately obvious how the notion of 'authenticity' and the opportunities for transfer from real world to classroom can be maintained to the extent that this can be done for speaking and listening skills.

These two issues – the possibilities for reflecting communicative criteria, and the treatment of the skill of writing resulting from its general educational role – have been significant ones in the development of materials and methods. We shall now go on to look at how writing has been handled in English language teaching, attempting as we do so to pick out the major trends.

The titles, with dates, of several popular writing courses are listed below. Pause for a moment to look through the list. Then, as you read the rest of the chapter, ask yourself what significance the titles might have. For example, can you discern a shift in the approaches to the teaching of writing? Do the dates of publication approximately parallel what you know of changing perspectives on language and language learning? (It might even be interesting to compare your ideas here with the similar task in chapter 8.)

These are speculative questions, and we certainly do not wish to suggest that there is a rigid relationship between a title, a date, and a 'movement' in language teaching. We shall make a few comments in the conclusion to this chapter.

> *Guided Composition Exercises* (1967)
> *Frames for Written English* (1966/1974)
> *Guided Course in English Composition* (1969)
> *Guided Paragraph Writing* (1972)
> *From Paragraph to Essay* (1975)
> *Think and Link* (1979)
> *Communicate in Writing* (1981)
> *Writing Skills* (1983)

Pen to Paper (1983)
Freestyle (1986)
Word for Word (1989)
Outlines (1989).

'Traditional' writing activities

There are a number of types of writing task that most of us will be familiar with, both as teachers and from our own language learning experience. Simplifying for the moment, they can be listed under three broad headings:

1   *Controlled sentence construction*   If the focus of a language programme is on accuracy, then schemes for controlling learners' writing output will obviously predominate. The range of activity types is considerable, and typical approaches include:

● Providing a model sentence and asking students to construct a parallel sentence with different lexical items

● Inserting a missing grammatical form

● Composing sentences from tabular information, with a model provided

● Joining sentences to make a short paragraph, inserting supplied conjunctions (but, and, however, because, although . . .)

2   *Free composition*   Apparently at the other end of the spectrum, a 'free writing' task requires learners to 'create' an essay on a given topic, often as part of a language examination. Sometimes students are simply invited to write on a personal topic – their hobbies, what they did on holiday, interesting experiences and the like. Other materials provide a reading passage as a stimulus for a piece of writing on a parallel topic, usually with comprehension questions interspersed between the two activities.

Although 'controlled' and 'free' writing appear to represent very different approaches, they are not in fact mutually exclusive, and many writing schemes lead learners through several stages from one to the other. A typical example is provided in Jupp and Milne's *Guided Course in English Composition* (1969): each 'composition' begins with structure practice, continues with a sample composition, and then uses this material as a basis for students' own compositions.

3 *The 'homework' function* Particularly in general coursebooks (as distinct from materials devoted specifically to the skill of writing), it is quite common to find writing tasks 'bunched' at the end of a unit, either as supplementary work in class or set for homework and returned to the teacher for later correction.

This brief and generalized summary indicates several trends in the 'traditional' teaching of writing from which current views have both developed and moved away:

• There is an emphasis on *accuracy*

• The focus of attention is the *finished product*, whether a sentence or a whole composition

• The teacher's role is to be *judge* of the finished work

• Writing often has a *consolidating* function

In other words, in many earlier materials the 'product' did not on the whole reflect the kind of real-world writing discussed earlier, and the 'process' was not really the concern of anyone except the writer: certainly it was not given much explicit attention. Byrne, however, rightly points out that 'many such schemes were carefully thought out and, although no longer fashionable, produced many useful ideas on how to guide writing' (1988: 22). This is well borne out by Moody, who devised one of the better known schemes (*Frames for Written English*, 1966/1974). Moody argues that the advantage of controlled practice is that it leads to automaticality in grammatical usage, and he certainly does not claim that a structured scheme provides a comprehensive view of writing. Furthermore, we should note that these approaches to writing drew on key language teaching and educational traditions: as such they fulfilled important pedagogical and practical functions. We shall also find that many of them contain the seeds of later developments.

This said, materials have gradually come to reflect both the diversity of written texts and the ways in which writers approach a piece of writing. We shall take each of these in turn.

The Written Product

We commented earlier that any piece of writing we do can be seen from a number of different perspectives which clearly take us beyond a concern for accuracy alone. Whilst few teachers are likely to be satisfied with written work that is full of grammatical mistakes, at the same time notions of 'correctness' are now felt to have a broader base, and to be embedded in a more integrated view of the skill of writing. Raimes' suggested techniques for teaching writing 'stem from the basic assumptions that writing means . . . a connected text and not just single sentences, that writers write for a purpose and a reader, and that the process of writing is a valuable learning tool' (1983: 11). She lists nine areas of relevance: excluding 'process' considerations, the concern of our next section, these are:

1   Syntax (sentence structure)
2   Grammar
3   Mechanics (handwriting, spelling and so on)
4   Organization (paragraphing, cohesion)
5   Word choice
6   Purpose
7   Audience
8   Content

A comparable approach is taken by Hedge, who refers to the production of a piece of writing as 'crafting', 'the way in which a writer puts together the pieces of the text, developing ideas through sentences and paragraphs within an overall structure' (1988: 89). She uses the term 'communicating' to examine specifically the need for a writer to develop a sense of audience.

We shall now look at some selected examples of activities to be found in materials for the teaching of writing: many more examples will be found in the books listed under 'further reading' at the end of the chapter. Within the overall framework of the need for an awareness of purpose, we shall modify Raimes' and Hedge's catego-ries and use just the headings of (a) levels of writing and (b) audience.

Levels of writing

Look back again at your personal list of writing activities. Most teachers, for example, write comments on student work as a regular part of their jobs. You may well recognize this style:

> This is quite a good summary, but it would have been a good idea to include more of your own opinions. Think more carefully about tenses. Your handwriting is also sometimes difficult to read.

From a different sphere, in a letter home from holiday you will probably include something about what you have been doing, details of people and places, and perhaps some information about travel arrangements. As you write, you will certainly have been operating on a number of different and interacting levels, not necessarily consciously, of course, and moving between 'top-down' and 'bottom-up' strategies discussed in chapter 6.

We saw in chapter 2 how the advent of the 'communicative approach' had far-reaching implications, including an extension of the size of language stretches that can be dealt with from sentence to discourse level. The two outer layers on figure 9.1 will certainly require consideration of both 'cohesion'– linking devices – and 'discourse coherence' – the ways in which a text forms a thematic whole. Such criteria are now well-established in the teaching of writing. Typical

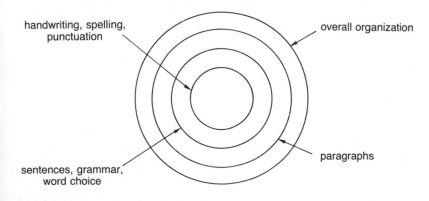

Figure 9.1

organizational principles for materials include paragraph structuring, particularly related to functional categories, and the use of a range of linking devices. Sentence-level and grammar practice is not omitted but, as the diagram suggests, is set in the context of a longer and purposeful stretch of language. Writing, then, is seen as primarily message-oriented, so a communicative view of language is a necessary foundation.

Some of the trends in the teaching of discourse-level writing, and the techniques used, are readily discernible from a glance at many of the published materials of the last ten years or so. Functional categories include:

> Sequencing; chronological order
> Comparison and contrast
> Classification
> Cause and effect
> Description: of objects, and processes
> Definitions
> Writing instructions; narrative; discursive essays
> Predicting and speculating

Linking devices covered include the various connectives associated with these functional categories, and the notions of lexical cohesion, referencing using pronouns and the article system, ellipsis and substitution that we looked at in chapter 2.

The techniques used are many: you will notice that they usually require learners to understand the overall purpose of a piece of writing, not just the immediate sentence-bound grammatical context. Here is a small selection of some of the possibilities:

- Providing a text to read as a model for a particular function

- Answering questions on a text, then using the answers as the basis for a piece of writing

- Using non-verbal information in many forms. This may be a simple visual, such as a picture or a drawing; or a table, a graph, a diagram. Alternatively, the overall structure of a text may be represented visually, as an 'information-structure' diagram. The last of these is particularly common with classifications

- Selecting appropriate connectives in a paragraph

- (Re-)constructing a paragraph from sentences given in the wrong order, or a whole text from a set of jumbled paragraphs. This technique is usually referred to as 'unscrambling'

- Paragraph or story completion, which can be done by adding an ending, but also a beginning or a middle section

- Parallel writing

- Choosing an appropriate title for a piece of writing, such as a newspaper article

Many other techniques are developed from pre-writing tasks carried out in the classroom: we shall look at these a little later in this chapter.

Audience

Byrne (1988) is one of several authors on writing skills who makes the important point that writing is a process of *encoding* (putting your message into words) carried out with a reader in mind. Certainly the outermost layer of figure 9.1 – the overall organization – is best considered in relation to audience and purpose. The degree of 'crafting' that needs to be done, and at what level, will also be determined to some extent by the addressee. Stylistic choices, in other words, depend on why and for whom we are writing.

It is likely that, in the great majority of situations, our students still write primarily for their teachers, or perhaps for an examiner, both acting in the role of evaluator. Grant (1987) makes the very useful point that, although transferring real-life writing directly to the classroom is problematic, what we should be aiming at is at least the creation of 'plausible contexts'.

Would you say that your students do most of their writing for their teacher, or are there other 'plausible contexts' that you have introduced into your classroom? When you have read through the following suggestions for extending the range of possible recipients for your students' writing, consider to what extent your own materials or classes could be adapted to accommodate them.

As we have noted several times, the classroom has its own purpose and structure, and is not simply a reflection of the outside world. In this sense, we can think of writing activities both from the 'instrumental' perspective of what is useful for external purposes, but also in terms of their educational function and the reality of the classroom itself. The following audience suggestions reflect this dual aspect. We have listed addressees along with a few suggested topics, but of course the possibilities are considerably greater than this. Our students, then, can write

- To other students: invitations, instructions, directions

- For the whole class: a magazine, poster information, a cookbook with recipes from different countries

- For new students: information on the school and its locality

- *To* the teacher (not only *for* the teacher): about themselves, and the teacher can reply or indeed initiate. (See Rinvolucri, quoted in Hedge (1988), who suggests an exchange of letters with a new class to get to know them.)

- For themselves: lists, notes, diaries (for a fuller discussion of diary writing see chapter 12)

- To penfriends

- To other people in the school: asking about interests and hobbies, conducting a survey

- To people and organizations outside the school: writing for information, answering advertisements

So far we have looked at the 'what' of writing, particularly at the nature of text and the importance of writing with a readership in mind. Writing continues to serve as a vehicle for language practice, and necessarily so, but this function is integrated into a broader and more diversified perspective. As Byrne puts it, teachers need to make students aware that 'any piece of writing is an attempt to communicate something: that the writer has a goal or purpose in mind; that he has to establish and maintain contact with his reader; that he has to organize his material and that he does this through the use of certain logical and grammatical devices' (1988: 14).

We now turn to the 'how'.

The Writing Process

One of the aims of this book is to trace the changes of focus in materials and methods for English language teaching, and to show how different approaches have gained prominence at different times. A characteristic of the last decade in particular has been a growing interest in what a language *skill* entails. Initially, attention was focused on the receptive skills, especially reading: more recently, research into writing – much of it concerned with writing in the mother tongue – has become more accessible to second-language teachers, and is beginning to have a significant impact on the design of materials and on attitudes to teaching writing. Stylistic factors, whether grammatical, discoursal, or lexical, are now set alongside a concern for how writers go about the performance of the task itself. A detailed discussion of the research base is outside the scope of this chapter: readers interested in pursuing the L_1/L_2 parallels further are referred to Freedman et al. (1983); descriptions of some of the procedures used to elicit information from writers, such as retrospective reports, behaviour protocols, directed reports and thinking aloud protocols are described in Hayes and Flower (1983). We shall now look at the writing process from the two related points of view of the writer and the classroom.

The writer's perspective

Try to note down the various stages that you think you go through when producing a piece of continuous text, such as a letter, a report, an essay, a story and the like.

Except perhaps with something as straightforward as a shopping list, it is unlikely that your text will appear directly on the page in its final form without any intervening stages. Even with a shopping list you may decide to re-order it, and categorize items in terms of different types of shop or different sections of the supermarket. Writers, it seems, do a great number of things before they end up with the final version – the 'finished product'. For instance, they jot down ideas, put them in order, make a plan, reject it and start again, add more ideas as they go along, change words, re-phrase bits, move sections around, review parts of what they have written, cross things out, check through the final version, write tidy notes, write on odd pieces of paper as thoughts occur to them, write directly into a typewriter or a word processor if they are lucky enough to have one, look at the blank page for a long time, change pens, refer back to something they have read – and many more things, some of them quite idiosyncratic.

If all this is what writers do 'naturally', then Raimes (1983) is right to refer to the English language writing class as very often 'anguish as a second language'. This 'anguish' must be particularly severe if students are expected to turn in a perfectly polished piece of work. Even if accuracy is an important and legitimate requirement, it is only achieved after a rather untidy and stumbling set of procedures, and the nature of the process itself needs to be acknowledged. We shall return to this point from a different angle when looking at attitudes to the correction of written work.

Hedge refers to all the components of the process taken together as 'composing' (taken alongside 'communicating' and 'crafting'). She suggests the following as a representation of the stages of writing:

Getting ideas together ◗ planning and outlining ◗ making notes ◗ making a first draft ◗ revising, re-drafting ◗ editing ◗ final version. (adapted from Hedge, 1988: 21)

Byrne (1988) has a similar set of steps:

List ideas
Make an outline ('scaffolding')
Write a draft
Correct and improve the draft
Write the final version.

For most of us, this is rather idealized: as Hedge points out, writing is more like a 'recursive', even messy, activity, where we move around among the different stages and carry out each stage several times, with great personal variation. However, although 'stage' is in principle contrasted with 'process', for pedagogic purposes it is useful to use the 'stage' idea as a framework for teaching, because of the need for a systematic procedure in the classroom context. Some researchers have also tried to isolate the strategies used by 'good' writers, but for our purposes it may be more useful to think of 'typical' strategies for attacking a writing task, rather than the less accessible ideal.

Nevertheless, out of the complexity and untidiness a set of procedures emerges which for teaching purposes can be reduced to three (following Hedge):

1 Pre-writing: jotting down ideas and preparing provisional plans.
2 Drafting and re-drafting, involving reviewing and revising; in other words, working out what to say and then how best to say it.
3 Editing the pre-final version, including assessing clarity for the intended reader and checking accuracy.

Materials for teaching writing are increasingly beginning to incorporate these process-based insights in various ways. An early example can be found in *Writing as a Thinking Process* (Lawrence, 1972), a course aimed mainly at people studying English for academic or professional purposes and based on a view of writing whereby learners are able to articulate their own thought processes. The emphasis is on paragraph construction in functional categories, and students are expected to manipulate data and make inferencing statements according to explicit cognitive criteria. For example, a task on chronological sequencing may require learners first of all to arrive at a correct sequence, then to make deductions by relating the different stages in that sequence. It is only much more recently, however, that the broader 'process' spectrum that we have been discussing here is taken more fully into account. *Outlines* and *Perspectives* (Hopkins and Tribble, 1989; Hopkins, 1989), for instance, include drafting, checking, improving for a second draft, editing and re-writing as central activities in each unit.

Writing in the classroom

Writing, like reading, is in many ways an individual, solitary activity: the writing triangle of 'communicating', 'composing' and 'crafting' is usually carried out for an absent readership. However, we must remember that our students are language learners rather than writers, and it would not be particularly helpful to have them spend all their time writing alone. Although process research points to a need to give learner-writers space and time to operate their own preferred individual strategies, the classroom can be structured in such a way as to provide positive intervention and support in the development of writing skills. We shall comment only very briefly here on possible classroom activities – they look directly ahead to the next chapter on the integration of language skills, and to the management of class-rooms that will be the focus of the third part of this book.

The classroom can provide an environment for writing at each of the three main stages of (1) gathering ideas: pre-writing and planning, (2) working on drafts, and (3) preparing the final version. The primary means by which this can be done – leaving aside for the moment the teacher's role of marking and commenting – is by establishing a collaborative, interactive framework where learners work together on their writing in a 'workshop' atmosphere. A few typical examples, all involving oral skills, must suffice:

- 'Brainstorming' a topic by talking with other students to collect ideas

- Co-operating at the planning stage, sometimes in pairs/groups, before agreeing a plan for the class to work from

- 'Jigsaw' writing, for example using a picture stimulus for different sections of the class to create a different part of the story (Hedge, 1988: 76–7)

- Editing another student's draft

- Preparing interview questions, perhaps for a collaborative project

In the multi-dimensional view of writing explored in this chapter, there are clearly a number of different possibilities available for the sequencing of materials and activities. We can reduce these to three:

1   Varying/increasing the size of the linguistic 'building blocks', from single lexical items ⟡ sentences and sentence joining ⟡ the construction of paragraphs and finally ⟡ whole texts. This requires attention to all levels of language, from sentence and text structure to a sense of the coherence of a completed piece of writing. This is related, of course, to the more traditional

progression through a writing scheme from 'controlled' to 'guided' to 'free', though we now have a much wider range of descriptive tools available for the language material.

2 Paralleling the stages in the process of putting a whole piece of writing together. Although writing processes have little in themselves to do with proficiency – an elementary learner can in principle plan, draft and re-draft, and edit as well as an advanced one can – the degree to which the process can be put to use obviously does have.

3 Task complexity. It can be argued – although it is a point that needs further exploration – that personal (expressive) writing is in some sense 'easier' than its institutional or professional counterpart. A letter to a friend, or a short story, while they obviously have their own structure, nevertheless are not as constrained by rules as, say, a business letter or a report or an essay.

Correcting Written Work

What is your usual and preferred method for correcting student work? What do you see as your main role in relation to the writing your learners produce?

Obviously teachers' attitudes and methods are determined to a certain extent by their approach to language teaching (whether chosen or imposed), and by the whole educational climate in which they work. We commented earlier that the most common role for the teacher is to be a judge, a critical evaluator of the finished product. Work is returned to students with mistakes indicated or corrected: the legendary red pen has always been a tool of the teacher's trade. However, the approaches to writing that we have looked at, from the perspective of both 'product' and 'process', inevitably lead to a much more varied view both of the role of the teacher and the classroom environment, and of the criteria for marking and assessing students' written work.

Firstly, process considerations suggest the usefulness of intervention at all stages of writing, not just at the end. It is unlikely that a draft will need to receive a grade, so the teacher, by commenting and making suggestions, becomes a reader as well as a critic. The feedback given to students is in this view both 'formative' – concerned with a developmental process – as well as 'summative' – the evaluation of the end-product. Raimes suggests no less than thirteen stages, from topic selection to the assignment of follow-up tasks (1983: 140–1). Secondly, this feedback, whether summative or formative, takes place at a number of different levels of writing, and sentence grammar is not the only subject of attention. We also need to take into account the appropriacy of the writing to its purpose and its intended audience as well as topic and content criteria. Several marking schemes along these lines are now used by individual teachers, in materials, and by some examination boards. A useful example is proposed as a 'writing profile' by Hopkins and Tribble (in *Outlines*, 1989) under the headings of:

> Communicative quality
> Logical organization
> Layout and presentation
> Grammar
> Vocabulary
> Handwriting, punctuation and spelling.

You might like to 'weight' these in terms of their importance in your evaluation of your own students' writing.

Thirdly, the red pen method is inherently negative, but there is no reason why feedback should not be positive as well. The *Outlines* scheme, for instance, commends as well as criticizes ('communicates effectively', 'excellent control of appropriate vocabulary' and the like). The issue here is what we see to be the overall function of correction. A distinction should be made between 'mistakes', when learners are not using correctly the language they already know, and errors, which, as we have seen, are largely the outcome of a learner's developing competence. Mistakes will require direct feedback and remedial treatment, and will largely relate to language points already covered; errors may be more appropriately used for the planning of future work.

Finally, there are implications for the role of people other than the teacher in the feedback process. Using other class members as addressees, and the classroom as a co-operative working environment, automatically means that students are involved in the production of each other's written work. There is then a natural extension to peer editing and revision, as well as the more established procedure of peer 'correction'. Clearly all these aspects will only be effective with guidance and focus, but potentially they can help students to develop a critical stance towards their own work as well. Several other procedures might be developed to involve learners in what is presumably the ultimate aim of *self*-monitoring and *self*-correction. These include marking schemes that indicate mistake type, leaving the learner to identify the specific problem; the establishing of personal check-lists which of course change as proficiency grows; and the technique of 're-formulation', in which the teacher suggests another wording for what the student is trying to express. It is important to recall that self-evaluation too will require different criteria at different stages in the writing process: there is little point in too great a concern for accuracy when gathering ideas, formulating a plan and establishing readership, whereas correctness has a vital role as the final draft takes shape. Hedge (1988) prefers to think of 'correction' under the more general heading of 'improving', a cover term which stresses the interacting of marking procedures with processing categories.

Conclusion

Earlier in this chapter we asked you to consider the titles of some published teaching materials to see if any trends were discernible. Although it is much too simplistic to suggest that the date of publication can be directly linked to a particular approach, it is probably true to say that there is a gradual shift from guiding learners through grammatical patterns against the background of 'composition' requirements, to a concern with paragraph and text structure from a communicative perspective, to titles that reflect ways in which we think about the activity of writing – 'outlining', 'putting pen to paper' and so on. Materials for the teaching of writing, then, do not neglect the basic skills, but are increasingly likely to see writing in terms of purpose, audience, and the development and organization of thinking, for real-world, for learning and for educational purposes.

Consider the Units provided here from as many angles as possible, for example: subject-matter; 'authenticity'; level; types of writing task; sequencing of activities; suitability for your own students. If they are not suitable, what would you wish to change?

UNIT 6 APPLYING FOR WORK

1 Context

- Look at the texts below and answer these questions:

  1 Where are the texts from? How can you tell?
  2 Which jobs are best for young women; for young men? Which jobs are suitable for both?
  3 Which job is probably for more than a few weeks?
  4 Which jobs are not suitable for someone who wants to work only in August?
  5 In which jobs would a knowledge of French and English be useful?
  6 What information will you give about yourself if you apply for any of the jobs?

- Discuss your answers with a partner and make a list of the information you would give about yourself.

Au pair

Anglo-French family requires au pair for August to help look after children: 4, 6, 9 and 12. Must be flexible, fun-loving and energetic. Lovely holiday home in Scotland. References required. Write: H. Pillet, Box 56.

Volunteer diggers required for Roman excavations in Bath. Start 1st July for 6 weeks. Daily expenses paid. Self-catering hostel available. Reply Box 88.

Nanny/home help required from 1 July for professional couple in London. Baby girl, 16 months, and boy, 4 years, dog and general help. Live-in, own room, TV. Responsibility, flexibility and hard work sought. References required. Write: Mrs Lowe, Box 67.

Holiday Camp

Keen, energetic and responsible young helpers needed for international holiday camp for children aged 8-16. Must have good organizing ability and be good with children. Knowledge of French, Italian or Spanish an advantage. Start August 1st for 4 weeks. References required. Write: Peter Herford, Administrative Assistant, Euroschools, Box 87.

---

2 Sentence practice

1 **Describing events begun in the past and continuing up to the present**

We often use the present perfect continuous with *since* and *for*.

I have been	studying English living here playing the piano working here collecting records	since 1980. for five years. since 1979. for two years. for several years.

- How long have you been studying English? attending your school? living at your present address? playing your favourite sport? watching your favourite TV programme? Write several answers.

2 Describing past experiences with present effects

We generally use the present perfect, eg:

I *have given* Sarah the message, so she knows about it.

- Find the parts A and B that go together, and write out complete sentences.

Part A

1 I have visited England twice
2 I have seen that new film
3 I have heard their latest record
4 I have written to my pen friend

Part B

and I like the tune.
and I think it's great.
and I want to go a third time.
and he knows about my plans.

- Write present perfect sentences about

1 your visiting Italy twice before.
2 your sister going to see that film for the third time.
3 your hearing the new single by Last Gasp.
4 your inviting Anthony to dinner for tonight.

3 Reporting past actions done at a specific time

We always use the past tense, often with a **past-time adverb.**

I *went* to England **last year.**
Sarah *saw* it **last week.**
Damon *heard* it **last weekend.**
I *wrote* to Jean-Luc **yesterday.**

We often combine several statements in a sequence, like this:

We *have been studying* French **for some years** (period of time)
and we *have been* to France **several times.** (number of times)
We *went* there **two years ago.** (specific time)

- Unscramble these sentences to make six correct sentences, three about Sarah and three about Damon:

Sarah He She Damon He She	has been has been learning has been studying went failed has taken	it the driving test German there to Germany to drive	for six months. twice. once. last week. for five years. last summer.

4 Describing ability

We often use *can* + verb:

I *can* start work on 1st August.
I *can* speak French.

Or *can* + *not* + verb:

I *cannot* drive a car.
I *cannot* speak Spanish.

● What can you do? What can't you do? Discuss with a partner and write four sentences.

3 Parallel Writing

● Here is Marie-Claire's letter.

1 Add the missing verbs.
2 Add the extra sentences at appropriate points in the letter.
3 Write out the complete letter.

23, rue d'Arpence
27000 Evreux
France
February 24ᵗ 19___

Dear Mr Pillet,

I wish to apply for the position of au pair which you advertised recently.

I am a French student aged 18, and I _____ English for six years. I _____ England twice, and last year I _____ friends in Reading.

I like looking after children. Last year, I _____ some young cousins while their mother _____ in hospital.

If you _____ a reference, you _____ to my English friends :   Mr and Mrs John Henderson
22 Kenton Avenue
Reading , Berks

I hope to hear from you soon regarding my application.

Yours sincerely,
Marie - Claire Lefèvre

Extra sentences

They were then aged 8, 6 and 2.
I am coming to England in July for a holiday with my English friends.
I can start work on 1st August.
I am doing my Baccalauréat this year.
Although it was tiring, I enjoyed looking after them.

4 Follow-up

- Either: Write Jean-Luc's application for the job at a holiday camp. Use the information below.
  Or: Write a letter of application for yourself for any one of the jobs in the advertisments.

Jean-Luc Raymond

Age:	19
Education:	Baccalauréat last year
	English 8 years at school
Sports:	volley ball, skiing, wind surfing, climbing
Interests:	photography, bird watching, old buildings
Availability for work:	1st August
Referees:	Mr & Mrs J. Henderson, 22 Kenton Avenue,
	Reading, Berks
Experience:	2 years helping in a 'colonie de vacances' in
	the French Jura
Previous visits to	
England:	2 years ago, 5 years ago

Source: R. V. White, *Writing Away*, Unit 6, pp. 21–4, copyright R. V. White. Lingual House, 1986.

| UNIT *1* | # Improving Your Writing |

Discussion

1 How do you decide if a piece of writing is successful? There is an obvious minimum standard for things like handwriting or typing, for example, it must be possible to read the writing, but what else are we judging when we read a letter or an essay?

1.1 Work with a partner and think about the five points given below. Then tick (✓) the two points you think are the most important for you when you are assessing a piece of writing. There is no single correct answer here, but some points are much more important than others.

CORRECT GRAMMAR	
APPROPRIATE VOCABULARY	
GOOD SPELLING	
CLEAR ORGANISATION	
CLEAR, APPROPRIATE LAYOUT	

1.2 Below and on the next page you will find two versions of the same letter. Letter B was written first but it is not as effective as it should be. Letter A is an improved version. Read Letter B carefully and compare it with the corrected version.

1.3 Work with a partner and decide what sorts of mistake the writer of Letter B has made; are they mistakes of:

LAYOUT (L)	VOCABULARY (V)
PLANNING (PL)	SPELLING (SP)
STYLE (ST)	PUNCTUATION (P)
GRAMMAR (G)	

Some of the places where there are mistakes have been marked with a number. Write the type of mistake in the box at the side of the letter.

Letter A

18, Cambridge St.
Hebden Bridge
Calderdale
W. Yorkshire
December 11th 1988

Dear Mr Reeves,
I am writing to ask if you can help me with a problem.
A few weeks ago I bought a radio-cassette recorder from your shop but yesterday it stopped working properly. When I put the tape in and pressed the 'play' button it simply didn't move. I tried other buttons but unsuccessfully. I thought it must be the tape, so I put another one in but the same thing happened. It was worse than the first time because when I tried to take it out the tape rolled itself round a little wheel inside the recorder.
I would be grateful if you could repair the recorder. I enclose a copy of the guarantee and my receipt.
I look forward to hearing from you soon.
Yours sincerely,
R.C. Samoes.

8

Letter B

¹ <u>December, 11th 1988</u>

² W. Yorkshire
18, Cambridge St
Hebden Bridge
Calderdale

³ <u>Mr Reeves,</u>
A few weeks ago ⁴ <u>I've bought</u> a radio-cassette recorder but yesterday it stopped working properly. When I put the tape inside it and pressed the 'play' button it simply didn't move. I tried the other buttons but ⁵ <u>unsucesful</u>. I ⁶ <u>though</u> it must be the tape, so I put another in but the same thing happened. It was ⁷ <u>worst</u> than the first time ⁸ <u>cos</u> when I tried to ⁹ <u>get it back</u> the tape ¹⁰ <u>enrolled</u> itself on a little wheel inside the recorder.

I'm ¹¹ <u>writting</u> to ask if you could ¹² <u>do the necessary repairs on it</u>. I enclose a copy of the guarantee and my receipt.

¹³ <u>Please fix it.</u>

¹⁴ _____
R.C. Samoes.

1	
2	

3	
4	

5		6	
7		8	
9		10	

11		12	

13	
14	

**Improving Your Writing –
A checklist**

2 An important way of improving your writing is to have a clear idea of things that you should check before you finish your work. The list given below covers most of the points you should check in a first version of a piece of writing. It is very important and you will be asked to use it in many of the units in this book. It is designed to help you produce clearer, more effective writing.

IMPROVING YOUR WRITING

FIRST CHECK | **Check that your writing makes sense**
- Is it correctly organised on the page?
  (Writing models in each unit will help you check this.)
- Is the information presented in a clear, logical order?
- Have you put in all the information your reader needs?
- Have you put in unnecessary information?

SECOND CHECK | **Check that you have used the right words**
- Have you used any words that are too formal or informal?
- Can you replace any of the words in your writing with more precise or more appropriate vocabulary?

Check spelling and punctuation
- Have you made any spelling mistakes?
- Have you punctuated your writing correctly?

Check the grammar
* Have you made any grammatical mistakes?

ESPECIALLY
* Subject/Verb agreement

    s
(She *live* in Frankfurt.)
* Verb forms   *have been living*

(We *are living* here for 5 years.)

                                arrives
(I will meet you when train *will arrive*.)
* Countable and uncountable nouns

(We need more *information* about this.)
* Correct use of articles

(They went to *the* New York)
* Word order

(I bought a *red* beautiful dress.)

Using the checklist

3.1 Check that the writing makes sense
The following short report is very badly organised. Work with a partner and rearrange it so that it is easier for the reader to understand. The following writing plan will help you.

* History
* Company structure
* Organisation
* Strengths and weaknesses

A. Our production centre is in Wodenswil, the main grain business is in Samstagern and we have big stores in Olten and Au. We also have a small water-mill (although this is not very important for the company) and we have about 200 employees.

B. The only problems that the firm has are that it is rather dependent on the value of the dollar and that sometimes there is too much work to do. At such times our workers are seriously overloaded, but they receive extra payments during these periods and the company continues to do well.

C. Our company makes glue and glucose and is also involved in the grain business. It is 130 years old and has different sections in various parts of the country.

D. The organisation of the company is quite simple. It buys wheat, maize and barley from overseas suppliers and from some local farmers and has eight vans that it uses to deliver glue and glucose to its customers. We don't do a lot of advertising for our products and only advertise in local newspapers.

3.2 Check that you have not used the wrong words
Many of the words in the following pieces of student writing contain words that
have been used incorrectly. Work with a partner to improve the text by putting in
correct vocabulary for this context. Select words from the list given below.

Describe someone you have seen recently

He opened the door to the library, stepped in and looked towards the tables
where <u>persons</u> sat studying and <u>slammed</u> the door carefully behind him.
   He was a man of middle height, <u>clothed</u> in a blue coat which looked a bit
<u>unmodern</u>, but still <u>went</u> him well. He was in his twenties, had a hard-looking
face with dark eyes and thick eyebrows. His hair was brown and short.
   As he walked through the library he looked around him as if <u>seeking</u> for
somebody. When he <u>glanced</u> the person he was looking for, his severe
expression disappeared and was <u>removed</u> by a warm smile.

---

dressed   old-fashioned   people   replaced
searching   shut   noticed   suited

3.3 Check that you have written in an appropriate style
Like the other passages in this unit, the short composition below contains many
usage and vocabulary mistakes. The writer has tried to write a formal essay but
some of the language is too informal and some of the vocabulary is inappropriate.
Work with a partner and use the words and phrases given in the box under the
text to replace those that are underlined.

Are factories spoiling our rivers?

Nowadays <u>a lot of</u> factories are very irresponsible. Not only do they use a <u>lot
of</u> clean water but they poison the rivers with their chemicals. Moreover,
since <u>they haven't cleaned</u> the rivers the water system is <u>getting dirty and
dirty</u>. Therefore, we cannot swim and drink any water of the rivers. In
addition, <u>we cannot see any fish which can</u> be eaten. As a result fish is very
expensive.
   There was a <u>matter</u> in Japan a long time ago. A lot of people who ate the
fish <u>got</u> ill. This was because the fish had a disease.
   In conclusion, we can say it is dangerous to <u>pour</u> filthy water into rivers.

---

a great deal of   became   becoming more and more polluted   dump
many   problem   they have failed to clean   from
fish from the rivers cannot

3.4 Check that spelling, punctuation and grammar are correct
The text below contains many grammar and punctuation mistakes. Work with
your partner to improve and rewrite it.

I think one of the best way to learn a language is to stay and life in the
country where it is spoken because then have you to speak in every situation
in this language, you have to try to make understand so you can get it in a
short time. You must study not so long like you must study when you take an
evening course every evening in your own country.

Source: A. Hopkins and C. Tribble, *Outlines*, Unit 1, pp. 8–11, copyright Longman,
1989.

Further reading

1 Byrne, D. (1988): *Teaching Writing Skills.* A well-illustrated text introducing current views of the skill of writing in the second language classroom.

2 Hedge, T. (1988) : *Writing.* A rich source of ideas for the teaching and learning of writing skills, using a framework that includes both 'process' and 'product' considerations.

10   Integrated Skills

Introduction

So far in this section of the book we have been devoting a chapter to
each of the four language skills in order to give each one some
in-depth treatment. In this final chapter of part 2 we consider some of
the different ways in which these language skills may be taught in an
integrated way in the classroom. Some of the natural overlap of the
language skills has already been examined in chapters 6 to 9,
particularly with regard to speaking and listening and to reading and
writing, although there are situations where either three or all four
language skills can be integrated effectively, and in this chapter we
intend to examine some of these. We start by examining situations
which require an integration of skills in order for them to be
completed successfully. After this, we consider some different
approaches to the integration of language skills in materials. Finally,
we look at skills integration in the classroom by discussing a broad
range of different materials from the teaching of general English to
the teaching of English for academic purposes. We also consider
project work and role play/simulation in relation to the concept of
integrated skills.

Let us begin by trying to clarify the concept of integrated skills by
looking at the definition provided by the Longman Dictionary of
Applied Linguistics. According to Richards, Platt and Weber (1985:
144) it is 'the teaching of the language skills of reading, writing,
listening and speaking in conjunction with each other as when a
lesson involves activities that relate listening and speaking to reading
and writing'. If we look around us in our daily lives we can see that we
rarely use language skills in isolation but in conjunction, as the

definition above suggests and, even though the classroom is clearly not the same as 'real' life, it could be argued that part of its function is to replicate it. If one of the jobs of the teacher is to make the students 'communicatively competent' in the L_2, then this will involve more than being able to perform in each of the four skills separately. By giving learners tasks which expose them to these skills in conjunction, it is possible that they will gain a deeper understanding of how communication works in the foreign language as well as becoming more motivated when they see the value of performing meaningful tasks and activities in the classroom. As Morrow (1981: 61) states in his second principle of communicative methodology, 'One of the most significant features of communication is that it is a dynamic and developing phenomenon. In other words, it cannot easily be analysed into component features without its nature being destroyed in the process. It is of course possible to identify various formal features of the way language is used communicatively, and these can be studied individually. But the ability to handle these elements in isolation is no indication of ability to communicate.'

Situations Requiring Skills Integration

Let us now examine some situations which require an integration of at least two language skills in order for the task to be completed successfully.

As you are reading, note down the different language skills which are involved at each stage.

From the skills integration point of view the situations may be quite limited – such as speaking on the telephone and taking down a message or taking part in a conversation – or, alternatively, they may be much longer and involve more skills integration, as we can see in the following examples:

1   We may read about a film or a concert in a newspaper or magazine:

We ask a friend if they would like to go
We 'phone the box office to reserve tickets
We drive to the cinema/concert hall with the friend
We ask the clerk for the tickets
We watch the film/concert
We discuss the film/performance with the friend on the way home

2   We may need to read lecture notes/articles/a paper in order to write a composition or an essay

We discuss it with other learners/the teacher
We compose a draft
We rewrite it until we have a final version
We read the teacher's feedback
We speak to other learners/the teacher about the feedback

The two situations that we have illustrated above show how, in our daily lives, we are constantly performing tasks which involve a natural integration of language skills. They also show that in a real sense none of these stages are completely predictable. For example, in the first situation described above, all the seats may have been sold for that particular performance or our friend may reply that she cannot go to the film or the performance on that particular evening for whatever reason. However, at each stage there is a particular *reason* for using that particular skill.

Exposure to this type of 'natural' skills integration will hopefully show learners that the skills are rarely used in isolation outside the classroom and that they are not distinct as such, but that there is considerable overlap and similarity between some of the sub-skills involved (for example, in previous chapters we saw how the sub-skills of reading and listening involved purpose and anticipation).

The notion of 'appropriacy' will hopefully be developed in learners if they can see how the four skills can be used effectively in appropriate contexts. As we said earlier in the chapter, overall competence in the foreign language is going to involve more than performing in the four skills separately, it will also involve them in effective, combined use of the skills which will depend on the nature of the interaction taking place. We might also argue that as integrated skills materials are more likely to involve the learner in authentic and realistic tasks, their motivation level will increase as they perceive a clear rationale behind what they are being asked to do.

Let us consider one more example of the integration of skills in a real life situation: we may see an advertisement for a product that interests us in a newspaper or in a magazine, then we may wish to talk to a friend about it to see if they think that it would be a good buy. If after some discussion they think not, we might decide to leave it there, or we may decide to phone the company offering the product to get further details. Next we might write a letter enclosing a cheque which will be read by somebody at the company who will despatch the product, possibly with a covering letter.

We can break this down into the different language skills that it would generate: reading, speaking/listening, writing, reading, writing. Again, one important point to note is that none of the events in this particular scenario is entirely predictable, but will depend very much on individual circumstances as to how and when the outcome will be reached.

If you teach integrated skills in your own situation, pause for a moment and think about how you do it. In what ways are your integrated skills activities similar to/different from the ones outlined above?

Byrne (1981), with respect to integrated skills, makes a useful distinction between skill integration viewed as synonomous with 'reinforcement' on the one hand, and skill integration where the four skills are introduced and established naturally, or as naturally as is possible within a classroom context, on the other hand. In the former, integration typically involves linking the language skills in such a way that what has been learned and practised is reinforced/extended through further language activities. In some cases this would involve a focus on listening and speaking first, followed by reading and writing, as this would provide a convenient class-plus-homework pattern. However, this would not expose learners to contexts where the four skills are established naturally and could deny learners the opportunity to use the four skills with a measure of appropriacy. Let us look at how this might occur in an example from a typical EFL textbook where a writing activity is rather artificially 'grafted on' to the rest of the unit as an extension activity rather than being designed to fit in with the rest of the unit as a whole as illustrated below:

MAN: What do you do Miss Jones?

SALLY: I'm a secretary.

MAN: Oh, a secretary.

SALLY: That's correct.

MAN: Where?

SALLY: At Midtown Council.

MAN: I see.

SALLY: I'm looking for a small one-bedroom flat near my office.

MAN: Now let's see. Ah yes, here's one. It's in Billington road, and it's a one-bedroom flat.

SALLY: Billington Road? Where is Billington Road exactly?

MAN: Here, look at the map. Billington Road is just here, next to the Town Hall.

SALLY: Oh, that's wonderful.

MAN: Yes. Well here's the address and the telephone number. 23, Billington Road, London, NW7. 234-8181

SALLY: Thank you very much. Goodbye.

MAN: Goodbye.

MAN: (phones) Hello, hello! 234-8181, Mrs Johns? A young woman called Sally Jones is coming to view the flat this afternoon. She's a secretary at Midtown Council. Thank you Mrs Johns. Goodbye.

And the extension:

Sally's mother, Mrs Jones, is in London. She wants to see Sally for lunch. Sally invites her for lunch. Sally writes her a message:

Mum, Please meet me outside the Shakespeare pub at 1pm. You can't miss it. It's next to the Odeon cinema.

Love, Sally.

If we contrast this example with those that we examined earlier in the chapter it does not really focus the learner on examples of authentic skills integration.

Recently, however, some materials have been produced which aim to provide learners with a balanced approach to integrated materials which are graded from elementary through to advanced. The Integrated Skills series from Heinemann (Bell, 1990), for example, claims to offer 'a new approach to skills teaching, in which integrated skills activities bring together reading, writing, listening and speaking in a natural and realistic way, and provide a balanced method for students to practise and develop their language skills.' Ten units form the basis of each book, each unit containing three lessons linked to the main theme of the unit. Typical themes in these units are: health, earning a living, the unconscious mind, education, protecting wildlife.

Look at the materials provided on pp. 207–10 from one of the textbooks in the series. The section giving information on the breakdown of the skills from the map of the book has been deleted.

From your reading of the materials, try to decide which skills are being practised at each point. What language is being practised at the same time? Do you feel that there is a natural progression of skills through the unit?

Integrated Skills in the Classroom

Nunan (1989) suggests how an effective language lesson can incorporate a range of different factors into it which ought to maximize language learning potential: he calls it 'the integrated language lesson'. Developing a unit of material to practise the integration of language skills in the context of a restaurant, he includes the following seven design principles:

1 *authenticity*: A tape containing authentic interaction between a waiter and a restaurant customer for learners to listen to.
2 *task continuity*: One activity builds on what went before; for example, listening leads on to reading and discussion.
3 *real-world focus*: The materials make an explicit link between the classroom and the 'real' world.
4 *language focus*: Learners are systematically exposed to the language system and are encouraged to identify patterns and regularities through discovery learning.
5 *learning focus*: The tasks develop the skills of self-monitoring and self-evaluation.

7 Which Job?

1 Look at the list of jobs below and choose the one that you would most like to do and the one that you would least like to do.

nurse
journalist
shop assistant
manager of a football team
policeman/woman
air steward/stewardess
cook
car mechanic
disc jockey
farmer

Compare your choices with another student and explain your reasons.

2 Which of the following qualities do you think are important in an air steward/stewardess?

good looks
intelligence
knowing several languages
good eyesight
physical fitness
a technical knowledge of aeroplanes
smart clothes
the ability to swim
patience
knowing how to look after babies
a knowledge of First Aid

3 Listen to Mark's conversation with the recruitment officer at Virgin Atlantic, an airline which carries passengers from London to America. What are the job requirements? Fill in the chart below.

Age
_____

Height
_____

Other requirements
_____

4 Read the article opposite in which an air stewardess talks about her work. Match the titles below with the right paragraph.

Training
The Route and my Job
Getting the Job
Working Hours
Introducing Debbie Mason
Social Life and Family Life
Health Problems

WORK MATTERS

There's more to being an air hostess than serving packaged meals to overweight businessmen.

❊ ❊ ❊

Debbie Mason, 24, has risen through the ranks to become an in-flight purser (head stewardess) with Virgin Atlantic. She told Sue Wheeler about her life on Richard Branson's airline and what it takes to get on in this high-flying job.

❊ ❊ ❊

Some time ago I was working in an office when I saw a picture of Richard Branson and read about him starting a new airline, Virgin. I sent him a letter saying I was interested in working for him. After a successful interview with a recruitment officer, I began their four-week training course. The personnel officers say it's usually obvious at the start whether somebody has the right qualities or not. Personality is very important. You have to be flexible, attractive, very well-groomed and able to smile when duty calls – even if you don't feel like it. Obviously you don't need airline experience, but nursing, or other work with people, is useful.

❊ ❊ ❊

The training course is really common sense although the practical side includes things like life-boat sessions in a swimming pool, fire fighting in a smoke-filled room and learning how to deliver a baby. In reality, though, you end up dealing mainly with travel sickness. The point is you have to be prepared for everything.

I had to pass exams in safety equipment procedures and first-aid which are required by the Civil Aviation Authority (CAA), plus Virgin's own cabin services course.

❊ ❊ ❊

I work on flights from Gatwick to New York or Miami. And I'm definitely not a glorified waitress! Only 10% of my work involves serving people. The emphasis is on safety and that's what we're here for. Before every flight there's a briefing where the crew are asked questions on first-aid and safety.

❊ ❊ ❊

I think this job ages you. On flights to New York I'm on board from 2.15 in the afternoon until nearly midnight our time. I'm supposed to drink eight pints of water per flight to prevent my body from dehydrating, but it's nearly impossible to get through that much. So my skin is probably suffering. But I think these are minor disadvantages. When we go to New York it's only 6.55 pm American time and we usually go out and have a party!

❊ ❊ ❊

I fly about four or five times in a 28 day roster, which means I work hard for two or three days, then take time off. I get at least eight days off every month, so it doesn't feel like most other full-time jobs. I get four weeks holiday a year, three of which have to be in the winter. But as one of my perks is being able to fly with any airline for 10% of the normal cost, I can afford to go to far away places in search of winter sun.

❊ ❊ ❊

It's a sociable job on board and off. There are only 220 crew members in total so we do know each other pretty well. This means things are very friendly and I think it's obvious to the passengers that we're having a good time, which helps them relax. When people leave Virgin to work for other airlines they often miss the intimacy of a small company and come back. But although the social life with Virgin is fabulous, outside it's non-existent. Friends and family know my time off is precious, but even at home I'm sometimes on standby. The job puts a strain on any romance. Happily my boyfriend works for Virgin too, and we chose to work a 'married roster' which means we fly together all the time. It's either this or take a chance you'll bump into each other once in a while.

---

5 Decide whether the following statements are true or false. If they are false, correct them.

  a She enjoys working for Virgin Atlantic.
  b Serving food takes up most of her time.
  c Virgin Atlantic recommends that she drinks a lot of water during flights.
  d She has less free time than people do in most other jobs.
  e She can get cheap flights on any airline.
  f She doesn't see her boyfriend very often.

H OMEWORK

Choose the job that you would most like to do. Write a paragraph describing the requirements for the job and what the job involves.

Map of the book

	TOPIC	SKILLS

UNIT 1 LIVING

LESSON

1 Around the World	Different lifestyles Hobbies and interests	Reading: Getting specific information from a magazine article Vocabulary: Finding synonyms in a text Speaking: Discussing hobbies and interests Writing: Writing a profile
2 Living at Home	Home life Relations with parents How to bring up children	Speaking: Answering a questionnaire Listening: Listening for gist Writing: Drawing up a set of rules for parents
3 Another Country	The problems of living abroad Impressions of Britain	Speaking: Discussing why people live abroad Reading: Reading a magazine article for gist Listening: Making notes from an interview Writing: Writing first impressions of a country

UNIT 2 THE POLICE AT WORK

4 Missing People	Reporting a missing person Physical descriptions	Writing: Predicting questions Vocabulary: Labelling a diagram Listening: Listening for specific information: physical descriptions Writing: Writing a physical description for a poster
5 Accident	Car accidents	Reading: Deducing meaning from context Speaking: Discussing accidents and how to reduce risks Writing: Writing a report of a road accident from notes
6 Burglary	Protecting your house Describing objects	Vocabulary: Objects found in the house Identifying objects from descriptions Listening: Listening for specific information: detailed descriptions of objects Writing: Writing a list of instructions

UNIT 3 JOB

7 Which Job?	Different jobs An air stewardess talks about her work	
8 Applying for a Job	Choosing holiday jobs Applying for a job	Reading: Reading intensively: job advertisements Listening: Listening for specific information: choosing a job Writing: Writing a letter of application
9 The Interview	Going for an interview	Speaking: Discussing interviews Reading: Making notes from an article Listening: Predicting questions. Making notes from interviews

	TOPIC	**SKILLS**

UNIT 4 HOLIDAYS

LESSON

10 Going Places	Holiday advertisements	Listening: Listening for gist and for specific information Speaking: Interviewing people about holidays Writing: Writing a holiday advertisement
11 Ballooning	Dangerous sports A ballooning holiday	Speaking: Discussing sports Reading: Reading for specific information Vocabulary: Labelling a diagram (parts of a balloon)
12 Complaining	Making complaints about a short holiday	Speaking: Discussing reasons for complaint Listening: Making notes from a phone conversation Writing: Completing a letter of complaint

UNIT 5 PEOPLE

13 Choosing Partners	Marriage partners Personal activities and interests	Speaking: Discussing what makes a happy marriage Reading: Reading an advertisement for specific information Writing: Writing a description of an ideal partner
14 Judging People	Character	Vocabulary: Character adjectives Speaking: Expressing opinions about people Writing: Writing a character outline Listening: Listening to voices and matching them with photographs
15 Predicting Character	Analysing character Psychological tests	Listening: Listening for specific information Speaking: Discussing methods of character analysis Writing: Writing horoscopes

UNIT 6 SURVIVAL

16 In the Antarctic	Survival in the Antarctic Going on expeditions	Vocabulary: Labelling a diagram Reading: Reading for specific information – intensive reading of extracts. Writing: Writing a leaflet advertising a trip
17 Ky Ho	The escape of a Vietnamese boat boy	Reading: Reading a newspaper article for specific information Deducing meaning from context Listening: Listening for specfic information Making notes from an interview Writing: Writing a newspaper article
18 Castaway	Survival on a desert island Favourite things	Vocabulary: Labelling a diagram (things on an island) Speaking: Discussing how to survive on an island Listening: Listening to a radio interview for specific information Writing: Writing a message

UNIT 7 HOUSE

19 Renting a Room	Having lodgers House rules	Speaking: Discussing renting a room Establishing the house rules Listening: Making notes from a conversation Listening for details Writing: Writing instructions

Source: B. Milne, *Integrated Skills: Intermediate,* Map of the Book, and Unit 3, pp. 14, 15, copyright Heinemann, 1991.

6 *language-practice*: The activities give the opportunity to learners to (for example) have controlled oral work practice.

7 *problem solving*: Learners work in pairs or in small groups to try to facilitate language acquisition.

As teachers we thus have a variety of ways of integrating the language skills in the classroom and in this section of the chapter we shall be examining some of the possibilities for different types of EFL classroom. We shall begin by looking at examples of general EFL materials; then we shall look at an example of skill integration from some EAP (English for Academic Purposes) Study Skills materials. Then we shall proceed to look at suggestions for developing listening and note-taking skills, giving oral presentations, project work, and role play and simulation.

General materials

In chapter 3 we looked at how *The Third Dimension* and *The Fourth Dimension* (1989) cultivate the dimension of 'expressivity' in language, and how these materials are designed to allow learners to express what they want to say and to give some depth to expressing it. From the integrated skills point of view the 'read, think and discuss' sections of a unit as the one illustrated on p. 212 build up the learner's sense of anticipation through a reading passage which moves on to a listening exercise and then moves on to discussing (speaking plus listening). One skill is dependent on another skill being practised before a full outcome can be achieved. The materials lead the learner, while reading the passage, to build up some anticipation which can only be satisfied by listening to an interview to find out the full picture. Hence, the skills are integrated across topics which the authors have attempted to 'personalize' for a wide range of learners.

EAP materials

Materials practising the integrated skills of listening and note-taking (writing) can be very useful in a number of academic and educational contexts, particularly for English for Academic Purposes students who will be going on to study their specialist subject through the

READ, THINK AND DISCUSS

What do you think she is talking about?

This is part of an interview with a young woman. Can you guess what she is talking about?

It was always the same. Always. I was in a house, a strange house, and I knew somehow that I shouldn't have been there; that I shouldn't have gone in. But there was some strange force, pushing me. There were some stairs ... very steep stairs ... and I started climbing them, and ... and then quite suddenly I fell. Then, when I was at the bottom of the stairs, I suddenly realised that there was someone ... or something else there in the house with me, and that these eyes had been watching me all the time, and ... I knew then that something terrible ... something awful ... was going to happen to me ... that I was going to be punished ... because I'd done something I shouldn't have done. I didn't know what it was I'd done; only that it was wrong, very wrong. Then I could hear it ... this thing ... whatever it was in the house with me ... coming closer in the darkness, because everything was dark, you see ... and it came closer and closer. And there was nothing, absolutely nothing I could do to avoid it ... nothing. I was trapped! Trapped in that dark house at the bottom of the stairs. There was no way out!

What do you think?

Choose the answer you think is best. Then give your reasons for the choice. She must be talking about:

a some terrible thing that really happened to her.

b a dream she had more than once.

c something she only imagined but which never really happened.

LISTEN AND FIND OUT 🖅

Now listen to the full interview. Then answer these questions:

1 What was she talking about?
2 What was she really afraid of?
3 How did she find out what her real fear was?
4 Have you ever had the same kind of fear?

FREE STYLE

In what kind of situation would you be afraid? It doesn't have to be a situation you have really been in. For example, it could be like this:
'I think I would be very afraid if I was walking down a dark street late at night all alone and suddenly I heard footsteps behind me.'

Then see if you can describe it to someone else.

Source: R. O'Neill and P. Mugglestone, *Third Dimension*, p. 64, copyright Longman, 1989.

medium of English. Materials such as the *Listening Comprehension and Note-Taking Course* (James, 1979), *Panorama* (Wilson, 1982), *Study Skills for Higher Education* (Floyd, 1984) and *Campus English* (Forman et al., 1990) are based on target analysis of needs and are designed to try to replicate as far as possible the skill areas that learners will find most useful in educational/academic contexts. Some of these materials focus directly on the types of study skills learners will need. For example: using your time effectively; dictionary skills; library skills; reading skills; note taking skills; writing skills; quoting skills and examination skills. Others attempt to integrate the four skills into topic areas which have a 'wide angle' appeal to EAP learners. Such topics might include the legal system; renewable energy; food for thought; our brave new world; health and the world of education.

Look at the following instructions based on materials from a section of *Campus English*. Decide which language skills the instructions require and consider the extent to which the skills are integrated in this section. (From Unit 8: 'What's it all for?', section 1: 'The World of Education'.)

A   *Consider the following questions*:
     Why are you continuing your education?
     What benefits will your education bring you?
     Try listing them in order of importance
     How do you see yourself in ten years time?
     What influence will your education have on this?
     Discuss your ideas on these questions with other students. Can you pinpoint any common objectives?

B1   *Tomorrow Talking* A television team conducted a survey recently to find out the attitudes of pre-university students in Britain.
     a) Read through the beginning of the report on this survey and note how it was organized in terms of target group selected and the way it was organized.
     b) Read on through the report and make a note of the actual questions that were posed by the interviewers.

B2   To find out more about the attitudes of students in your learning environment towards today's society, it might now be interesting to conduct a similar survey.
     a) Decide on the composition of the group you want to investigate.
     b) Decide on the manner in which the survey is to be conducted.

    c) Decide on the areas to be examined and the questions to be posed.

    d) Decide on the way in which you will collate and interpret the data.

B3   Conduct the survey and present the results in an appropriate way.

B4   Write a brief report on the findings.

Listening and note-taking using audio/video materials

It is possible for teachers wishing to incorporate listening and note-taking skills into their classrooms to use audio/videotape material which is available on the market or, if recording equipment is available, to record a short sequence on a topic which would be relevant to the needs of their own learners, thereby motivating them further. As Kennedy (1983) writes, this would then provide a realistic context in which the activity of note-taking could take place. It may be possible to work within the framework of existing materials by developing this principle to fit in with the ideas/topics covered in a particular textbook (we refer the reader to chapter 5).

Think about how a lesson based on audio/video input might proceed.

One suggestion might be to ask learners what they know or think about the topic in the first instance, clearing up any ambiguities or terminology beforehand. Next, the teacher can play a short sequence (5–10 minutes) of the tape and ask them to take guided notes on a sheet provided, or ask them to note down the most important points that they hear/see. When they have finished, the learners can be asked to compare their work with that of other students. A natural follow-on activity from this would be discussion work where learners should be asked to discuss points that they found interesting or, if the material is suitable, some aspects of the tape which may be more open to question (as happens in 'real' life). Then the students could be asked to reconstruct the overall 'message' of the tape from their own notes. A transcript of this section of the tape can be handed out afterwards for immediate feedback and self-correction. Natural integration of skills – primarily listening, note-taking (writing) and speaking, but also reading through notes to reconstruct the text – can thus be achieved.

Oral presentations

Preparing learners to give short oral presentations in class to the rest of the group is another useful way of achieving skills integration in the classroom. One way to begin this activity is to take cuttings from newspapers, magazines and topics presented (but not developed in this way) in existing teaching materials. In some cases reading material can be used as an initial stimulus and the activity can be graded so as to give lower proficiency learners an opportunity to work with less exacting materials. The learners can then take notes and try to pinpoint aspects of what they have read which will be worth discussing. They are then given time to prepare a short talk in front of the class and are encouraged to use maps, diagrams, charts and overhead projector slides if these can help to make the talk clearer to the group. During the presentation, the other learners are required to take notes so that they can ask questions and/or raise pertinent points during a plenary discussion after the talk has finished.

As teachers we can sometimes experiment with student assessment at this stage by asking the students to assess each other's work (peer assessment). It is possible to devise a fairly rudimentary evaluation sheet where small groups of students are asked to answer questions which might cover: what they thought of the presentation; was it well organized and were they able to follow the main points; could they summarize the talk for someone who was not present; did the speaker make effective use of visual support material; what advice would they give to the speaker for future presentations. This activity can thus inter-relate the reading, writing, speaking and listening skills in a motivating way.

Project work

Projects with integrated 'themes' which entail integrated skills can provide a pertinent way of giving learners an effective forum in which to develop these skills. Let us consider an example which takes the

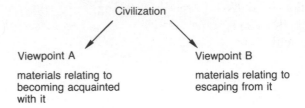

Figure 10.1

overall theme of 'Civilization' as its starting point and examines how it may be seen from opposing points of view. Viewpoint A is concerned with becoming better acquainted with it; viewpoint B is concerned with escaping from it, as shown in figure 10.1 above.

One possible suggestion for reading materials for viewpoint A would be magazine articles or books and booklets on the 'Grand Tour', a popular phenomenon in the eighteenth-century, when certain young men visited classical areas and cities in Europe. For viewpoint B, materials from magazines and newspapers on 'getting away from it all' and 'living on a desert island' could be provided. The reading component could be designed so that a 'jigsaw' pattern is established (see chapter 6) which would enable learners to piece together information from both parts to get a complete picture of the theme.

Possible listening activities might include interviews with a man on his reactions to the 'Grand Tour' and a woman/group on living a communal experience on a desert island. Speaking could involve discussion prompts such as: 'what problems do you think that people would have on a Grand Tour/desert island?' (reference might be made to health, money and safety for example); and 'is living on a desert island escaping responsibility?' The level of difficulty and amount of guidance offered could be varied according to the level of the learners.

Think of some ways of integrating writing skills into the project work outlined above.

The scheme outlined above is relatively teacher-led. In some cases it may be possible to allow learners to work on projects by collecting data themselves and, where they have access to native speakers, to devise questionnaires and interviews which they can then feed back into the group. Skills integration should develop naturally from the tasks that the learners are asked to complete.

Role play/simulation

Role play and simulation activities are often thought to be one of the most effective ways of integrating language skills in the language classroom. Though the terms 'role play' and 'simulation' have been interpreted in many different ways by both teachers and textbook writers, both activities offer a flexible yet principled way of tailoring integrated skills to learner needs.

What are the advantages to learners and to the teacher of using role play/simulation activities in the classroom? Are there any potential problems to using them?

It is generally the case that role play activities involve the learner in 'role assumption'; in other words, the learner takes on a different role (and perhaps identity) from his or her normal one by 'playing the part' of a different person. Role play is used more frequently in the general EFL classroom, that is, in the teaching of English for General Purposes (EGP), where the ultimate goals for learning the language are not necessarily specified in advance, if at all. It may be desirable, however, to give learners more practice in language 'use', even though it may be argued that the communication which ensues is not entirely natural, as the learners may not really empathize with the character whose role they have been asked to assume.

Simulation work, on the other hand, usually requires the learners to take part in communication which involves personal experience and emotions. Because of this, simulation is often seen as being central to English for Specific Purposes (ESP) situations where the task/s to be worked upon can be related directly to the learner's actual or intended occupation. As a consequence, the learner will not only learn more about the communicative use of language in the L_2, but will hopefully learn more about the setting/scenario relevant to their occupational field. For example, as well as building up competence in the use of the foreign language, a business person taking part in a meeting may well learn more about negotiation strategies in an international context.

Both types of activity clearly have their place in the classroom – be it for general purposes or for learners with more specific goals in learning the language – as they offer a flexible approach to integrating the skills, and actively involve learners at all stages by stimulating their creativity and responding to their particular needs and interests. According to Jacobs (1988:99) these types of group activity encourage positive student attitudes towards the target language, their peers, and the teacher, since 'the mutual dependence that co-operative structured activities require would lead to more communication among students because they need to exchange information and advice in order to succeed in achieving their goals'. They can also release the teacher from the centre stage position for a lot of the time, thereby allowing the possibility of more individual help if necessary. If we manage the activity effectively we hopefully can overcome problems of introversion and lack of fluency in learners by designing tasks that all learners can participate in. A model for structuring simulation (and role play) activities in the classroom is offered by Herbert and Sturtridge (1979). Their structure incorporates the flexibility mentioned above with respect to how tasks can be graded, the role of the teacher during the activity, and to the type of material to be used. They suggest a three-phase sequence for staging a roleplay/ simulation in the classroom. In the first phase learners are given the informational input and/or the linguistic input necessary to carry out the simulation. In the second phase the learners work on the activity by discussing the task or the problem set. In the third phase the teacher gives learners feedback on the activity just performed, possibly discussing errors and suggesting follow-up work if necessary.

In the first phase, for example, the informational input can either be in the form of a memorandum to read or perhaps it could be listening based. The linguistic input can be graded so that preliminary work can be done on the material in class before the role play/ simulation activity proper or, if the teacher thinks that the learners have had enough training, they can be presented with a 'deep end strategy' in which they are given informational input but then move straight into the second phase, the language work being dealt with as an 'outcome' in the third and final phase.

As an illustration of this, let us consider a role-play/simulation in which learners have to discuss some cost-cutting measures in their firm, company or school – a fairly typical situation. A task for the first phase of the simulation may involve the reading of a memorandum regarding an imminent meeting for the heads or representatives of different divisions/departments/sections in the company or school. The participants can be divided up into small groups for each division or section (or run separate simulations), and are given a memorandum to read and think about, plus some notes which summarize the present situation in their own division.

However, all participants could be given different information about their respective divisions and a 'jigsaw' is thus established which will be pieced together when this information becomes disclosed during the second (main) phase. For example, what might be an effective measure to implement in one section of the school or company could prove disastrous for another section. Ensuing interaction is therefore going to focus heavily on negotiating suitable outcomes for as many parties involved in the discussions as possible.

The information that the other learners have will be similar with respect to some of the measures above, and very different in other cases. Hence much of the meeting will focus on the negotiation and management of potential conflict. In the first phase it may be an idea to 'tease out' some of the language that the participants will need in the second phase. In this second phase the simulation itself takes place and the main focus is one of fluency. The teacher may wish also to take notes, operate audio/video equipment, or intervene in the simulation if so required. At the conclusion of the meeting, one of the managers can be asked to write a report to head office summarizing the decisions that were agreed upon in the meeting. This type of simulation is thus a highly effective way of integrating reading, listening, speaking and writing skills.

The third phase, the 'feedback' phase, has to be handled carefully so as not to become a negative account of what went wrong. For error analysis it might be possible to give a report on general types of mistake that were made in the group, or where and how communication broke down, as well as giving individualized feedback to learners. The simulation should also provide many ideas to the teacher for future language work. Other types of role play/simulation work might include setting up a committee to consider the applications of several candidates for a grant or scholarship which only one of the candidates can obtain. In another type of activity, students could enact roles in an imaginary courtroom by trying to solve a particular crime.

If your textbook does not provide any material for role play/simulation work, would you be able to incorporate some of the above suggestions into your lessons? Please refer back to chapter 5 if necessary.

Conclusion

This chapter has attempted to unify some of the issues raised in previous chapters by considering different permutations of integrating language skills in the classroom. First of all we attempted to define integrated skills, and the advantages to the learner of working with integrated skills materials. We saw that some tasks and materials only develop the skills in an 'additive' way and are somewhat removed from the ways in which we might use the skills in the 'real world'.

Finally we considered some class activities which offer different permutations of the skills: listening and note-taking using audio and video based materials; making oral presentations and role play/simulation activities. This chapter concludes the second part of the book. In part 3 we shall examine different ways of organizing the resources and management of the classroom.

In chapters 6–9 we looked at each language skill in turn. Review these chapters and see what implications there are for the integration of skills across the chapters.

Further reading

The following provide background discussion to integrated skills with some practical examples.

1   Byrne, D. (1981): 'Integrating Skills'. In Morrow, K., K. Johnson (eds), *Communication in the Classroom.*
2   Herbert, D. and G. Sturtridge (1979): *Simulations.*

Part III

Aspects of Classroom Methods

11   Group and Pair Work

Introduction: Structure and Content

One of our key themes in the earlier part of this book has been the effect of 'communicative' approaches on the design of materials for English language teaching. Provided that the term is not taken to imply a single methodology, it is clear that the development of a broader view of the nature of language and language learning has permeated language teaching over the last 20 years or so. From the perspective of methods used in the classroom, asking students to work in groups or pairs has come to be taken for granted as a natural, integral part of language learning behaviour and of communicative methodology. Most teachers are now familiar with these kinds of instructions in their coursebooks:

'Practise the dialogue with a partner'
'Ask your classmates . . .'
'Work in a group of four . . .'
'Give your story to someone else in the class to read'
'Do the quiz in pairs'
'What could happen next? Discuss in groups'
'Discuss your answers with other students'
'Choose a question, and ask as many other students as you can'

We shall see later that, although the relationship between materials and methods is in a sense an obvious one, it is not quite as clear-cut as it might seem, as indeed some of the examples just quoted here imply.

We can consider not only the frequency with which a particular activity is used in the classroom, but also to what extent that activity grows out of the materials themselves.

Check through the coursebook you most frequently use. How often are learners expected to work in pairs or in small groups? What kind of language material is being practised during pairwork and groupwork activities? For example, is it a written dialogue? grammar? free speaking on a given topic?

It will be useful at this point to make a general distinction in language teaching between *content* and *structure*. By 'content' we here mean the materials themselves – the language items selected for practice, whether structural or functional; whether subject-matter, situations and so on. 'Structure', on the other hand, is concerned with how classes are managed, and thus with decisions about various classroom options as to who works with whom and in what possible groupings. In Richards' words (1990: 10) : 'Classroom management refers to the ways in which student behaviour, movement and interaction during a lesson are organized and controlled by the teacher to enable teaching to take place most effectively'. Wright (1987) makes a three-way distinction between 'language data' (e.g. topic), 'method' (e.g. practice) and 'classroom organization' (e.g. 'work in groups') but we have chosen to put the last two together for the purposes of this chapter. 'Structure', in other words, is procedural, and can be thought of as being content-independent.

This chapter is the first of a pair in which we look at a variety of organizational possibilities for the classroom and the first one in a part of the book in which we look, very selectively, at aspects of classroom methods. Here we discuss, first, the functions of group and pair work. We then go on to consider the implications of various classroom structures for patterns of interaction between teachers and learners, and of learners with each other. The final section will examine possible advantages and disadvantages in different styles of classroom management. The first part of the chapter is mainly descriptive; the second part, evaluative.

The Classroom Setting: the Functions of Group and Pair Work

The social organization of the classroom

Managing classes so that learners 'work in pairs' or 'divide into groups' is now so much part of the everyday professional practice of large numbers of English language teachers that the instructions leading to these activities sometimes seem to be 'switched on' automatically, occasionally with a frequency that is difficult to justify. It happens with all kinds of content – dialogue practice, sharing opinions, reading aloud, comparing answers to questions, doing grammar drills, formulating questions in an information-gap task – the list could be extended considerably.

While all these can undoubtedly be practised in a number of different ways, at least two kinds of objection can be made. The first is the possibility that imposed classroom structures may not always be congenial to the learning styles of individuals in the class: we shall come back to this point in the chapter on individualization that follows this one, and again when considering how teachers, by observing what actually goes on in their classrooms, can become more sensitive to their students' preferred ways of working. The second objection is that a mechanical organization may pay insufficient attention to the relationship between an activity and its purpose. For example, it may be unhelpful to practise reading aloud in groups or pairs if students are unable to check each others' accuracy. If, however, the aim is to encourage learners to discuss a topic more freely, then a paired format may be the most useful one. As Morrow (1981: 59) writes: 'A consistent methodology is more than just a collection of activities or techniques. It requires an underlying set of principles in the light of which specific procedures . . . can be evaluated, related and applied'. Brumfit (1984) is similarly critical of a methodology that sees groupwork as a mere management device, preferring it to be a means of developing real communicative competence. (We shall comment on a possible modification of this view below.)

A more coherent picture of management structure is provided by the notion of the classroom as an aspect of 'social organization'. Seen from this perspective, any procedural decision by a teacher – asking students to work in pairs, or to divide themselves into groups, or nominating group membership directly – leads to a specific set of interaction patterns and to control of those interactions. The classroom, as we saw in chapter 1, does not operate in a vacuum, and this patterning is closely related to the role relationships of teachers and learners, and of learners with each other; and thus by extension to the nature of the school and to the whole educational, even socio-cultural, context. We shall need to bear this wider setting in mind when discussing the pros and cons of pair and groupwork. Wright (1987) explores the social organization of the classroom in detail, focusing particularly on organizational patterns, social relationships and role differentiation in relation to pedagogic purposes and out-comes.

Functions of groupwork and pairwork

As we have just noted, Brumfit is typical of many writers on language teaching methodology who see a necessary connection between the organizational structures available to teachers and a 'communicative' methodology. In many ways it is logical to assume a natural link between the learning of functional aspects of language use and a classroom-based behaviour that requires class members to exchange and share information and ideas. Such a link, for instance, may mean that students learn how to give and follow instructions in a paired format; while to respond appropriately in a typical range of practical social situations, or at a more advanced level, may involve the exchange of opinions within a small group.

We can, therefore, take communicative purposes to be a valid and important aim of group or pairwork. However, it would be limiting to think of this as the sole function of such 'alternative' methodological patterning. We need to remind ourselves that the language classroom does not only exist as a reflection of the 'real world' or, to be more precise, the world outside the school: it has its own rationale and frame of reference. As such, Morrow's criterion of a 'consistent methodology' can comfortably encompass the use of various patterns of interaction, firstly, for language practice and problem-solving activities within a modified communicative framework. Issuing invitations to one's classmates, reaching a conclusion in discussion using roles assigned by the teacher, or working with a partner to book a hotel room (as in Watcyn-Jones' *Pairwork*, 1981, for example) obviously require as much a linguistic as a social outcome. Secondly, such procedures can also allow for work on language content that is not functionally based at all: in a large class, practising drills will give individual learners more chance to speak than they might otherwise have. Wright gives the example of a blank-filling task that can become interactively interesting 'if groups of learners are instructed to identify correct answers and to speculate on the reasons for the incorrectness of the other alternatives in a multiple choice exercise' (1987: 143–4).

This takes us directly to the final point to be made here. The classroom is clearly a place where people have to work together, essentially requiring a compromise between their own individuality and the dynamics of the whole group. In other words, it is ideally a co-operative environment where structuring activities in different ways (quite apart from the primary language learning function) can allow for the establishment of a cohesive and collaborative working atmosphere. Wright (1987) captures this distinction by referring to both the 'instructional' and the 'enabling' functions of classroom organization.

Pairwork and groupwork

Pairwork and groupwork are not synonymous terms: just as they obviously reflect different social patterns, so the ways in which they are adapted and applied in the classroom also have distinctive as well as similar functions. Pairwork requires rather little organization on the part of the teacher and, at least in principle, can be activated in most classrooms by simply having learners work with the person sitting next to them (although other kinds of pairing – for example, according to proficiency – may be more suitable depending on the task). The time taken for pairwork to be carried out need not be extensive, and there is a very large range of possible tasks throughout the whole spectrum of functions we have identified, from fully communicative, 'simulated', structure and vocabulary practice, to those where an important aim is to set up co-operative working habits. Chapter 8 of this book ('Speaking Skills') has a number of examples, as does Harmer (1983: chs. 7 and 8) and Littlewood (1981: chs. 4 and 5).

A group, on the other hand, even though it can have a comparable range of functions, is by its very nature a more complex structure, which will probably require greater role differentiation between individuals as well as a certain amount of physical re-organization of the classroom. This role differentiation may refer to 'assumed' roles, particularly in a 'communicative' setting (having learners enact a courtroom scene with a variety of 'characters', for example, or 'pretend' to be a town council trying to negotiate a decision about building priorities), or to the structure of the group itself, with members being assigned tasks of chairperson, reporter/note-taker, and so on. The timescale often needs to be more extended, to allow for the greater number of interacting participants.

Finally, groups and pairs are not mutually exclusive, and there are a number of variations that bridge these two basic structural activities. For instance: individuals out of a pair can re-form to make a different pair; or pairs can 'snowball' by joining other pairs until eventually the whole class may have re-formed.

At this point in the chapter, it will be useful to briefly consider these two issues, one of which summarizes the discussion so far, the other of which looks ahead:

a) Looking at your comments on the first task in this chapter, to what extent does the use of pair and groupwork in your own materials reflect the different functions we have discussed? Try to distinguish particularly between 'co-operative' purposes and different kinds of language practice, as well as between pairs and groups.

b) How much flexibility do you have in your own teaching in the 'management' of your classroom?

Interaction and Classroom Structure

Arranging the class

Readers may well recognize one or more of the following possibilities for the physical arrangement of their classroom, as shown in figure 11.1 (where T = teacher, S = student, and the lines = main directions of interaction). Not all possibilities can be covered here,

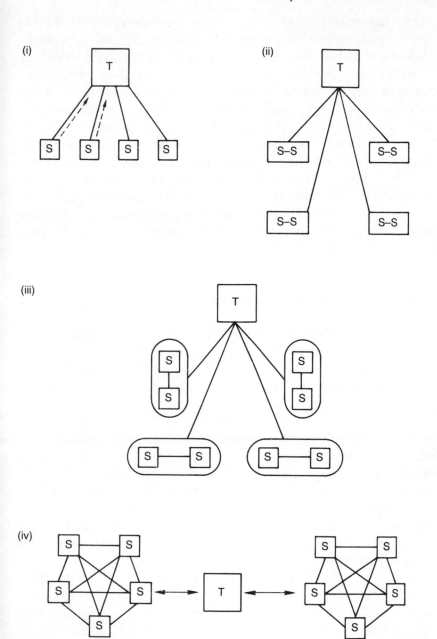

Figure 11.1

but we have tried to show a representative sample. Wright (1987: 58) sets out patterns in a comparable way, but also includes the relationship of individuals, pairs, groups and the whole class to the product, or learning outcome. He also sets out the layout in more detail. These arrangements are not necessarily static, and in a flexible classroom may change during the course of one lesson, both physically as well as in terms of roles and interaction. There may, of course, be straightforward physical restrictions on the possibilities, such as room size or the nature of the classroom furniture (tables, benches, worktop space, mobility). Space considerations not only act as obstacles to the establishment of a more communicative and co-operative classroom: a room that is too small for the number of students may actually force participative working patterns even where they are not appropriate.

Interaction patterns in the classroom

Just as a great deal has been written about different organizational structures in everyday classroom practice, so there is a large and rapidly growing research literature concerning the effects of various types of patterning both on aspects of classroom behaviour and on learning outcomes. The research comes particularly from studies in the psychology of second language acquisition, and from work in social psychology and the sociology of small group behaviour. Here we can only set out very selectively a few of the topics of potential interest to teachers, just to give a flavour of the debate. The bibliography gives several references which go into these topics in more depth, and teachers themselves may well wish to evaluate the relevance of these studies to their own classrooms (and ways in which the nature and requirements of research converge and diverge from those of teaching and learning).

The 'lockstep' class   The area that has received by far the most attention to date is that of the quantity and quality of verbal interaction in the plenary class as opposed to the smaller group setting. The former is represented in simple terms by figure 11.1. (i) The principal researchers have been Long and his colleagues (for example 1975, 1985; Pica and Doughty, 1985), whose basic premise is that *pedagogical* reasons for group work can be supported by *psycholinguistic* research.

These researchers make a basic distinction between, on the one hand, a 'lockstep' organization of classroom interaction, where activities are 'teacher-fronted', and, on the other, a small group format. Lockstep is explained in terms of a simple sequence of teacher stimulus ◊ student response ◊ teacher evaluation of student response (a traditional pattern of teacher question – student answer – teacher comment). This is, in other words, a situation where the whole class is moving along together, 'where all the students are "locked into" the same rhythm and pace and . . . activity' (Harmer, 1983: 205), and where the teacher is the primary, even the only, initiator. Long (1975: 216) comments more critically: 'The teacher who attempts to conduct a large, heterogeneous group of . . . 30 secondary age EFL students through a language programme as one unit is obliging all students to cover the same ground at the same time, at the same pace, via the same approach, method and technique, and using the same material'. In such a context, he argues, 29 out of 30 people will be 'unemployed' at any one time, at least as far as observable learning behaviour is concerned.

It follows from this that breaking the class down into smaller size units (groups, pairs) should in principle lead to a greater amount of language being spoken by each individual, and to a wider variety of language functions being used as a result of increasing role differentiation. Long quotes research by Barnes on 'exploratory' language in the small group setting, though whether L_1 use can be assumed to have direct relevance for the learning of a foreign language is debatable. Finally, Malamah-Thomas (1987: 7) isolates 'action' and 'reaction' as characteristics of traditional lockstep arrangements, and stresses the need for 'interaction', 'a constant pattern of mutual influence and adjustment', whether between learners, or teacher and learners. We shall comment in a little more detail on the implications for teaching of this kind of research in the next section.

Group structure   Discussion of the nature of classroom organization also draws on very extensive research into the 'social' structure of groups of participants working on specific tasks. It is interesting to speculate what might happen if we simply tell the whole class to divide into small groups in any way they choose: will they do so randomly, or with friends, or with people of similar proficiency? Furthermore, if we imagine giving a free discussion topic to a sub-group consisting of, say, six or seven of our students, and we then leave them to talk with only a small amount of monitoring, it is probable that some will talk more than others, one or two will want to dominate and control, others will react by withdrawing into silence, and so on.

These kinds of 'natural' grouping, and relatively spontaneous speech and behaviour patterns within an unmonitored group, are clearly quite different from the other end of the spectrum of control, where the teacher specifies both the group and the nature of the task in detail (a dialogue rehearsal, for example). The majority of classes fall somewhere between the naturally occurring and the completely structured. Jacobs describes how he investigated co-operative behaviour in small groups in his writing classes, and relates it to research in social psychology on 'goal structure'. He found it necessary to *construct* groupings to achieve a co-operative rather than a competitive or an individualistic goal structure, on the argument that 'when I put students into groups, I hoped they would just naturally co-operate with each other. But my experience . . . showed that *groups* did not necessarily equal *co-operation*' (1988: 97). Wright (1987) cites more detailed research on how natural groupings evolve, and identifies four stages:

Forming
Storming (conflict behaviour in the group)
Norming (group cohesion starts to develop)
Performing (the group solves a task)

Learning styles

It is often argued that, in lockstep classes, learners are unrealistically assumed to learn what teachers choose to teach them, leaving no room for the kinds of individual differences that we touched on in chapter 3. We can, however, make a general distinction between overt behaviour – what learners appear to be doing, whether in groups or in the whole class – and covert learning processes that are not so easy to observe directly. Clearly as teachers we would wish to bring these two aspects in line as closely as possible: research on learning styles is a developing area that is beginning to contribute to our understanding, and one to which teachers, with their rich knowledge of classrooms and learners, have much to contribute.

One basic distinction in learning style research is between 'cognitive' factors (to do with the way people think) and 'affective' factors (to do with emotions and what we feel). There is some attempt to relate these to different types of teaching. Although there is an assumption that all learners will do better if they are in a setting where learning by discovery is encouraged, it is not clear that such preferences are universal. There is now quite a long research tradition on the strategies apparently used by 'Good Language Learners' (Naiman et al., 1975), and on the various cognitive and personality types that affect learning (Skehan, 1989). A number of writers are now trying to relate methods, not just to ideas about the nature of communication, but also to what is known about these kinds of psychological variables. Willing (1988), for example, directly relates cognitive style to methodology by looking at research into 'field-dependent' and 'field-independent' learners, claiming that the former will be more likely to prefer team problem-solving situations in groups, whereas the latter tend to favour situations that call for more individual work. This is only speculation, but it does point to the direction in which research on learning is moving. There are still many questions that have to be answered: it is not clear whether styles are teachable, nor how preferences might affect the practical organization of a class.

So far, we have looked at group and pairwork in the classroom from a number of angles as a procedural, organizational concept, and at some of the related research background. It is now time to turn to an examination of the potential advantages and disadvantages of such procedures.

Groupwork and Pairwork: Benefits or Drawbacks?

Before you start to read this section (and looking back at some of your comments earlier in this chapter), consider the feasibility and appropriacy of groupwork and pairwork as 'organizational frameworks' for your own classroom. What are the possibilities and limitations? And to what extent do you need to take into account external views and guidelines, rather than organize your class according to your own particular preferences?

We must be clear that any discussion of the advantages and disadvantages of particular methods is relative. There can be no absolute pros and cons, and we say again that what is appropriate in Mexico may well not be appropriate in Japan. This is why the headings in this section are all printed with a question-mark against them, to indicate the difficulties of making generalizations. We have stressed many times that any individual teacher with a single class has to be seen in the wider context of the school and its educational and social environment. In many parts of the world, and in the perceptions of many people, the status of 'teacher' commands great respect, and it would not be regarded as appropriate behaviour for the teacher to take a strongly interactive role. In other words, there are many different notions of 'authority' and 'social position', and the expectations of behaviour that go with them. Wright (1987) comments that such expectations directly affect our awareness of 'social distance', and points out that, on the whole, the greater the assigned status, the greater the sense of social distance and therefore the likelihood of a very formal working framework. The implications of this for whole class versus small group work in the language classroom are clear.

Again, it is often the case that 'knowledge' is regarded as content to be transmitted, so that language becomes a curriculum subject similar to history, or physics. In such a context it is unlikely that exploratory, problem-solving activities will fit naturally into educational philosophy and practice. The picture can become very complex when teachers and learners with different backgrounds and preconceptions meet in the same classroom. Consider, for example, the mutual difficulties of a teacher trained in the 'communicative' tradition with an instinctive preference for small group work, and a learner who believes that a teacher's role is to be an explicit instructor. Neither side is right or wrong, but a process of adjustment will certainly be necessary.

At the same time, we have also noted that 'the wider context' will include not only local conditions but also the English language teaching profession as a whole. From this perspective, research and practice are not static, and what is appropriate at a particular point may well be superseded a few years later. Wright (1987) reminds us that such concepts as 'power' and 'distance' can in certain circumstances vary even during the course of a single lesson. To deny the possibility of change, then, is to assume that all development is irrelevant. Neither position – the universal application of certain methods on the one hand, or a lack of openness to new ideas on the other – is very realistic.

A final consideration in setting out the framework for discussing the pros and cons of group and pairwork is the question of whose perspective is taken into account. Clearly any teacher will have a view; but so will learners, parents, colleagues, head-teachers and education authority personnel, and these views will not always necessarily be in harmony.

We now enumerate, first, some of the more frequently heard points in favour of groupwork and pairwork, and then some of the points against. There is insufficient space here to present argument and counter-argument for each of these points, and readers are invited to consider each argument critically and from their own perspective.

Advantages?

Our earlier discussion of the research base put forward a number of reasons why getting learners to work in sub-groups in a plenary class is often to be preferred to 'lockstep' (while also acknowledging that certain kinds of practice may best be handled with the whole class paying attention at the same time):

1 In a lockstep framework, there is little flexibility. Students are frequently 'observers' of others, and work to an externally-imposed pace. In small group and pairwork, on the other hand, the possibility of an individual's learning preferences being engaged is correspondingly increased. (We shall see in the next chapter how the individualization of instruction can take learners even further along this path.)

2 Groupwork in particular is potentially dynamic, in that there are a number of different people to react to, to share ideas with and so on: exchange of information is sometimes more 'natural' in smaller-scale interaction. The extent to which this is so, however, clearly depends closely on the nature of the task set.

3 Different tasks can be assigned to different groups or pairs. This may lead to a cohesive whole-class environment if these tasks can be fitted together, perhaps in a final discussion. Alternatively, a teacher working with a mixed proficiency group may have the flexibility to allocate activities according to learners' levels.

4   Each student has proportionally more chance to speak and therefore to be actively involved in language use. Furthermore, the more varied the types of activity, the greater the variety in types of language used. This takes us back to Long's earlier point concerning improvement in both quantity and quality.

5   Groupwork can promote a positive atmosphere or 'affective climate' (Long and Porter, 1985), as distinct from the more public and potentially threatening 'performance' environment of the lockstep classroom. Motivation, too, is often improved if learners feel less inhibited and more able to explore possibilities for self-expression. Arguably, too, co-operation in the classroom is encouraged. These are undoubtedly positive factors, but the individual classroom still needs to be 'in tune' with its educational environment.

6   There is some evidence that learners themselves favour working in smaller groupings. Student opinions recorded on the *Teaching and Learning in Focus* series of videos (Thematic module: *Learners*) claim to like group work, because it provides 'variety'; interestingly, less enthusiasm is shown for pairwork in some cases, one student saying that she does not feel she can 'take enough' from just one other person. Willing's (1988) research in Australia on learning styles amongst adult migrants to the country bears out these comments: from a long list of learning styles, groupwork was rated as best in 35 per cent of questionnaire responses as against only 15 per cent for pairwork. Nunan (1988), commenting on Willing's work, gives teachers food for thought by showing how much *teachers'* ratings of the usefulness of activities differ from *learners'* preferences. For instance, although 'conversation practice' is rated as 'very high' on both sides, pairwork comes out as 'very high' for teachers but low for learners. It has to be stressed here that published research data are somewhat patchy, and different contexts might well produce differential results. In chapter 13 we shall be looking at some of the small-scale investigations that teachers can carry out in their own classrooms, and the theme of 'learner preferences' provides us with a good example.

Disadvantages?

Many readers will recognize these kinds of stated objections to groupwork and/or pairwork, and as usual they must be evaluated critically and according to context. Some of them are practical and straightforward classroom management problems, whereas others are deeper in the sense that they impinge on attitudes to teaching and learning and the whole cultural setting of the classroom.

1   There is some concern that other students will probably not provide such a good 'language model' as the teacher, though this problem, of course, has to be balanced against the richer interactive possibilities that a non-lockstep environment can provide. Certainly feedback from the teacher requires a more complex arrangement when multiple groupings are involved, as does the necessary 'control' to ensure that quieter students are not dominated by more talkative individuals.

2   There are several possible institutional objections to re-arranging the classroom and to an increased communicative environment. Furniture, for example, may be impossible to move around or may encourage static interaction patterns (such as students sitting in rows on long benches fixed to the floor). Sometimes, too, school authorities or other colleagues may react negatively to what they perceive to be the increased noise levels that come from an active class.

3   Some monolingual classes readily use their mother tongue instead of the target language, particularly where discussion is animated and even more so when the teacher shares the same L_1. It is not surprising that interacting in English in these circumstances may initially be perceived as artificial.

4   Learners – as Willing's research shows – often have strong preferences, and it is not unusual to find a stated wish for teacher control and direct input of language material. It is even an expectation in many cases, and there is a point at which a teacher's doubts about its pedagogical effectiveness need to be matched by learners' perceptions of the 'best way' to learn.

5   If the class is divided into smaller units, there may be problems of 'group dynamics' where, for example, students may not wish to work with those of their peers assigned by the teacher to the same

group. This may be compounded by feelings of being 'better than' or conversely 'worse than' others.

6 By far the most commonly heard objection to 'alternative' class-room arrangements, and in some ways underlying all the others listed here, is that of class size. It is all very well, the argument runs, to conduct group and pairwork if you only have a small, multilingual class of co-operative adults working in a comfortable, modern environment, but 'try doing it with a class of forty!' This is the title of an article by Nolasco and Arthur (1986), in which they try to meet the 'large class' objection head on. Using their experience of teacher training in Morocco, they first of all list nine reasons for teacher resistance to what were perceived as 'new' ideas and techniques. These reasons, some of which we have already met, were as follows:

> Students not interested in unfamiliar materials and methods
> Discipline problems
> Physical constraints
> Problems of duplicating material
> Students prefer grammar and exam practice
> School administration objects to noise
> Students talk in L_1 in pairs
> Students complain they are 'not being taught'
> Enthusiasm causes problems of class control

The authors are sympathetic and sensitive to these objections, and they go on to sketch out a phased plan whereby teachers and learners can gradually be introduced to the advantages of group and pairwork. The plan starts from the basis of familiar materials and working patterns, and slowly increases learner responsibility, initiation and control. A more detailed discussion by the same authors of the direct relationship between the large class and communicative methodology can be found listed in the 'Further reading' section of this chapter: the perceived problems are wider than just the methodology of group and pairwork.

Conclusion

In this chapter we have tried to show that dividing a class into small groups, asking learners to work in pairs, or, by implication, any kind of 'structuring' decision by the teacher, are not merely a set of alternatives that can be mechanically applied. However sound their justification in principle, all such arrangements have to be assessed in terms of the teaching situation in its widest sense – the existing syllabus and materials, expected roles of teachers and learners, the practicalities of physical space, the institution, and the whole educational system. At the same time we would wish to argue again that no teaching environment can be regarded as fixed for all time. New syllabuses are introduced, often in line with shifting perceptions of national and international needs; attitudes of teachers and learners to materials, methods and to each other change; the expectations of individuals develop, both for themselves and alongside wider social changes. As we shall see in the remaining chapters, all these considerations have direct implications for the training and development of both teachers and learners.

Draw up a table for your own classroom of the things you like about group and pairwork, and the things you don't like. You will probably be able to think of more points than we have included in our discussion here.

If possible, compare your ideas with those of a colleague – it would be particularly interesting if you could work with someone from a different background to your own.

What factors do you think influence your opinions? It may be the materials you use; your learners' attitudes; school policy; your view of your own role; and so on.

Further reading

1 Nolasco, R. and L. Arthur (1988): *Large Classes*. As indicated in the chapter, this discusses many practical issues to do with large classes, referring particularly to communicative methodology.

2   Nolasco, R. and L. Arthur (1986): Try doing it with a class of forty! Gives a specific example of the introduction of group and pairwork techniques to a group of teachers who at first thought such techniques would be inappropriate and difficult to use.

3   Wright, T. (1987): *Roles of Teachers and Learners*. Explores the different possibilities for teacher and learner roles in the classroom, relating them to the wider context. This can usefully be read alongside Malamah-Thomas *Classroom Interaction* (1987).

12 Individualization, Self-access and Learner Training

Introduction

In the last chapter we considered some of the different possibilities of structuring the classroom with groups and pairs of learners in mind. In this chapter we shall be looking at the concept of individualization in language learning and the extent to which this can be implemented both inside and outside the classroom. We shall begin by thinking about why we may wish to individualize the classroom. Then we shall examine some possible definitions of individualization, self-directed learning and self-access and try to relate them to actual learning situations. Finally, we consider the emerging area of learner training in relation to individualizing the classroom.

Any real growth in the phenomenon of individualization began about twenty years ago and was nourished by the Threshold proposals of the Council of Europe (Richterich and Chancerel, 1980) and the notion of 'Permanent Education', or Education for Life, with respect to which pioneering work was undertaken at CRAPEL (Centre de recherches et d'applications pedagogiques en langues), a language teaching and research centre at the University of Nancy, France. Individualization in language learning is also symptomatic of the development of interest shown in the learner and the learners' needs, particularly, but not exclusively, in the realm of Languages for Specific Purposes, which has grown apace over the past two decades. Skehan shows how these developments represent a significant move away from the behaviourist, psychological approaches to language learning in the 1960s to a renewed interest in cognitive approaches to learning which emphasize 'the active, hypothesis forming nature of the learning process' (1980: 28). The phenomenon has grown to such an extent that entire conferences are now devoted to it. (See for example ELT Documents 131 *Individualization and Autonomy in Language Learning* (1988), and *Autonomy in Language Learning*, Language Centre, University of Florence (1989).

Why individualize the classroom?
Before reading further, think of some reasons why classroom teachers may wish to individualize language learning.

First of all, it is clear that language learning normally takes place in groups and, as Bowers suggests, 'a major question therefore becomes that of ensuring that the place of the individual in planning and participating in the learning process is not suppressed by the built-in constraints of the group context' (1980: 72). Every class is composed of individuals each of whom will have different capabilities and general work rates, and among these heterogeneous groups it can obviously be a problem for the teacher to allow for the variety of pacing which will be necessary if all students are to learn effectively. We sometimes speak of 'teaching up' to some students or, conversely, 'teaching down' to others. It is quite common to hear other teachers speaking about 'teaching to the middle range of the group' hoping that this will best satisfy students' needs. In this context individualization can help to break the lock-step of the classroom (the teacher assumes that all learners have assimilated the same amount of material by the end of a particular class when, in most cases, they will not have done). As a concept, individualization is not just limited to language learning either. 'Open learning' centres are sometimes used in industry as part of an in-service or professional development programme for workers which may be tailored to their own individual needs and to the pace at which they prefer to learn.

Many practitioners believe that all learners can make satisfactory progress in learning a foreign language if they are given sufficient time, plus the possibility of developing their preferred learning styles and habits. It is clear that some learners work better in groups whereas others prefer to work alone. Some learners have a preference for a particular time of the day, and for many the place of study can be very important, be it in class, in the language laboratory or at home. In some learning contexts it can be very difficult for learners to attend classes regularly, perhaps because of other commitments, and in these situations an individualized programme may prove to be an effective mode of learning. As Dickinson suggests (1989: 35) even though these practical reasons are important, individualization is also important for educational reasons: 'firstly, at its broadest, to help people to develop into independent individuals, able to think for themselves, and secondly, more narrowly, to prepare people to learn. That is, helping people learn how to learn. Thus, at the end of a successful educational process, the student should be capable of designing and managing his or her own learning projects.'

In sum, individualization as a concept in language teaching and learning aims at providing as many permutations as possible to the learner in order to break the traditional lock-step of the classroom.

How do you cater for individual learner needs in your classroom at present?

Individualization: Possible Definitions

To some practitioners, individualization is a term which is used to cover all topics which focus on the learner as an individual. Geddes and Sturtridge (1982) start from this viewpoint. Brookes and Grundy (1988) also see it as a widely applicable concept, which has learners at its centre irrespective of whether they work with or without the help of a teacher. Chaix and O'Neil (1978) comment on how individualization involves the adaptation of criteria such as goals for learning, content, methodology and pacing to a particular individual, although whether this is determined from the perspective of the teacher or of the learner would need to be ascertained.

Brumfit and Roberts (1983: 193) argue that individualization involves: 'the organization of learning and teaching in such a way as to allow the abilities, interests and needs of the individual learner to be enhanced as effectively as possible; with the consequence that the traditional notion of the "average student" and "aiming for the middle" in teaching is abandoned.'

The mention of the *organization* of teaching and learning above leads us to consider the notions of autonomy and self-directed learning in relation to individualization. Autonomy and self-directed learning entail individualization, but as Trim (1976: 1) has shown, 'it is possible to pursue individualization within a highly authoritarian framework. The teacher looks at the individual's problems, but decides herself how different types of individual should be treated.' If we consider the implications of Trim's statement, then an individualized programme in this sense would be the very antithesis of self-direction and autonomy. There is consequently an issue between freedom and control, between autonomous, self-directed learning and externally (teacher) directed learning. It may therefore be useful to see the totally externally directed mode and the totally self-directed mode as two polarities in individualizing language teaching, with the majority of programmes occurring somewhere between the two extremes (see figure 12.1). It is probably fair to state, therefore, that total autonomy is only pertinent if it results in an efficient and satisfying mode of learning for that particular individual.

Individualization is also a partial response to the belief that direct teaching in the classroom does not always result in learning taking place. Teaching can take place without learning, whereas learning can often occur without any formal teaching. As Riley (1982) points out, learning cannot be done *to* or *for* learners, it can only be done by them, and this is one of the basic principles in the definitions of individualization: that learners will assume some responsibility for their own learning at some stage in the process.

Individualization does not necessarily mean that the students will be working on their own either. In some cases individualization can

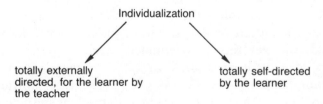

Figure 12.1

take place in small groups or pairs where students work on a similar task. At other times the learner may work with a teacher or in a solitary mode.

It is useful to see individualization not as a method *per se*, but as a possibility of re-organizing the resources and management of the classroom environment and, as such, has many implications for the teacher. Sheerin (1989: 3) quotes Strevens, who suggests that 'it takes better teachers to focus on the learner', and clearly individualization may involve some teachers in hitherto unknown roles such as 'guide', 'helper', 'facilitator'. How we get learners to work in an individualized mode may well depend on how much structure we wish to give them. It seems clear that all language learners need to feel some purpose to be successful in their learning, and to help in the achievement of this Dickinson (1989) suggests analysing the language needs of the learner and then establishing a 'contract' with each of them. Points in each individual contract may include agreement between teacher and learner on learning objectives in relation to different language skills, the level of improvement aimed at, and how and when this may be achieved. After this, it is up to the teacher and learner to decide exactly how to proceed from here. They may decide to allow the learner more or less total autonomy in trying to attain the objectives set, as a teacher from Italy reported to us: 'Ideally I wouldn't interfere with what the students select at all, but during the explanation of the materials I would suggest to students that they choose material in areas where they feel they have problems or which are their weakest areas. But after that, I wouldn't interfere at all. . . . they can select what they want and proceed with it themselves. . . . they know where their weak areas are. Generally students select the material that's most appropriate to their problems.'

Implementation Inside and Outside the Classroom

It is quite common to hear teachers complain about the many reasons why they feel that they cannot individualize their classrooms. These arguments sometimes relate to the fact that they are non-native speakers; that they are under-resourced in general; that the syllabus is strictly controlled; that class size is too large (perhaps even more reason for needing to individualize); that materials are 'fixed';

furniture is screwed to the floor thereby restricting movement of learners; that they work in a school and not a university. In other words, all the variables and constraints that we mentioned in chapter 1.

In this next section we hope to show that the provision of a measure of individual choice need not entail a full-scale reorganization of the classroom and resources and that individualization may be started in a relatively modest way.

One way of attempting to provide a measure of individual choice in the classroom is to use self-access activities where learners choose the tasks and activities that they wish to pursue with or without the help of a teacher. For example, learner X might have problems with reading skills and may opt to do extra work in this area. Learner Y may have a need to do some extra listening work. Of course self-access does not have to be remedial (implying that one is asking the learners to begin from a linguistic lack); some learners positively want to work in areas that they enjoy and where they wish to enhance their performance. Some teachers programme self-access work into their weekly time-table – perhaps for two sessions a week to begin with – and build up from there. Self-access might be offered as integral to a particular course, or in a supplementary mode in a resource or self-access centre (see later in this chapter).

Something to note at this stage is that a self-access operation does not have to be a full-scale one to begin with. Where resources are limited, it is possible to set up the classroom as a mini self-access centre with different parts of the room being used for different activities – perhaps reading in one corner, listening with cassettes and headphones in another, and some computer assisted language learning (CALL) in another. As materials and hardware can perhaps be stored easily and transported on a trolley, a small-scale beginning may enable teachers working within administrative constraints or working with sceptical colleagues to start a self-access operation with the hope of extending it later. As teachers we all have to prepare materials for lessons and provide feedback to our learners anyway – either in class or through marked homework assignments (homework is in any case often set and marked on the lock-step principle that we outlined above). One positive suggestion therefore, might be for two colleagues to collaborate over a mini self-access project by building up a small 'bank' of self-access materials.

Consider your own teaching situation. What kind of self-access activities would be appropriate for your learners and, if they do not exist already, how could they be set up within your institution?

As an illustration, reading is one area which provides ample scope for developing self-access work. Teachers can either design their own self-access boxes, perhaps working with other colleagues as we suggested above, by dividing materials into different levels according to topic and level, or can use and adapt some commercially available materials, depending on the type of students in the group, their proficiency level, the purpose of the course and so on. The British Council (1983) reports on how colleagues at a British Council teaching centre in Mexico worked together designing boxes of authentic materials for their learners; the Centre for British Teachers (CBT) has produced a well utilized reading laboratory for use in German secondary schools. (For teachers interested in this idea, *Reading Choices* by Jolly (1982) provides many suggestions for reading activities.) Developing a reading laboratory for individualized classroom work is another possibility for teachers who may be working with limited resources. Stoller (1984) outlines the features that such a laboratory might usefully contain. Ideally it should:

- accommodate a wide variety of student reading levels

- have a large variety of reading selections at each reading level

- have a selection of high interest topics appropriate to the learners

- allow for systematic progression from one level to another

- permit students to progress at their own pace

- include a self-correction system

- include charts and graphs for easy record keeping

- include a placement test for accurate level assignment

- include exercises that require students to practise a variety of reading skills and strategies

Let us examine how this may work in practice. During the self-access class learner X decides to read a passage on ecology more or less at 'intermediate' level, which could be level 3 (level 5 being the highest). She goes to the reading laboratory at the front of the classroom, looks through the level 3 materials, selects the appropriate passage from the alphabetical index and takes the passage away to read. She may make notes on vocabulary and expressions, and has the option of answering the questions provided with the passage and checking them with a self-correcting key.

She notes down what she has completed in her contract or record book, and may or may not enlist the teacher's help depending on individual circumstances.

After working at this level (say level 3) the learner herself may decide to progress to the fourth level in the next class. In other words, the learner is exercising a good deal of individual choice and responsibility in what materials she selects and how she chooses to deal with them.

Look at the self-access material in the extract on p. 249 which appears in Sheerin (1989). Think about how it could be set up and used with your learners. Would any adaptations be necessary and if so, what would they be?

Walker (1987) gives an account of how she individualized a reading programme by getting the students themselves to bring along self-selected reading materials and making use of a 'standard reading exercise' which she adapted from elsewhere. In order to become part of an individualized language learning programme, self-access materials should enable the learners to: decide what work they want to do; find the material and work through it; correct/assess answers where necessary; have work evaluated when desired. For many learners in educational contexts where the teacher alone is perhaps expected to dispense all knowledge, it is advisable to lead students in gradually, make sure that they are satisfied with working in this particular mode, and that they understand the rationale for the type of material they will be studying. Well-designed materials should make the learner secure enough to work alone.

Earlier in the chapter we mentioned that self-access work can be done on a larger scale outside the classroom, and where the latter is

3.3 Introducing Sherlock Holmes

CLASSIFICATION   R.CO/1 = Reading. Comprehension activity/1

LEVEL   Lower intermediate

AGE   Adolescent/young adult

ACTIVITY TYPE   Comprehension activity

AIM   To read and look closely at the most important parts of the text and to check comprehension.

PREPARATION   Look up the following words in a dictionary if you don't know them: *a wound, to heal, a client.*

INSTRUCTIONS   Read the text below and say whether the sentences which follow are true or false.

TASK SHEET

For many years, I shared an apartment in London with my
friend, Sherlock Holmes,
My name is Doctor Watson. I worked as a doctor in the
British Army for several years. While I was in the army, I
5   travelled to many strange and interesting places. I had   5
many exciting adventures.
Then one day, in Afghanistan, I was shot in the shoulder.
My wound was deep and took many months to heal. I
nearly died from pain and fever. At last I got better, but I
10   could not work in the army any more. I retired from the   10
army and came back to England.
That is why I was living in London with Sherlock
Holmes. I had known my friend for many years. Our
address was 221B, Baker Street, in the centre of the city.
15   I enjoyed sharing an apartment with Holmes. My friend   15
was a very clever man. He was the most famous private
detective in London. He helped to solve crimes and catch
criminals.
When people were in trouble or needed help, they came
20   to Holmes. Sometimes the police came to Holmes and   20
asked for help in catching a criminal.
Sherlock Holmes did not care if his clients were rich or
poor. He enjoyed solving their interesting problems. He
was very happy when he was working. It was the most
25   important thing in his life.   25

From *The Sign of Four* by Sir Arthur Conan Doyle, retold by Anne
Collins.

60　　　　　　　RECEPTIVE SKILLS

True or false?

1 Sherlock Holmes and Doctor Watson lived in the same place.

2 Doctor Watson was a soldier in the army.

3 Doctor Watson came back to England because he was tired of the army.

4 When Doctor Watson came back to England, he got to know Sherlock Holmes.

5 Sherlock Holmes was a detective in the police force.

6 Sherlock Holmes helped people in trouble whether they could pay or not.

7 Sherlock Holmes liked using his mind.

KEY

1 True (lines 1/2 and lines 13/14).

2 False. He was a doctor in the army (lines 3/4).

3 False. He 'retired from' (= 'left') the army and came back to England because he could not work. He could not work because he had been very ill (lines 7/11).

4 False. He knew Holmes before he went to Afghanistan (line 13).

5 False. Sherlock Holmes was a private detective. He sometimes helped the police but he did not work for them as an employee (lines 16/17 and 20/21).

6 True (lines 22/23).

7 True (lines 23/25).

FOLLOW-UP 1

If you got fewer than 4 answers right, try a comprehension exercise at elementary level.

If you got between 4 and 6 answers right, try some more comprehension exercises at this level.

If you got all the answers right, try a comprehension exercise at intermediate level.

FOLLOW-UP 2

If you are interested in Sherlock Holmes, read the rest of the story.

Comments to the teacher

1 Students can gain more from such activities if the relevant line reference to the text is given after each answer.

2 Note that students can be advised to move to a lower or higher level depending on how many answers they got right. This technique can be used with many other activities.

3 Many published Readers contain examples of this kind of activity which it is possible to adapt for self-access.

Source: S. Sheerin, *Self Access*, pp. 59–60, copyright Oxford University Press, 1989.

the case, the self-access or resource centre should ideally contain the following software and hardware:

- resource room/s incorporating all materials
- consultation room/s for individual counselling
- listening (self-monitoring) section or laboratory
- computer assisted facilities with programmes on vocabulary, testing, reading and communication games
- video facilities
- wall charts analysing at a quick glance all materials available
- classified folders, drawers or boxes containing all the materials available in the centre
- answer sheets, or self-correcting keys where appropriate.

Sheerin (1989) gives a full account of how the centre can be equipped depending on the space available in the institution. Quiet activities such as reading, vocabulary work, grammar practice and general browsing for materials and cassettes should be located at one end of the centre, and 'noisier' activities such as self-access speaking, watching TV, video programmes, and doing CALL activities in pairs should be housed either in adjoining rooms or in side bays away from the main thoroughfare. The entrance and supervisor/librarian's desk should also be situated in a noisier part of the centre if at all possible away from the quieter more 'studious' activities.

Let us now look at an example of a wall chart on p. 252 which offers an overview of all the different materials available to learners in one resource centre (adapted from Sheerin, 1989).

If learners are interested in using some of the CALL programmes that the centre has on offer then they can refer to a more detailed sheet in the centre which lists the materials available with corresponding proficiency levels. The layout of a CALL reference sheet, devised by A. Sinclair for a class with overseas students at the University of Essex, is reproduced on p. 253. Learners are given the possibility of choosing their own programme within the skill area and level provided and can work either by themselves or with a colleague. A member of staff is available to offer administrative help, guidance

Reading, general	*Listening*	*Writing*
Intensive reading, short texts, extensive reading in specific areas.	Intensive listening/short texts, social English, extensive listening, e.g. listening to lectures.	Spelling, punctuation, controlled activities, guided writing, free writing topics, text types, e.g. letters, report writing.

Speaking	*Grammar*	*Vocabulary*
Pronunciation, sounds, stress patterns. Communication tasks, oral interaction activities.	Verbs, nouns, adjectives, tenses review, prepositions, use of modals etc.	Using the dictionary, text and topic based work, idioms, word building and associations.

Social English	*CALL*
Functions; requests, apologies, suggestions etc. Life in Britain, briefing on/study in Britain.	Vocabulary, grammar, reading practice.

and feedback to each learner. Each learner is also responsible for keeping a record book of all the programmes completed and new items of language that were learnt.

It is common practice for an institution to offer a general orientation worksheet to a resource centre so that learners can quickly obtain an overview of the way the centre is organized and which permits them to explore and think about some possible 'routes' that they may take in order to satisfy their needs. On p. 254 is an outline of a typical worksheet which can be handed out to learners so that they can familiarize themselves with the facilities available:

CALL Programmes available for you to use

(Level: E=Elementary, I=Intermediate, A=Advanced.)

1 Vocabulary Practice
   Crossword Challenge (1 or 2 players)   I/A
   Vocab (which word or skullman)   E/I/A
   Criss Cross Quiz (2 players)   E/I/A
   Screentest First Certificate (word formation)   I
   Screentest Proficiency (key words)   A
   Cambridge First Certificate (gap filling)   I/A
2 Grammar Practice
   Screentest First Certificate (sentence transformation)   I
   Screentest for Proficiency (sentence transformation)   A
   Choicemaster   E
   Criss Cross Quiz (2 players)   E/I/A
   Cambridge First Certificate (sentence rewriting)   I/A
3 Reading Practice
   Storyboard Plus   E/I
   Storyboard   I/A
   Clozemaster   E/I/A
   Speedread   I/
   Screentest First Certificate (space filling)   I
   Screentest Proficiency (space filling)   A
   Cambridge First Certificate (reading) Cloze passage   A
4 Writing Practice
   Screentest First Certificate (dialogue building &   I
   sentence completion)
   Screentest Proficiency (sentence completion)   A
   Wordstar (word processing)
   Cambridge First Certificate (letter/dialogue)   I

Self-Access-Centre
Orientation Worksheet

The questions on this sheet are designed to help you find your way around the materials and facilities that we have available in the self-access centre. Please ask your teacher or the librarian if you run into any difficulties.

1. In which part of the centre would you find (i) English language magazines, (ii) today's newspapers?
2. Where would you find the English Dictionaries? Write down the reference number.
3. There are some materials that you cannot borrow from the centre. What are they? Write down their reference numbers.
4. You would like to work on the microcomputer with a colleague. Which programs might be of interest to you?
5. What do you have to do in order to borrow a cassette tape?
6. When and where can you listen to the tape?
7. Write down the names of any tapes in your subject area that you would like to listen to.
8. You are interested in finding out more about the English language today. Which section would you look in?
9. Find the 'readers' section and note the titles of three books that you would like to read during the course of the term.
10. How many books can you borrow at any one time? How do you sign them out and how long may you keep them?

If you do not have the possibility of either setting up or using a self-access centre in your institution, think of some of the ways open to you for reorganizing your resources in small ways to try and individualize your classroom more effectively. If you do have a self-access facility, think about some of your learners and their individual characteristics and devise a plan of activities for each learner who will visit the centre for up to six hours per week on three separate occasions.

Once students have found their way around the centre then they can begin to devise an individualized plan which may, for example, include listening to general, social English, listening to lectures, some intensive reading (both general and perhaps subject specific), CALL practice and video listening with note-taking practice.

Many variables are clearly involved in the setting up of a centre of these proportions, not least of which will be a whole range of staffing and budgetary issues. Materials will have to be prepared and written; the centre will have to be maintained and regularly added to, perhaps by learners themselves in some cases; the centre will have to be supervised and students will have to be advised/counselled.

What we have attempted to do here is to show the different proportions that self-access activities might take. As we suggested earlier, it is possible for an institution or even an individual teacher to start off in a small way to begin with and to develop the facility as and when circumstances permit.

Advantages and shortcomings

Operating a self-access system will offer learners a wide choice of material and the possibility of becoming much more self-reliant and less teacher dependent. Hopefully learners will begin to understand more about their needs and how they prefer to learn. On the other hand, it has to be stressed that setting up a self-access system will involve a lot of time and work, usually on the part of the teaching staff, and that institutional constraints may mean that a full-scale centre will never become operational. However, if it is at all possible, the end result is worthwhile.

From the materials point of view, there is a danger in providing too much that is related to classroom work: the materials become 'further practice' or 'follow up activities' rather than allowing the students to explore and learn new things by themselves.

Focus on the Learner Through Diary Studies

In recent years some EFL teachers have been exploring the advantages offered by learner diaries as yet another way of focusing on the learner as an individual with certain needs. There is now a growing awareness of how these diaries can establish an effective channel of communication between teacher and learners.

The process works as follows: the teacher enters into an individual 'contract' with each learner in the class whereby the learners keep a daily record of events which happen to them. The teacher will only discuss contents of the diary in private with learners, who are free to develop the diary in whatever ways they wish. It may include observations of what they did on a particular day; observations and feelings about classes, teachers, peers, landladies; thoughts on how they feel they are learning with respect to a task, a class or the whole course. It is important for learners to understand the rationale behind the diary writing and the following example of guidelines developed for learners can be useful in establishing this:

LEARNER DIARY

The diary is a very important part of your studies here and will be of most help if you write it regularly. Your diary will enable you to express your opinions on all the classes that you take, and will help you to understand exactly what you need in your studies, as well as keeping a record of all the work you do. It will also give you valuable extended writing practice.

For the next few weeks we would like you to write each day about the lessons you have taken. There is no limit to the amount you can write, but we suggest that you spend at least 20 minutes a day on the diary. Your tutor will ask you to hand in the diary weekly; it will then be corrected, returned and discussed in tutorials.

It would be useful if your diary could include *some* of the following information:

date / lessons followed
how you think you performed
what difficulties you had
how you think that you might overcome these difficulties
what you found most enjoyable / least enjoyable
what you found most useful / least useful
what you feel about a specific lesson / the course / group / teacher / yourself
what you did in your spare time to practise your English
any other thoughts, feelings and experiences relevant to your personal progress on the course

Please look upon the diary as an exercise in writing fluently: your diaries will not be graded or strictly corrected, but frequent and important language errors will be pointed out to you. All diary entries will be treated confidentially.

Diary entries are often highly individual and allow learners to report on a range of different observations according to the needs and wishes of each learner. Some learners may offer a simple account of what they have done during a particular day from a general point of view. Other learners, however, prefer to focus on particular classes that they have attended or a specific learning issue, such as how they feel they are progressing with vocabulary or with listening.

Diary writing can be very useful for learners. What sort of information for future work do you think the teacher might be able to get from reading the diaries?

As well as giving each student authentic written practice, these diaries can help the teacher with counselling the learner on specific learning problems that may not have surfaced in the classroom. They can sometimes offer a teacher a fresh insight into the study techniques of a particular learner, which, again, are not always apparent in the classroom, especially when the teacher may be dealing with large numbers. As a result of reading the diaries it may also be possible for teachers to make corrective adjustments to materials and methods and to rearrange group dynamics in subsequent classes. For teachers wanting to investigate particular issues within their own classroom, they offer numerous possibilities of looking at the ways that individuals approach tasks and how they conceptualize and categorize teaching and learning events. By adding other data as well, it may be possible for the teacher to do a longitudinal study of a particular learner or small group of learners over a period of time – perhaps four to six months – in order to see what sort of learning/study profiles emerge for these particular learners.

Learner Training

We have examined individualization and some of its possible ramifications, such as using self-access activities both within and outside the classroom. We now start to look at other concrete possibilities for helping learners to learn more effectively by making them aware of their different language learning needs. As teachers, many of us have been involved in some aspects of learner training to a greater or lesser extent, by giving suggestions for organizing vocabulary books to using dictionaries more effectively, to how to exploit the environment outside the classroom for learning the target language wherever possible. As learner training can only really work effectively if we have some account of what a 'good' language learner actually *does*, let us briefly examine the background to some of this research. Attempts to develop systematic learner training during the last decade can be traced back to research which was originally carried out in Canada in the 1970s by Naiman, Fröhlich and Stern into the strategies of thirty-four adults known to be 'good' language learners. (Readers are also referred to the work of Rubin and Thompson, 1982, for an account of the good language learner. See also chapter 3, which raised several of these issues.)

Before reading further, what do you feel would be the characteristics of a 'good' language learner?

From Naiman et al. (1975) the following generalized strategies emerge as being of most importance. Good language learners:

- are aware of their own attitudes and feelings towards language learning and to themselves as language learners

- realize that language works as an organized system and is a means of communication and interaction

- assess and monitor their progress regularly

- realize that language learning involves hard work and time and set themselves realistic short term goals

- actively involve themselves in the L$_2$ and learn to take 'risks' in it

- are willing to experiment with different learning strategies and practise activities that suit them best

- organize time and materials in a personally suitable way and fully exploit all resources available

Taking these basic strategies as a starting point, Ellis and Sinclair developed what they called 'systematic' learner training during the 1980s; the final product was a published course in learner training entitled *Learning to Learn English* (CUP: 1989). Their systematic approach is designed to help learners to assume more responsibility for their own learning by providing tasks which include a focus on learning styles, self-assessment of needs, advice on how to use a self-access centre and strategies designed to improve each language skill. It is open to both teacher and learners to decide whether to integrate the course with the language learning materials that they are currently using, or to have distinct learner training periods during the course. The extract on pp. 260–1 aims at getting learners to analyse and prioritize their own needs:

Let us finish this section by looking at the following quotation from an EFL teacher being interviewed by Nunan (1991: 185) whose remark neatly encapsulates the feeling that a growing number of practitioners have with respect to the importance of learner training on their courses: 'As a teacher I see my role as being twofold. One is, yes, I am teaching the language, but I feel my other very important role is to assist the learners to take a growing responsibility for the management of their own learning. Within our programme, learners are with us for only a relatively – a short time, and we have to prepare them so that their learning can continue outside, erm, the length of their course.' On the whole evidence tends to suggest that teachers are becoming increasingly aware of the various opportunities that individualizing the language classroom can offer to both learners and teachers alike.

Consider the concept of learner training in your own teaching situation and the extent to which it would be feasible to incorporate it into your regular classes.

1.3 Why do you need or want to learn English?

1 Analysing your needs

Before you start your course, it is a good idea to think carefully about what you need or want English for. You could analyse your needs like this.

a) Decide on your *main purpose* for learning English e.g. for work.
b) Make a list of the *specific situations* where you need to use English
   e.g. speaking on the telephone, answering enquiries, giving information, writing business letters.
c) Decide which *skills* you need for each situation: extending vocabulary, dealing with grammar, listening, speaking, reading or writing.

You should then have a better idea about which skills you need to work on and be able to establish your priorities.

Here is an example of how one learner analysed his needs. Stig is a Swedish Youth Hostel warden who needs English for his work. He filled in the following chart. You will find a blank chart on page 109 in the Appendix, which you could use to analyse your own needs.

Situations	Skills					
	Vocabulary (✓)	Grammar (✓)	Listening (✓)	Speaking (✓)	Reading (✓)	Writing (✓)
Youth Hostel Reception Desk						
-welcoming new guests	✓			✓		
-giving YH information	✓			✓		
-explaining regulations	✓	✓		✓		
-answering enquiries	✓		✓	✓		
-putting up notices	✓	✓				✓

1.3   Why do you need or want to learn English?

2   Prioritising your needs

How much do you know / can you do already?

Stig used an assessment scale from 1 to 5:
1 = this is the standard I would like to reach – my goal.
5 = I can do very little. I am a long way from my goal.
He considered each skill that he needed and circled the number that he felt
represented his position on the scale, as follows:

Extending vocabulary	Dealing with grammar	Listening	Speaking	Reading	Writing
1	1	1	1	①	1
2	2	2	②	2	2
3	③	③	3	3	3
④	4	4	4	4	④
5	5	5	5	5	5

He was then able to see more clearly what he needed to improve most.
You will find a blank self-assessment scale in the Appendix (page 110) for
your own use.

What are your priorities?

Stig then gave each skill a priority rating from 1 to 6:
1 = highest priority
6 = lowest priority

I thought I needed to improve my
speaking, but now I realise that it
is mainly vocabulary that is
missing. My speaking is quite
good, in fact. I also realise that I
need to concentrate on my
listening and writing. I can read
English quite well – I don't need
to do it much, anyway.

Stig, Sweden

Skill	Priority rating
Extending vocabulary	1
Dealing with grammar	4
Listening	2
Speaking	5
Reading	6
Writing	3

You could prioritise your own needs in the same way. If you do this, it will give
you a clearer idea about which sections in Stage 2 of this book would be most
useful for you. It will also give you a basis for negotiating the content of your
course with the other members of your class and your teacher. You will find a
blank record of priorities in the Appendix (page 110).

Source: B. Ellis and G. Sinclair, *Learning to Learn English*, pp. 10–11, copyright
Cambridge University Press, 1989.

Conclusion

We began this chapter by looking at the concept of individualization in its broadest sense by examining some definitions of the term and have suggested various ways of implementing it both inside and outside the language classroom by incorporating combinations of self-access work, diary writing and learner training. We have tried to show that the most appropriate way of implementing individualization will depend, to some extent, on the *context* of the teaching operation that we work in. We have also attempted to illustrate that individualization is one way of re-organizing the management and resources of the classroom to try to maximize learning potential for as many people in the class as possible.

Further reading

1 Dickinson, L. (1987): *Self-instruction in Language Learning* provides a helpful introduction to this topic.
2 Sheerin, Susan (1989): *Self-Access* is a more practical account with useful suggestions on setting up individualized activities both inside and outside the classroom.

13 Observing the Language Classroom

Introduction

In this chapter we shall be looking at language classrooms in order to try to analyse in some detail what actually occurs in them. We shall begin by considering why the classroom might be a useful place to observe. Then we shall move on to examine, as teachers in the classroom, some of the different issues that we might want to look at which can help us to become better informed about our own practice, and hopefully to improve our own teaching. After this we shall look at some of the different methods that have been used by teachers/researchers to gather data from classrooms. Our final aim in the chapter is to make some suggestions for observation tasks that could be of use to teachers working in a wide variety of classrooms, and to apply these tasks to transcripts of actual classroom interaction. We hope this analysis will help teachers to become further informed about their own practice.

Why Focus on the Classroom?

Allwright and Bailey (1991) quote Gaies (1980), who comments that the classroom is essentially a crucible and that when language learning occurs, it is as a result of the combinations of the different elements of the teacher–learner, learner–learner relationships which are embodied in the numerous interactions which take place in the classroom. We noted in the previous chapter that what we teach does not necessarily result in learning taking place, nor does the best prepared lesson plan result in that plan being followed absolutely in the classroom. As Allwright and Bailey (1991) suggest, this would be tantamount to a 'play reading' rather than a language lesson as such, and may well impose a framework upon the class that some learners could find restricts rather than aids their learning. Because of this, what is often noticeable about classrooms is that they are not necessarily neat, organized places, while interaction patterns which occur in them can be highly erratic and variable: genuine interaction cannot be completely planned for and requires co-operative effort. Allwright and Bailey also suggest that the co-operation required in the classroom setting involves everyone (teacher and learners) in managing many things at the same time, including: who gets to speak?; what do they talk about?; what does each participant do with the different opportunities to speak?; what sort of classroom atmosphere is created by learners and the teacher? For us as teachers, it is important to have the opportunity to observe the interaction within the classroom because it can determine the actual learning opportunities that students get. We might also suggest that learners do not learn *directly* from a syllabus but what they actually learn, or not, is the result of the manner in which this syllabus is 'translated' into the classroom environment, in the form of materials but also of their use by the teacher and learners in the class.

What to Observe

Think about your own classroom situation. If you had the chance to observe your own or a colleague's class, what sorts of things would you want to look at?

As we mentioned in the previous section, the classroom is the basic focus of the teaching and learning process, and there are literally hundreds of different permutations of classroom processes that we may wish to focus on: some of them perhaps very 'macro' or wide-ranging – such as how a particular teacher/group of learners use a textbook during a class – and some very 'micro' – such as how a teacher elicits responses with a given class or how a particular learner or small group of individuals initiate turns in an oral skills class. We may wish to classify the information that we get from observing the classroom into different areas such as information which focuses primarily on the teacher; the interaction patterns of learners in general; interaction of learners in pairs and/or groups; and the interaction of certain individuals with the teacher. If we wish to focus on the teacher, the following criteria could be offered as factors for observation. We may wish to investigate each one in turn or we may decide to focus on some or all of them during a particular lesson:

- the amount of teacher talking time (TTT) contrasted with student talking time (STT) during the course of a particular class

- the type of teacher talk that takes place in a given class and where it occurs in the lesson

- the teacher's questioning/elicitation techniques

- how the teacher gives feedback to learners

- how the teacher handles 'digressions' in the classroom

- the different roles a teacher takes on during the class ('manager', 'facilitator' etc.)

- the teacher's use of encouragement and praise with learners

- the technical aids and materials a teacher uses to create learning contexts, and how the teacher involves the learners in these activities

- how 'tightly' a particular teacher corrects the learners' work.

There are many more possibilities, of course.

Think about other criteria which may be of interest to you as a teacher and add them to ours.

Nunan (1990) reports on a teachers' workshop where one of the groups participating in the workshop offered the following criteria as aspects of the class that they would like to look at. These were:

wait time; repair techniques; 'fun'; questioning; materials; student–teacher interaction; scope of student response; amount of direction offered; class organization; lesson objectives; student and teacher talk time; control and initiative; who asks questions; context for language practice; how language is practised; methods used; digressions; variety of activities; interaction between students; lesson cohesion; teacher language; eliciting techniques; evaluation possibilities.

It is possible, of course, to extend these criteria, or combinations of them, to different classes in order to gain comparative data. For example, we may wish to compare the metalanguage (the language the teacher uses in the classroom to explain things) of the same teacher across a range of different classes – perhaps of different proficiency levels – in order to ascertain what similarities and differences exist across the various groups; or we may wish to observe how different teachers who teach the same class use the textbook or set of materials with that class. Some teachers feel that it would be useful to observe classes with a fundamentally different focus, such as a 'traditional', grammar based class, in contrast to a more 'communicative' one, to see which could be deemed more successful from the learners' point of view. In a similar vein, we may wish to observe various things that occur in a given classroom with the learners themselves.

Kumaravadivelu (1990) writes how the teaching act has been the subject of much classroom observation, perhaps at the expense of the equally important tasks of observing the learning act and trying to understand learner perceptions of classroom events. It may be useful to observe the group dynamics of a particular class during a language lesson in order to observe the interaction patterns that occur as a result of the exercises/tasks that the teacher sets up and manages. We might observe how well the learners seem to work together as a whole group, in small groups, in pairs or, indeed, if some learners prefer to work individually. Allwright (1984, 1988) comments on the idiosyncratic nature of the language classroom and the fact that from the same lesson different learners will take away very different things. Analysing and perhaps contrasting two or more different learners in a class can help us as teachers to understand how these learners are using the classroom context to maximize their own learning potential, if at all.

To further illustrate the essentially puzzling nature of language learning in different classrooms, Allwright (1992) offers the following comments from teachers and learners, in different contexts, on what *they* found was particularly bewildering about language learning in their classrooms:

Teachers:

> Why do students feel that they have to know all the vocabulary in order to understand a text?
> Why do students use so little English in group work?
> Do students work better in small groups or pairs?
> What do students really want to learn from our lessons?

Learners:

> Nobody ever explains the purpose of the exercise
> I don't understand why I don't understand English
> We try to understand the words not the lessons
> Teachers expect us to remember what we did in the last lesson but we don't operate like this
> Why does a teacher only ask me a question when I don't know the answer?

Being armed with an awareness of these factors can make classroom observation highly fruitful in that we may be able to make corrective adjustments to classroom teaching and management as a result of analysing the data we collect.

Different Approaches to Classroom Observation

Having decided on the criteria that we would like to observe in the classroom, we than have to decide which method we would like to use to gain access to the classroom for observation purposes. Allwright and Bailey (1991) list three main approaches which classroom observers have typically used in classroom observation. The first of these is an experimental observation in which the teacher/researcher exercises a high degree of control over the classroom and purpose-fully becomes involved in the setting to try and discover the effects of the intervention. A control group would typically be set up. This 'scientific' approach to observation usually implies a one-way, (usually) top-down approach to classroom observation, since the teacher and class will be observed from the 'outside' by a linguistic 'expert' who will probably distinguish theoretical issues from actual classroom practice. The second main approach is called 'naturalistic enquiry' and may involve observers as participants either in their own or in someone else's class to 'see what happens'. The essential feature of this approach is to act as a 'fly on the wall' and, where possible, not at all to influence normally occurring patterns of instruction and interaction.

Another way of implementing the approach is to video a class or to have one's own class videoed. However, sitting in on a class and/or videoing the experience are never neutral, because an unaccustomed presence in the class is bound to cause some disruption and alter the normal patterns of interaction. One particular advantage of this approach is that data from different classrooms can easily be seen and compared.

The third approach, an increasingly popular one, may well be of more interest to practitioners as a whole as it is performed by teachers themselves from *within* the classroom. Wajnryb (1991) comments how classroom observation up until the recent past has often been perceived in judgemental terms of assessment, evaluation or experi-mentation. Assessment and evaluation through observing the class-room are still an integral part of many teacher training programmes across the world and are deemed useful, especially where it is thought that the trainee may benefit from the evaluation and feedback of a more experienced teacher or trainer. Today, however, there is a growth of emphasis on extending knowledge and understanding of what happens from *inside* the classroom (perhaps with some small-scale intervention). This is done by teachers themselves, perhaps collaborating with a colleague, either as part of a teacher development or classroom research project. (Classroom research by teachers is explored in the following chapter.) In this third approach, observation may include some naturalistic observation (perhaps of a colleague's class), but will typically involve teachers in the setting up of some small-scale intervention which will then be monitored by the teachers themselves over a period of time. Topics for this type of classroom research may be the development of oral competence of a learner/ learners; why the content of certain materials appears not to stimulate students; or, whether 'active' tasks actually improve the language learning.

Although the data for the observation may be gathered over a period of time, the teachers' observations are 'recycled' or fed back into the classroom process. Hence, within this framework, classroom observation does not occur from the outside but instead the impetus comes from within the classroom in a 'bottom-up' fashion which allows the teachers themselves to decide which areas they wish to investigate. The observation involved in classroom research can be quite small-scale; it does not have to run to the dimensions of a large project.

If you have been involved in any type of classroom observation, think about the approach that you used. What were the advantages/ disadvantages of this approach?

Using video recordings

If we are interested in understanding classrooms through observation in a co-operative way outside the realm of experiment/assessment (within a teacher development programme, for example), there are a number of advantages in using pre-recorded video tapes as a way of stimulating interest in the classroom for observation purposes. Sometimes various administrative constraints may make it impossible to work with colleagues or in a team, and in such cases video-taped classes can give teachers access to situations that they would not otherwise be able to observe. Videotaped lessons may also provide a springboard for the teacher-initiated research outlined above, in that the issues raised on the tape may have relevance to the observer's own classroom and could help in the formulation of an action plan for that particular teacher. The British Council produces a video package of edited lessons called *Teaching and Learning in Focus* (1983) which is relatively easy to obtain. Using video for classroom observation also has the advantage of being easy to set up – you do not have to disturb a class or organize one especially for the purpose, and you, the observer, have total control in that you may view, pause, replay and so on. Videotaped lessons are also useful to the extent that it is possible to focus on a single issue for one viewing, such as teacher talk, and then replay the tape to focus on a different issue, perhaps to observe how a pair of learners work together on an information gap activity. It can be very motivating to see how other teachers work in the classroom without the threat of being evaluated oneself. When videos are viewed as a group activity with other teachers, any difference in perception and/or opinion which occurs can be usefully discussed. There is sometimes a danger, however, that we might see these lessons as offering a perfect model or, conversely, be over-critical of what we may consider to be the shortcomings of a particular teacher, rather than trying to get as balanced a perspective as possible.

As with all media, there are drawbacks to using video. We can rarely see the whole class performing as the camera can only offer us a partial view of the classroom. As lessons are usually edited, this also results in the observer getting an incomplete picture of the whole lesson. Nevertheless, given its versatility as a resource, video-taped material can offer many possibilities for classroom observation.

Devising Classroom Observation Tasks

Earlier in the chapter we suggested that we may wish to observe the general 'macro' details of the classroom or we may wish to analyse a particular aspect in more depth – such as observing the teacher in as comprehensive a way as possible or looking at a sub-topic of this area, like the amount of teacher talk in a given class. In this section we shall offer some suggestions for analysing different aspects of one area – that of teacher talk in the classroom – and then consider some criteria that we might wish to include in a general observation task sheet which could be used as an aid to provide an initial 'overview' of a classroom. Later we shall apply some of these details to the analysis of transcripts of English as a Foreign Language classes to see how they might operate on 'real' data in practice. Teacher talk in classrooms has been an area of interest to researchers for a long time. What often surprises teachers themselves, as Nunan (1991) points out, is the sheer amount of talking that they themselves do in the classroom, sometimes up to 80 per cent of the total class.

Depending on the actual aims of a particular lesson, the amount of teacher talk may vary; for example, a teacher may wish to focus on the explanation of a certain function or structure in one class which will entail a high degree of teacher talk, to be followed on by a range of student centred tasks in the next class which will include a higher amount of student talk. In the late seventies, in the heyday of the communicative approach in Britain, it was generally thought that teachers should strive for a high degree of student talking time (STT) and a low amount of teacher talking time (TTT) in the classroom (see the account by Gower and Walters, 1983). However, some practitioners feel teacher talking time is useful, not merely for organizing the classroom, but also because it can offer useful and pertinent language practice, since the metalanguage used by the teacher can be considered as 'genuinely communicative' and may be of considerable benefit to the learners.

Consider your own teaching situation. Think carefully about how much time you spend talking in the classroom as a proportion of the total lesson. Does this surprise you?

We may wish to observe how the teacher talk relates to the specific function of the teacher in the class at that point in time. Stubbs and Delamont (1976) outline some of the functions of the teacher in the classroom which include: giving instructions; organizing seating arrangements; setting up and building up situations through questions; directing practice activities; giving cue-card prompts; using a student for demonstration practice in pairwork activities; correcting; setting written work; developing 'rapport'/showing a personal interest in the students.

Nunan (1991) adds a further dimension to Stubbs' and Delamont's perspective by outlining three factors that ought to be considered when assessing the appropriateness and quantity of teacher talk. These are: the point at which the talking occurs; is it planned or spontaneous, and if spontaneous, is the digression helpful or not; and the value of the teacher talk as potentially useful input for acquisition purposes. What actually constitutes appropriacy and quality may be thought of as matters of judgement and could be subject to considerable variation. Evidence also tends to suggest that the questions a teacher asks in the classroom can be extremely important in helping learners to develop their competence in the language. It is useful to observe if teachers put questions to learners systematically or randomly, how long they wait for a response, and the type of question asked, from that requiring a simple one-word reply to higher order referential questions where learners can provide information which the teacher does not know. Similarly, in the case of feedback and correcting learners, we can observe how and when the teacher does this and if all learners receive treatment systematically.

Thus far we have looked at some of the factors that we may wish to observe pertaining to the teacher in the classroom. We could also, for example, turn our attention to one learner or to a pair of learners to compare how each of them tends to individualize whole class instruction to their own benefit.

Let us now consider some of the general criteria that we may find useful in order to observe as many facets of the language classroom as possible in the context of one language lesson. We have set these out in the form of a general observation task sheet (adapted from Thickett, 1986) which can be used as a prompt for making notes during an observation session:

1. *Focus on Learners*
Group Dynamics. How well do they work together as:
a) a whole group
b) small groups
c) pairs. Do some prefer to work individually?
How well do they appear to relate and respond to the teacher?

2. *Focus on the Teacher*
a) What is the approximate amount of teacher talking time in the lesson. When does it occur? How much explanation/metalanguage is used? Is TTT all in the L_1, all in the L_2, or a mixture of both?
b) What are the different roles assumed by the teacher during the class?
c) How much encouragement is offered to the learners and how is it done?
d) If aids/materials are used what is their purpose in the lesson?

3. *Presentation and Practice*
a) How is a context for the lesson established?

b) Do all students get adequate practice? How does the teacher ensure this?

4. *Production Stage*
a) What activity/activities are the students asked to perform?
b) Do they seem to be pertinent/useful in realizing the objectives of the lesson?

5. *Classroom Management*
   Are the activities smooth and effectively managed?
   Do students seem to be clear about what they should be doing?

6. *Correction/feedback*
a) How 'tightly' does the teacher correct students at various stages of the activity/ies?
b) What type of feedback is offered to learners? Is it equally distributed?

7. *Motivation*
a) How would you characterize the atmosphere of this class? e.g. alert, hard-working, good humoured, keenly motivated etc.
b) Note down any particular motivating features of this lesson.

8. *Overall Comments/Observation*

If you have the opportunity, try this observation schedule with a colleague by observing each other's classes and producing feedback to each other. Add any other factors which you feel are important to you in your teaching situation.

Applying the Tasks to Classroom Data

In this section we intend to look at the application of some of the observation tasks discussed above to actual classroom practice. We shall analyse transcripts of three different language classes in order to see if we can ascertain with any degree of certainty what is occurring in each of them.

In this first extract we are going to examine two short sequences which occur in a classroom where the teacher is working with a small group of students who are about to comment on two pictures. Picture 1 shows a glass blower working in a factory, picture 2 shows two people running away from a fire in open country. The teacher is going to get the learners to work in pairs.

Sequence 1

Note how the teacher sets up this activity. Work with a colleague if at all possible.

T: So what I'm going to do is come round with the pictures and I'd like you to have a look at the pictures so that the person on the left describes the left hand picture to their partner and . . . just try to talk about it from as many angles as you can . . . and then the person on the right talks about the right hand picture to their friend. I'll come round and see what you're doing and help you if necessary. O.K. Any questions?

S: See the pictures?

T: Yes; you want to see the pictures first. (*laughter*) Everybody happy? Excellent. Good. (*The teacher distributes the pictures to each group.*)

T: Can you two work together? (*Hands out all the pictures. General noise.*)

T: What can you see in the picture? Describe it to your partner. You've got to use a bit of your imagination, . . . w . . . w . . . what's that's not clear?

S: This is fire, a fire?

T: Yes, and what do you think he's doing with the fire?

S: He works with glass. He's made of glass. (*Laughter, Noise.*)

T: He's made . . . he's not made of glass himself is he? He makes glass. Now please continue, in pairs, to describe the pictures as best you can.

Sequence 2

Read the sequence and think about how effectively the learners seem to be communicating with each other. What does the teacher do during this episode? Are errors corrected? Does this matter?

In this sequence from the lesson two learners are communicating about the pictures. They have described them to each other. Now they are comparing them.

S1: We haven't forest, it's wide open, no trees, its like desert, so this man to try . . . to keep to limit the fire, but it's out of control.

S2: Yes, this is make in this picture. In this picture thought this is destruct. There's a link – fire. He try to keep it in one place but . . .

T: He is not successful.

S2: Difficult for him to put . . .

T: Put . . . put out?

s2: Put out a flame. He's more afright because he knows danger near him. This one looks more calm (*pointing to picture 1*), but very concentrate on his work. Much control. He know what he doing.

T: (*Asking S1 about picture 1*) You've described this.

S1: This is a man who is going to work with glass, he's going to mould the glass.

T: Yes, mm, to mould the glass.

S1: . . . and here in the bottom, I think it's one bottle that he doed, he did and in the top I think that the glass is very red and hot and he is very careful, precise and concentrate on what he is going to do.

T: Right, right.

When you have completed the above, read the following transcript which was recorded from a third year Intermediate Class at the British Council Centre, Rabat, Morocco. The data is from a follow-up lesson on how to make and respond to polite requests, based on Unit 6 of *Developing Strategies* by Abbs and Freebairn (1981). The source of the transcript is: *Teaching and Learning in Focus*, Edited Lessons, The British Council.

Consider the following questions in relation to the transcript. Again work with a colleague if at all possible.

1 Analyse the four main activities that the teacher asks the learners to perform.
2 Observe what the learners appear to be doing during these activities. Analyse pair/group arrangements in relation to activity.
3 Do the activities seem useful in realizing the objectives of the lesson?
4 How much teacher talk is there in relation to student talk? What are the different functions of the teacher talk and when does it occur?
5 How much correction and feedback does the teacher provide? Does it seem to be equal for all learners?
6 Do you feel that this is a teacher or a student centred lesson? Why? Note what the teacher says himself.
7 Allwright and Bailey (1991) mention the 'atmosphere' that is created in the classroom co-production. How would you characterize the atmosphere of this particular class?

Transcript:

[16:00]   *   *   *   *   *   *

(Second Lesson)

T: Let's imagine now then that you're talking to your wife Boujemaa. What, what do you say to your wife here?
BOUJEMAA: Do you think – er – you could – er wa . . . er – no, wash the – the car for me please?
T: And how – how would you answer Matgozata.
MATGOZATA: If you want . . . (laughter) . . .
T: She's a lovely wife isn't she. OK . . . that's charming that is. Can we have another one – um. You're having dinner Mrs Khadraoui and you're feeling very, very tired so what do you say to your husband?

GHITA: I wonder if you'd mind washing up for me.

T: OK, what I would like to do now, I'm going to give you a few of these cards each if you could work 2 or 3 people together and just practise asking each other for things. OK? But first of all decide who you are. Are you friends or are you acquaintances. OK. If you could work with René. And if you two could, could work together perhaps. And if you two wouldn't mind working together. Or perhaps you three could work together here. OK. Good.

MATGOZATA: Oh thank you very much.

GHITA: Here you are.

MATGOZATA: Mine is broken.

GHITA: OK.

GHITA: Oh la have you got a screwdriver Matgozata?

MATGOZATA: Yes I have one.

GHITA: Could you – er – could you pass me yours. I . . . I . . . broked mine.

MATGOZATA: Yes of course . . . it's no problem.

MATGOZATA: . . . Oh . . . lovely . . . suitcase . . . can you . . .

RENE: Would you mind phoning to my wife please.

T: Would you mind phoning my wife please.

RENE: My wife please – yes.

BOUJEMAA: Certainly.

RENE: Yes – um – yeh. Would you mind – er – washing the dishes please.

BOUJEMAA: Um – that's difficult but – er – I going to do that.

T: Can I ask a little question here. Who are you talking to here a friend or – or – an acquaintance?

BOUJEMAA: Er . . . no . . . as . . . er . . .

RENE: It's not a friend.

T: Not a friend . . . somebody you know a little.

RENE: Yeh.

T: OK, excuse me, would you mind listening to me for the moment? OK – for homework last night I asked you to write some short dialogues for the pictures on – on page 47. If you remember, I hope you've done your homework have you? Done your homework Hilly?

HILLY: No.

T: Would you mind leaving the classroom. No I'm not serious. OK if you look at these 6 pictures now, for which some of you have prepared dialogues at home. Now could you just practise them with the person next, next to you first of all. OK and be very careful about who you are talking to again. OK. Just go through the 6 dialogues you've prepared for homework. But listen, just a second please, just a second. Before you start. Don't do all of them. If you could do the first two perhaps, and if you could practise the second two, and if you could practise the next two and if you could practise the first two again. OK. Carry on please.

[19:18]   *   *   *   *   *   *

s: Do you think – er – you would made me – do you think.
s: . . . er . . . open.
s: Yes . . . oh . . . ah . . . you could help me to open the car . . . er . . . because I have a lot of to carry.
s: Yes Mama of course.

[19:40]   *   *   *   *   *   *

T: OK now then. I'd like to listen to some of this homework now. – like er – could you do number 1 for me – er – Boujemaa or René.
BOUJEMAA: Yes, er . . . Do you think you could lift my suitcase down for me please?
RENE: Of course.

T: Now then, we're going to do something a little different now, you will all need pen and paper, we're going to do a little bit of dictation, but not the usual kind of dictation. I don't want you to write what I say. I want you to write what the characters in my story say. OK. The first thing I'll do is introduce you to the characters. There they are. Mary and Jane. Now Mary and Jane are two girls who live in the same street. They're very good friends and they're both typists and they work in a big office in the city centre. Now their boss is a man called Mr Smith, but we'll meet him later. Now I'm going to tell you the story and I want you to write what the people say. Whenever I want you to write I'll stop and give you time to write. All right? Before you write what a person says write the person's name as well. OK? So. One day Mary and Jane are working in the office and Mary asked Jane for a cigarette, so write what Mary says please.

[21:42]   *   *   *   *   *   *

T: OK so we've got Mary, Jane and Mr Smith.

S: The boss.

T: OK the boss yes. Could you shut your books. Let's try it again without the books. OK carry on.

GHITA: Have you got a cigarette Mary?

MATGOZATA: Yes, of course, here you are.

GHITA: Thank you.

DRISS: Why are you smoking in the office? You know that, that I hate it. Er – now – er – Mary do you – er – would you mind opening – er – the window please.

GHITA: Yes of course, I'm terribly sorry, sir.

T: She looks sorry too doesn't she. Alright good. So I've got a text here, it's all about Sandra but what I've done is I've cut the text up into little pieces and I want you to rearrange the pieces in sequence, so that what you have is one long story.

[22:45]   *   *   *   *   *   *

S: Do you agree.

T: Let's see what Wafaa thinks . . . what do you think Wafaa?

WAFAA: . . . I think . . . er . . er . . . you put it . . . er . . . now.

S: I think this is the . . .

S: You think . . . me too . . . me too . . . I think it is my place here.

S: I take another.

T: Shall, shall I bring some boxing gloves?

S: Yes.

T: Some boxing gloves for you two.

S: No . . . no problem.

T: Try and work it out together then.

DRISS: . . . . my boss . . . . by the way . . . . I thought my job was going to be really interesting . . . and – er.

GHITA: Well I'm called a programme assistant but I'm really secretary, I type the letters and make tea for my boss.

MATGOZATA: Yes, it, it's good and – er – and I, I've always wanted to work in the media but I'm a bit – er . . . now, my boyfriend, ah Mark also works there.

GHITA: Ah yes . . . video technician . . . yes . . . ah . . . that's right . . . yes.

(*inaudible*)

T: There it is yes thanks good. You carry on with what you're doing then. Good Driss, you're here, but I've got you as being absent yesterday too. Boujemma – Boujemma is not very good on the register is he.

DRISS: He's not . . . er . . . a true friend.

T: And Ghita you, you were absent as well yesterday . . . ah this is ridiculous. Good, and Mohamed – still away.

GHITA: Yes he, he has a lot of work.

T: Ah, very busy time.

GHITA: Yes very busy yes.

T: OK, and Matgozata.

MATGOZATA: Yes.

T: Good. You're here – how's – how's Farouk at the moment – how's Farouk – not well.

MATGOZATA: He's not very very well.

T: Is he working hard as well?

MATGOZATA: Yes.

T: OK. You carry on.

(Group of 3 men)

T: OK if you just stop for a second. Our time is almost finished, so we have to wind up here. If you want to see the correct sequence of the text, the text is on page 45 in your books. OK. Now we haven't got any time now but in the lesson tomorrow, well there's no lesson tomorrow it's the weekend isn't it? OK in the lesson on Monday I'll go over this text with you and we'll see if there – if there are any problems of understanding. OK, anyway thanks very much and I'll see you on Monday. Have a nice weekend all of you.

SS: Thank you . . . thank you very much.

T: They prefer the – um – the second kind of lesson, the lesson where they have control because the kind of English they're interested in is social English and they have very little opportunity for practising their English here in Morocco, so for them a – a large part of a lesson in fact is just to be in a situation and with people, so that they can speak English. In general I think a – a good teacher is one who can stimulate his class without dominating it and – er – create relaxed atmosphere without turning it into – er – an afternoon tea party.

[26:00]   *   *   *   *   *   *

Source: The British Council, *Teaching and Learning in Focus*, Edited Lessons vol. 2, pp. 22–5, copyright The British Council, 1983.

In the short transcript that follows, thirty Japanese high school students are in the classroom with two teachers, one of them a Japanese teacher of English, the other an assistant teacher of English. Look at the following questions and try to answer them as you are reading the transcript. Again, try to work with a colleague, if at all possible. (Key: IT = Japanese Teacher; AET = assistant English teacher, s = Student)

1 Look at the student interaction which takes place. What have the learners been asked to do?
2 Why might the classroom contain two teachers?
3 Look at the teachers in this episode. How do they react to the learners?
4 How do the two teachers handle error correction?
5 Think about the language classroom that has two teachers in it from the *learners'* point of view. In what ways might it be helpful and in what ways confusing?

S1: Please, can you tell me how to go to the train station?
S2: I don't . . . you take bus number 5 first to Fountain Square and then . . . to change to number 10 which take you there directly.
S1: Sorry. I didn't have that . . . bus 10 is it first?
S2: No, I repeat, bus 5 first to Fountain Square then at the

same bus stop you wait a number 10 which take you there
directly.

S1:   Thank you. You are very kind in offer information.

S2:   No problem.

S1:   Goodbye then.

S2:   Goodbye.

AET: Well done, good (*clapping*), that was fine.

JT: Any comments then, please?

AET: No? Something to notice however . . . (*draws on board*).
'You are very kind in offer information'. No. We don't say
this.

JT: What is wrong here?

AET: Anybody correct it?

S1:   You are very kind to offer information.

JT: Is that better then?

S2:   Yes.

JT: It was very kind of you to offer or to give me this
information.

AET: Or just thanks or thank you for the information.

Conclusion

In this chapter we have examined the reasons why classrooms are
useful sources of information about teaching and learning and have
considered some of the different criteria that we might want to
observe in them. After this, we moved on to look at some of the
different options which are open to us for observing the classroom.
We then suggested that we might wish to concentrate in some detail
on one particular aspect of the language classroom, such as teacher
talk, or that we may wish to observe several criteria together,
depending on our particular purpose. We then proposed a set of
general observation criteria that we might find useful in order to get
an overview of what is happening in a particular classroom. Finally,
we examined transcribed data from three different classrooms and
applied focusing tasks to this data to try to gain further access to, and
understanding of, what was occurring in these classrooms.

How might your approach to what you do in the classroom be affected as a result of reading this chapter?

Further reading

The following books give a useful overview of the area of classroom observation:

1. Allwright, R. L. and K. Bailey (1991): *Focus on the Language Classroom.*
2. Nunan, D. (1989): *Understanding Language Classrooms.*

14   Views of the Teacher

Introduction

Chapters on 'the teacher' are often, even traditionally, to be found at the end of books concerned with aspects of language teaching methodology. Such a format might well be criticized on the grounds of relegating teachers to last place on a scale of importance, with learners certainly, but also materials and methods, having primacy. In the present book, however, this is emphatically not the intention, and the position of this chapter is deliberate. It has been chosen because the teacher arguably represents the most significant factor in any language teaching operation. The teacher is typically a 'constant' in the throughput of different students in the institution, and works in different ways at the interface of several systems – the classroom, the school, the educational environment – all of which affect a teacher's professional attitudes and behaviour. A principal aim of this chapter, then, is to offer a view of the teacher as a synthesizer of all the aspects we have covered, as a professional who has to make sense of the decisions, opinions and perceptions of many different people. Certainly teachers will often experience this as pressure and conflict, which may be difficult to resolve. Nevertheless, we wish to stress the importance of a positive and active professional self-image, rather than a more passive and reactive one.

The chapter is broadly divided into three sections. In the first of these, we examine the concept of 'role' and explore its possible dimensions for English language teachers in general. We then go on to look particularly at the teacher's classroom role, focusing on the implications of innovation and change in materials and methods.

These two sections, in other words, will be concerned first, with contextualizing 'role' and, secondly, with differences over time. Finally, a number of issues to do with the training and development of teachers will be raised. We have included more activities and things to think about because of the nature of the topic and its reflective orientation, and the chapter finishes, quite intentionally, on an open-ended note.

The Teacher's Role

Make a few notes on what you actually do as a teacher in a regular working week. Keep the notes – we shall refer back to them later.

Our own list looks something like this:

> Preparing timetables
> Spending a certain number of contracted hours in class
> Preparing materials and handouts
> Seeing students individually
> Attending staff meetings
> Arranging out-of-class activities
> Writing reports
> Marking tests and examinations
> Planning courses and their associated teaching activities
> Liaison with outside bodies and other institutions.

There are two obvious points to be made here. The first concerns the fact that any job specification is part of a network of interacting and overlapping roles; secondly, and related to the first point, we do our job in the context of a whole 'environment'. This now takes us full circle, and we shall be referring back explicitly to the points first raised in chapter 1.

The concept of 'role'

Role theory is a very large topic on which a great deal has been written: it is, for example, a major research field in social psychology and related areas, including the investigation of behaviour in industrial and organizational settings. We can only touch on it here, and draw a few implications for the EFL teacher's work.

The list you have just made will show that you carry out a range of specified tasks within the social framework of an institutional structure. It is, then, self-evident that your work is not done in isolation, but that you need to interact, directly or indirectly, with a number of others – with students, obviously, with other teachers, with the headteacher (or Head of Department/Principal), with non-teaching staff, and so on. Both in your professional and in your private life you are a member of a *role set*, the group of people with whom you interact in any particular situation. Taking yourself as the 'focal person' (Handy, 1985), you may like to represent your own most important role sets in diagrammatic form as in figure 14.1 You could also do this with family and friends as the set, or alternatively for any leisure activity that you do regularly. Wright (1987) makes a further distinction between role set and *role network*, the latter signifying roles in some kind of hierarchical relationship to each other where each person accepts or at least understands the organizational chain of authority and accountability. One example of how this view works in practice can be found in the scheme organized by the British Council for inspecting and recognizing private language schools in the UK. As well as the obvious categories of 'teaching' and 'professional qualifications', the extent to which a school performs its central teaching

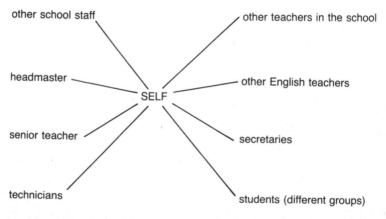

Figure 14.1

function is also evaluated in terms of the overall management structures, in addition to resources and the physical environment of the institution. Thus a classroom teacher may be accountable to a senior teacher and through him to the Principal, but also 'laterally', to colleagues with special areas of responsibility such as resource management.

A number of important points follow from these general features of the concept of 'role'. We shall take just three of them here:

1 We noted above the significant members of our own role set in any specific situation. The 'mirror image' of this, of course, is that *we* fulfil certain roles in the role sets and networks of other people: we are therefore at any one time colleagues, employees, perhaps authority figures in the classroom, somebody's superior, a casual acquaintance, and so on. There will also be differences in what is accepted as appropriate institutional behaviour, and great variation in patterns of power and authority.

2 There is arguably a great deal of truth in the assertion that 'we are as others see us'. In other words, our image of ourselves as professionals will be an amalgam of a whole range of perceptions and expectations, and this takes us beyond the idea of a role as simply a list of tasks to be carried out, or an officially issued job description. Bush (1984), for example, refers to the theatrical image used by several writers in which the actor plays out a role in accordance with the expectations of an audience. This implies, however, that the actor is rather a passive figure: Bush goes on to remind us that a role is not tidy and objective, but that 'in practice the role-occupant brings to the position his or her values, perceptions and experience and these will interact with other expectations to determine the way the part is played' (76). Moreover the notion of a 'network' indicates that different people's expectations will carry different degrees of importance: for instance, an organization with a powerful authority figure at the head may lead to a reduction in the weight attached to student views and needs.

3 Most writing in the field of role theory recognizes – as indeed the previous points imply – that people inevitably perceive their own role as multiple and complex. A number of secondary notions have therefore evolved which reflect this. Handy's (1985, ch. 3) list is comprehensive, and makes rather negative but probably realistic reading. He points out that a role occupant can experience one or more of the following, which are interrelated:

- Role conflict: for example, our role as a classroom teacher and as an institutional examiner may not be fully compatible

- Role ambiguity, defined by uncertainty as to what is expected at any particular time

- Role overload – not the same as work overload – where the focal person is not able to integrate roles that are too many and too varied. Many teachers who are required to take on increased administrative or external duties may experience this as a problem

- Role stress, which Handy divides into role pressure (positive, where synthesis of roles and expectations remains possible), and its opposite, role strain

Earlier in this section you drew up a simple 'role set' diagram with yourself as the focal person.

Consider now the range of roles that you play in your own institution. To whom are you responsible, and who is responsible to you? Do any of Handy's points match your own experience, for example as a result of increasing role diversification? In particular, is your own perception of your role(s) fully in line with what you take to be the expectations of others?

As Wright (1987: 5) briefly remarks, 'there is more to a role than just doing a job'.

The wider environment

Up to now, we have been thinking of teachers in the setting of their own institutions. However, crucial as that is, the concept of 'role' cannot be restricted to the institution in which we work, and in a sense, our workplace is a microcosm of the wider environment. In the first chapter of this book, we proposed a framework for thinking about materials and methods in which a number of contextual variables – management decisions, resource factors, types of learners, and many more – were considered. Here we re-examine them from the perspective of the teacher as a 'focal person', and taking into account

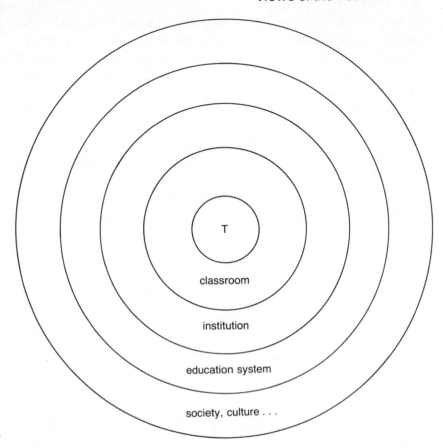

Figure 14.2

such factors as the teacher's potentially multiple roles, the expectations of others, and the inherent possibilities for conflict, pressure
and so on. We might represent the situation as in figure 14.2 to show
both the importance of the teacher as well as the direct and indirect
effects of all these different 'layers' on the teacher's role.

Beyond the immediate environment of your own institution/school, try to
enumerate from the outer layers in particular (a) the people (the other
'actors') and (b) the variables that you think have most influenced your
understanding of your own role.

You may have listed your family and friends, or your own tutors; your students' peer groups and parents; external inspectors or advisers; the authorities who draw up your contract and decide on your salary and conditions; the writers of commercially published materials; agencies and organizations sponsoring students to take your programmes. For example, low pay sometimes indicates low social esteem of the profession and even low self-esteem, and may in turn mean there is a need to take on extra work, leaving no time for any more than routine preparation of classes, certainly not professional development. Conversely, the combination of a consultative environment which considers the views of everyone involved both within and outside the institution, and a recognition that teachers may be more active and productive if they are given time to develop resources, for example, will clearly lead to a more positive working atmosphere.

A useful way of looking at these issues from the teacher's point of view is set out by Strevens (1979) in terms of the concept of 'control'. Apart from variables to do with the learner, which it is not necessary to list again here (except to note that our learners can exercise control, often legitimately, in a variety of ways), Strevens offers the two broad headings of *community-controlled* variables and *teacher-controlled* variables. A few representative examples are given here. Community-controlled variables include:

> Cultural norms and restrictions, for instance on materials or teaching styles
> Standards of teacher training
> Status of teachers in society
> Attitudes to target language

Under this heading he also includes institutional factors, such as class size, resources, time available and so on. Sometimes, of course, these may be directly within an institution's control; often they are not. Teacher-controlled variables include:

> Approaches to syllabus design
> Materials evaluation (and production)
> Choice of methodology, techniques, classroom organization (see next section for a fuller discussion)

You may well disagree with some of the details of where exactly the responsibility lies, but the 'control' notion is helpful in describing the many different facets of a teacher's role.

Teachers in the Classroom: Change and Innovation

The chameleon

The full title of the article that we have just referred to is 'Differences in teaching for different circumstances or the teacher as chameleon' (Strevens, 1979). This is a striking image, and your dictionary will tell you that a chameleon is a type of lizard whose most significant characteristic is 'its ability to change its skin colour to match its surroundings' (*Longmans English Larousse*). While we certainly do not wish to suggest that teachers merely change to conform, as a reaction to their working environment, this capacity to adapt to new circumstances, particularly over time, is a vital one. Strevens reinforces the point that we have made before, that no teaching/learning situation is really static. Political and educational circumstances change, as do resources available for teacher training; views of methodology change, as does the language itself; research is gradually disseminated; teachers develop; learners' expectations change; and there is a great increase in international travel. (The extent to which the elements of change can be considered positive is a separate issue, and is too context-specific to be examined in detail here.) Most of our discussion in this section will focus on the teacher's *classroom* role, picking up the key implications for teachers of the materials and methods examined in this book.

We would like you at this point to try to set out the most important changes in your own job, and role, over the last few years (5–10 years might be a useful period if you have been teaching that long). For example, do you have new areas of responsibility, either administrative or pedagogic? Have there been many innovations in the type of materials used? Have your students' attitudes to learning English changed in any discernible way? Are there any techniques that you have adopted in the classroom that you did not use a few years ago, or conversely, have you abandoned any? Some of the changes you identify will be concerned with your role within the classroom, some with your role outside. Insofar as they are separable, please take more time to think about the *classroom* context – learners, materials, methods.

Teachers will all have their own version of changing circumstances. The present writers, who teach English at most proficiency levels to adults coming to Britain for a variety of purposes, noted these general trends:

- Students will often have spent time in an English-speaking country already

- Classes have become increasingly participatory

- More detailed attention to needs and expectations is required of us, and for an ESP teacher this often includes some familiarity with learners' jobs or subject specialisms

- There is a great amount of published material now available, appropriate in varying degrees

- We spend more time engaged in various forms of individualized instruction

In sum, we think it likely that your role will have become more diversified on many fronts.

Before going on to identify some of the more specific aspects of classroom-based change, it is worth reflecting for a moment on the sources of innovation in language teaching. Prabhu (1987) makes a very valuable distinction between 'voluntary' change on the one hand, and 'statutory' or imposed change on the other. He writes: 'A new perception in pedagogy, implying a different pattern of classroom activity, is an intruder into teachers' mental frames – an unsettling one, because there is . . . a threat to prevailing routines and to the sense of security dependent on them. If, however, there is no compulsion to adopt new routines . . . the sense of security is largely protected and teachers' existing perceptions may then begin to interact with the new one and be influenced by it' (an influence which is likely to be beneficial). He goes on, 'Statutory implementation of an innovation, by contrast, is likely to distort all these processes and aggravate the tensions in teachers' mental frames', resulting in either outright rejection, or at least rejection of the rationale behind the innovation (105). In other words, the argument here is that statutory imposition may lead to conformity and routine efficiency, but will be less likely to become part of a teacher's own repertoire and to form the basis for personal development. Gaies and Bowers (1990: 170) suggest the following as examples of 'statutory' decisions:

- the adoption of new textbooks

- the introduction of pedagogical/methodological 'reforms' that teachers have not been trained to implement

- the establishment of new goals for a language teaching pro- gramme

- the prescription of new teacher–learner role relationships (as when a central authority specifies less 'teacher-fronted' and more 'learner-centred' work).

It will be useful, then, to regard Prabhu's distinction as implicit throughout this section.

Change, materials and methods

The main purpose of this book has been to survey current trends in materials and methods for English language teaching, to trace the sources and development of those trends, and to link our everyday practice as teachers with the principles on which that practice is based. Let us now briefly review some of the themes that have recurred with reference to the classroom context.

1 There has been a significant shift towards more 'communicat- ive, views of both language and behaviour. This in turn has led to, on the one hand

2 An analysis of language which includes, but also goes beyond, sentence grammar to the level of 'discourse' – of paragraph structure and longer texts – and the incorporation of such an analytic framework into teaching materials. And on the other hand

3   The acceptance and adoption of a variety of classroom 'management' techniques designed to allow for more realistic practice of language in use.

4   Syllabuses and materials are often based not only on one or two, but on several organizing principles linked together in quite complex ways: the 'multi-syllabus' idea tries to capture this complexity.

5   Research into the characteristics of language skills has contributed to gradual changes in the materials we use for teaching reading and listening comprehension, as well as the productive skills of writing and speaking. For instance, the range of possible activities has been extended a long way beyond the traditional procedures of reading/listening, followed by a test of understanding through comprehension questions. In other words, we can now work with a notion of *language strategy* as well as *linguistic content.*

6   Our methodology has also been affected by increased understanding of differences in learning styles, justifying the distinction between whole-class and smaller group work, and also allowing, where feasible, for the individualization of instruction in various formats.

Not all these developments have taken place simultaneously, of course: the various aspects of change have had differential impact and usefulness, and have naturally occurred at different times in different contexts, as you will be well aware from your own teaching situation. Note, too, that sometimes an innovation has direct implications for what a teacher in some sense needs to know (knowledge about text structure, for example, or the psychology of comprehension). At other times it influences attitudes and perceptions about appropriate roles and behaviour as well (such as re-structuring the classroom arrangement or introducing self-access material). We can now reflect on how these perspectives have contributed to the diversification of the teacher's role that we referred to a little earlier.

Consider this general point of Littlewood's (1981: 92): 'The concept of the teacher as "instructor" is . . . inadequate to describe his overall function'.

Do you agree with this statement? If so, what other concepts might be useful in contributing to a fuller picture of the teacher's overall role?

A number of writers on methodology and teacher training have proposed various ways of labelling the language teacher's potential roles. Harmer (1983: 200–4) offers these:

1   The teacher as *controller* of everything that goes on in the classroom
2   The teacher as *organizer* (classroom manager) of a range of activities
3   The teacher as *assessor*. Obviously the 'examiner' role is one of our traditional functions, but Harmer extends it to include the importance of giving regular feedback, as well as just correction and grading
4   The teacher as *participant* (co-communicator) in an organized activity such as debate or role play
5   The teacher as *resource* (consultant, adviser), most obviously as a language informant

Littlewood points out that these various roles can be put together under the 'umbrella' idea of the teacher as *facilitator* of learning. (He has a comparable list to Harmer, and his own terms are included above in brackets.)

Look back over the list of teacher functions that you made earlier: to what extent does it overlap with/differ from the (fairly representative) list that we have just set out?

Now try to put the individual points in order of importance for your own teaching circumstances. For instance, are you primarily an instructor/ assessor and only secondarily a 'resource' for your students?

If you are studying/working with other teachers, it will be interesting to compare your order of priority with theirs. Do colleagues working in the same situation necessarily have identical perceptions? And do teachers from different contexts see things differently from you?

As a short commentary on this activity, and to conclude this section, two observations can be re-stated. First of all, the roles and tasks that we perform result from a complex network of factors, and an objective definition, however necessary, will not be sufficient. They derive from our own perceptions, from the attitudes and expectations of many others, and not least from the language teaching materials that we are expected (or choose) to work with. Secondly, and finally, it should be remembered that this whole discussion has been based on the assumption that change and innovation are an inevitable part of our professional lives, and therefore no individual role description can be regarded as frozen in time.

Preparing the Teachers

The 'good language teacher'

The idea that it is possible to characterize the 'good language learner' is, as we saw in chapters 3 and 12, now quite well-established, and several researchers have investigated the types of learning strategies that successful learners appear to use. It would be logical to hope that teachers could eventually be described in a similar way, but the sheer number of variables involved in teaching will probably mean that this remains an impossible task. Even if we were to take the very straightforward criterion that a 'successful' teacher is one whose learners achieve good examination results, this in fact tells us rather little: we do not learn much about the relative importance of the teacher's preferred style and method, nor about the role of materials, and certainly nothing specific about the part played by different elements in an individual learner's success. Indeed this may have more to do with motivation, attitude, interest and so on, than with anything the teacher has to offer directly. Nevertheless, and despite the impossibility of precise measurement, most of us will have an opinion as to what constitutes a 'good language teacher'.

Assume that you have some responsibility for the selection of English language teachers for the specific context in which you work. Make a list of the qualities that you would be looking for in that selection process.

Your suggested list may contain some of the following, and you may well have others that we have not thought of:

> Knowledge of the language system
> Good pronunciation
> Experience of living in an English-speaking country
> Qualifications (perhaps further training taken, or in-service development)
> Classroom performance
> Evidence of being a good colleague
> Length of time as a teacher
> Ability to write teaching materials
> Careful planning of lessons
> Same L_1 as students, or a sound knowledge of it
> Experience of a variety of teaching situations
> Personal qualities (outgoing, interested in learners and so on)
> Publications
> Knowledge of learning theories
> Wide vocabulary
> Ability to manage a team of teachers

We should note here that this list includes factors of different kinds: some are specific to (English) language teaching, while others are more to do with the general qualities that might be expected of all teachers. Day (1990) formalizes this by referring to the distinction between *subject-matter* knowledge and *action-system* knowledge. In his words, the former 'refers to the specific information needed by teachers to teach content' (the language system, for example), and the latter to 'information dealing with teaching and learning in general, regardless of the subject matter. Included in action-system knowledge are such issues as classroom management and teacher expectations' (43). Although it is difficult to categorize our list of teacher qualities under one heading or the other in any precise way, Day's basic distinction is quite helpful when considering the 'training' of teachers, to which we now turn.

Teacher training, teacher education

In an obvious sense, opinions as to the necessary and desirable qualities of a teacher form the basis for the specification (whether by education authorities, training bodies, colleges and so on) of the goals of teacher training and teacher education programmes. Detailed design of such programmes will in turn derive from this setting of aims and objectives.

There is a large literature on the issue of 'training' versus 'education', and on the more concrete design specifications for a variety of training programmes for different levels of experience, different contexts, differing in duration and with varying degrees of generalizability. A few references are given in the further reading section at the end of this chapter. It has not been the purpose of this book to conclude with a detailed proposal for a particular kind of teacher preparation programme, a topic which is well covered elsewhere, but rather to trace developments and trends in materials and methods in our field and then to ask, in this final chapter, what might be the most appropriate perspectives on the role and training of teachers. With this in mind we look, first, at the relevance of the training/education debate, and secondly, invite you to formulate your own ideas for the in-service preparation of teachers.

Sometimes the notion of 'training' is used to refer to pre-service programmes for new teachers, with 'education' the preferred term for in-service work with experienced professionals. The idea here is that the narrower concept of training is more applicable to people who need to acquire a knowledge of the basic 'tools' of the job, whereas education implies a broader range of knowledge and skills. More usually, it is argued that *both* beginning *and* experienced teachers need elements of each, albeit with differing emphasis and depth. If we glance back at the list of possible teacher qualities, it is quite difficult to claim that some are relevant in pre- or, conversely, in-service situations. Pennington (1990: 134) relates the issue to the whole concept of professionalism, and argues that teachers require both 'a repertoire of skills' and 'judgement to apply these skills'. Richards (1990) puts forward a similar distinction with the terms 'macro' and 'micro' as approaches to teacher preparation. By 'micro' he means techniques – what teachers actually do that is directly observable and quantifiable (amount of teacher talk, questioning techniques, types of classroom tasks and the like). By 'macro' he means a 'holistic' approach which focuses on 'the total context of classroom teaching and learning in an attempt to understand how the interactions between and among teachers, learners and classroom tasks affect learning' (9). In other words, a macro approach is concerned with a teacher's ability to make judgements and inferences, to explore the relationship between different types of activity and their effect on learning, and to raise questions about one's own practice. It is both exploratory and generative. Clearly a teacher needs to be familiar with both kinds of approach.

We would like to ask you now to consider the design of a possible teacher preparation programme. In order to keep the task within manageable proportions, we suggest a number of guidelines.

Assume you have responsibility for planning an *in*-service course for teachers. Think in terms of a short programme of one or two weeks duration, and relate your planning to a teaching context with which you are familiar.

> What components would you wish to include?
> Approximately what proportion of time would you devote to each one?
> What would be your preferred methodology – lectures, workshops, discussion, observation of teaching?
> To what extent, if at all, would you give consideration to participants' personal proficiency?
>
> If possible, try also to decide whether you are more concerned with 'macro' or 'micro' approaches, and with 'subject-matter' or 'action-system' knowledge, as we defined them earlier in this section.

The present authors have worked with a number of different groups of teachers from many different countries, and we have also asked them to design a teacher programme along these kinds of lines. Some groups have chosen to work just on a specific area or theme. Examples would be 'Approaches to Skills Teaching and Learning'; 'The Development of Self-access Materials'; 'Communicative Methodology'. More often, these teachers have designed a broader-based programme, and the following content headings are typical (the points are not given in any particular order and are illustrative, not rules):

> Errors: analysis and treatment
> Syllabus design and lesson planning
> Materials evaluation
> Principles of learning
> Audio-visual aids
> Observation of teaching (using video if possible)
> Preparing supplementary materials
> Using English outside the class
> Sharing problems
> Test design
> Sound system of English

Suggested methodology of presentation is a mixture of lecture input and workshop-discussion, depending on the area under consideration. Our groups have placed particular emphasis on the importance of working out in advance the needs and interests of teachers on such an in-service course, and on the principle that a starting-point of enquiry in everyday practice will usually be more fruitful than a run-down of theory for its own sake, however stimulating.

Teacher Development

At several points in the preceding section we indicated the importance of seeing language teachers not only as carriers of knowledge about language and techniques, but as active and questioning professionals who are able to make generalizations and inferences from the basis of their own practice. Ramani (1987) refers to this as 'theorizing from the classroom': she proposes a teacher training procedure the starting-point for which is the sharing of subjective responses to various kinds of classroom data (see chapter 13 of this book for a number of examples). Just as 'training' is embedded in 'education', so this more exploratory perspective extends education itself into the idea of teacher *development*. This is a rapidly growing area of attention, and in this final section there will only be space to mention just two ways in which the term is understood.

First, there is a long tradition in general education – as distinct from language teacher education specifically – of encouraging classroom teachers to be *initiators* of research and development, as well as *recipients* of external investigation and results (for example by professional researchers or educational administrators). Research, in other words, is done 'by', not only 'on' or 'to' teachers, and is thus much more readily integrated into questions of practice. Hopkins (1985) offers a very clear overview of 'the teacher as researcher', and also introduces the closely related concept of 'Action Research'. The well-established Classroom Action Research Network (CARN) publishes bulletins that illustrate the kinds of topics that teachers are interested in investigating (see the end of the chapter for details). Here is a very small sample (1990):

Giving and receiving feedback in class
Initiating 'developmental' writing with children
Collaborative research with other teachers
Tape-recording pupil discussions
Do 'active' strategies actually improve the quality of learning?
Encouraging learners' questioning

The key point, in Hopkins' words (1985: 128–9), is 'the teacher's ability . . . to think systematically and critically about what he or she is doing. Central to this activity is the systematic reflection on one's classroom experience to understand it and to create meaning out of that understanding.'

Secondly, teacher development can also be equated with personal development. There are many activities that teachers can in principle engage in if they wish to extend their understanding of their role. They may, for instance, put themselves in the position of their students by learning another language. They may choose to attend courses or workshops, join a local teachers' network, go to conferences, write a regular teaching diary, learn something about educational management or counselling. Obviously each individual's working environment will determine to what extent these courses of action are realistic. This whole area has been incorporated into various teachers' organizations, one of the largest being the International Association of Teachers of English as a Foreign Language (IATEFL; see the end of the chapter). IATEFL itself has a number of Special Interest Groups ('SIGs'), one of which is on Teacher Development.

These three overlapping but distinct views of teacher preparation – training, education, development – are seen by Wallace (1991) as three models, which he terms (i) the 'craft' model, where a range of practical techniques is learned from an experienced person; (ii) the 'applied science' model, implying a one-way application, and often therefore separation, of theoretical research to practice; and (iii) the 'reflective' model, with the teacher as a 'reflective practitioner'. Wallace's own conclusion offers an appropriate ending to this book too, which has throughout attempted to encourage teachers to think critically about the major aspects of their own everyday professional reality. Wallace writes, 'An important aim of the reflective approach to teacher education is to empower teachers to manage their own professional development. Surely few things could be more conducive to raising the standards of teaching than a cadre of teachers who have the skills, ability and motivation to develop their practice . . . A second aim of this approach is to enable teachers to be more effective partners in innovation. In many situations teachers themselves are not recognized as possible agents of change . . . innovation is always a top-down affair . . . If foundations have been laid where, during their training period, at least some teachers have had an opportunity to be reflective and collaborative, then it might be possible for their professional expertise to be harnessed to implement innovation more effectively' (1991: 166).

We would like you to consider two final questions here relating to your own development as a teacher:

1) What kinds of activities have you done – or would you like to do – outside the daily classroom context that are of professional interest to you? A little earlier we gave just a few examples, which you might like to refer back to.

2) What are some of the issues that concern you as a teacher? For instance, would you like to have a clearer picture of the contribution of group work techniques to learning? Are you interested in the 'acceptability' to different people of the errors that your learners make? Would you like to compare your experiences of a particular class with those of a colleague? How useful are bilingual dictionaries, and do they affect a student's memory for vocabulary? Would it be useful to carry out a longitudinal 'case study' of an individual learner? How can we match

more closely the statutory teaching materials to learners' needs and interests?

But these only represent a few of *our* questions, and we leave you now to generate some of your own.

Further reading

1 Hopkins, D. (1985): *A Teachers Guide to Classroom Research*. This book was written in the context of mainstream education. The title is self-explanatory, as a way in to issues of professional development.

2 The following texts offer an overview of language teacher preparation:

Gower, R. and S. Walters (1983): *Teaching Practice Handbook.*
Harmer, J. (1983): *The Practice of English Language Teaching.*
Richards, J. C. and D. Nunan (eds) (1990): *Second Language Teacher Education.*
Wallace, M. J. (1991): *Training Foreign Language Teachers: a reflective approach.*

Organizations

CARN stands for the Classroom Action Research Network. It is based at the University of East Anglia, in the School of Education. (Address: University of East Anglia, Norwich NR4 7TJ, UK.) Its central aim is to improve the quality of education by promoting teacher research and professional development. Note that CARN is not specifically for language teachers.

IATEFL stands for the International Association of Teachers of English as a Foreign Language. It is the largest European-based organization. It holds a major annual conference, publishes a regular Newsletter, and includes a range of Special Interest Groups. (Address: 3 Kingsdown Chambers, Kingsdown Park, Tankerton, Whitstable, Kent CT5 2DJ, UK.)

Materials

Abbs, B. and I. Freebairn (1977): *Starting Strategies.* Harlow: Longman.

Abbs, B. and I. Freebairn (1981): *Developing Strategies.* Harlow: Longman.

Aston, G. (1982): *Interact: An Interaction Workbook.* Loughborough: Modern English Publications.

Axbey, S. (1989): *Soundtracks.* Harlow: Longman.

Bell, J. (1990): *Integrated Skills: Upper Intermediate.* Oxford: Heinemann.

Brewster, S. (1991): *Intermediate Listening.* Walton-on-Thames and Edinburgh: Nelson.

Cooper, J. (1979): *Think and Link.* London: Edward Arnold.

Davies, E. and N. Whitney (1979): *Reasons for Reading.* London: Heinemann.

Floyd, J. (1984): *Study Skills for Higher Education.* Harlow: Longman.

Forman, D., F. Donoghue, S. Abbey, B. Kruden, I. Kidd (1990): *Campus English.* London: Macmillan.

Geddes, M. and G. Sturtridge (1980): *Listening Links.* London: Heinemann.

Geddes, M. and G. Sturtridge (1982): *Reading Links.* London: Heinemann.

Goodale, M. (1987): *Meetings: Ten Simulations on International Topics.* Hove: Language Teaching Publications.

Hall, D. and M. Foley (1988): *Speaking Out.* Walton-on-Thames: Nelson.

Hedge, T. (1983): *Pen to Paper.* Walton-on-Thames and Edinburgh: Nelson.

Hedge, T. (1983): *Freestyle.* Walton-on-Thames and Edinburgh: Nelson.

Herbert, D. and G. Sturtridge (1979): *Simulations.* London: NFER.

Hopkins, A. (1989): *Perspectives.* Harlow: Longman.

Hopkins, A. and C. Tribble (1989): *Outlines.* Harlow: Longman.

Imhoof, M. and H. Hudson (1975): *From Paragraph to Essay.* London: Longman.

James, K. (1979): *Listening Comprehension and Note-Taking Course.* London: Collins.

Johnson, K. (1981): *Communicate in Writing.* Harlow: Longman.

Johnson, K. and K. Morrow (1978): *Communicate.* Cambridge: Cambridge University Press.

Jolly, D. (1982): *Reading Choices.* Cambridge: Cambridge University Press.

Jones, L. (1981): *Functions of English.* Cambridge: Cambridge University Press (2nd edn).

Jones, L. (1983): *Eight Simulations.* Cambridge: Cambridge University Press.

Jordan, R. R. (1982): *Figures in Language: Describe and Draw.* Glasgow: Collins.

Jupp, T. C. and J. Milne (1969): *Guided Course in English Composition.* London: Heinemann.

Jupp, T. C. and J. Milne (1972): *Guided Paragraph Writing.* London: Heinemann.

Keller, E. and S. Warner (1988): *Conversation Gambits.* Hove: Language Teaching Publications.

Lawrence, M. (1972): *Writing as a Thinking Process.* Ann Arbor: University of Michigan Press.

Lynch, M. (1977): *It's your Choice: Six Role Playing Exercises.* London: Edward Arnold.

Mackin, R., J. Webb, R. L. Scott-Buccleuch (1970): *OPEAC Oral Drills Workbook.* London: Oxford University Press.

Maley, A. and R. S. Newberry (1974): *Between You and Me: Guided Dialogues for Conversation Practice.* Sunbury-on-Thames: Nelson.

Milne, B. (1991): *Integrated Skills: Intermediate.* Oxford: Heinemann.

Moody, K. W. (1974): *Frames for Written English.* London: Oxford University Press.

Morrow, K. and K. Johnson (1980): *Communicate.* 2 Cambridge: Cambridge University Press.

O'Neill, R. (1971): *Kernel Lessons Intermediate.* London: Longman.

O'Neill, R. with P. Mugglestone (1989): *The Third Dimension/The Fourth Dimension.* Harlow: Longman.

Phillips, D. and S. Sheerin (1990): *Signature.* Walton-on-Thames and Edinburgh: Nelson.

Porter-Ladousse, G. (1983): *Speaking Personally.* Cambridge: Cambridge University Press.

Sandler, P. L. and C. L. Stott (1981): *Manage with English.* Oxford: Oxford University Press.

Spencer, D. H. (1967): *Guided Composition Exercises.* London: Longman.

Swan, M. and C. Walter (1990): *New Cambridge English Course.* Cambridge: Cambridge University Press.

Tribble, C. (1989): *Word for Word.* Harlow: Longman.

Underwood, M. (1975): *Listen to This!* London: Oxford University Press (2nd edn).

Underwood, M. and P. Barr (1980): *Listeners.* Oxford: Oxford University Press.

Ur, P. (1981): *Discussions That Work.* Cambridge: Cambridge University Press.

Watcyn-Jones, P. (1981): *Pairwork.* Harmondsworth: Penguin Books.

White, R. V. (1986): *Writing Away.* London: Lingual House.

Williams, R. (1982): *Panorama: An Advanced Course of English for Study and Examinations.* Harlow: Longman.

Willis, J. and D. (1989): *COBUILD English Course.* London: Collins.

Bibliography

Allwright, R. L. (1984): Why don't learners learn what teachers teach? The interaction hypothesis. In Singleton, D. M. and D. G. Little (eds): *Language Teaching in Formal and Informal Contexts.* Dublin: IRAAL, 3–18.

Allwright, R. L. (1988): Autonomy and individualisation in whole class instruction. In Brookes, A. and P. Grundy (eds): 35–44.

Allwright, R. L. (1992): Understanding classroom language learning: an argument for exploratory teaching. Talk given at Essex University, February 1992.

Allwright, R. L. and K. Bailey (1991): *Focus on the Language Classroom.* Cambridge: Cambridge University Press.

Anderson, A. and T. Lynch (1988): *Listening.* Oxford: Oxford University Press.

Bartlett, F. C. (1932): *Remembering: A Study in Experimental and Social Psychology.* Cambridge: Cambridge University Press.

Beaumont, M. (1983): Take it from the text: an approach to the teaching of reading. In Jordan, R. R. (ed.): *Case Studies in ELT.* London: Collins, 26–34.

Bowers, R. (1980): The individual learner in the general class. In Altman, H. and C. James (eds): *Foreign Language Teaching: Meeting Individual Needs.* Oxford: Pergamon, 66–80.

Breen, M. (1987): Contemporary paradigms in syllabus design. *Language Teaching,* 20/2, 81–92; 20/3, 157–74.

Breen, M. and C. N. Candlin (1987): Which materials? A consumer's and designer's guide. In Sheldon, L. E. (ed.): *ELT Textbooks and Materials: Problems in Evaluation and Development.* ELT Documents 126. London: Modern English Publications/The British Council, 13–28.

British Council (1983): *Teaching and Learning in Focus.* London.

Brookes, A. and P. Grundy (eds) (1988): *Individualisation and Autonomy in Language Learning.* ELT Documents 131. London: Modern English Publications/The British Council.

Brown, G. and G. Yule (1983a): *Teaching the Spoken Language.* Cambridge: Cambridge University Press.

Brown, G. and G. Yule (1983b): *Discourse Analysis.* Cambridge: Cambridge University Press.

Brumfit, C. J. (1980): Seven last slogans. *Modern English Teacher*, 7/1, 30–1.

Brumfit, C. J. (1984): *Communicative Methodology in Language Teaching: the roles of fluency and accuracy.* Cambridge: Cambridge University Press.

Brumfit, C. J. and J. T. Roberts (1983): *A Short Introduction to Language and Language Teaching.* London: Batsford.

Bush, T. (1984): Key roles in post-school management. In *Management in Post-Compulsory Education.* Block 3 Course Materials, Course E324. Milton Keynes: The Open University.

Bygate, M. (1987): *Speaking.* Oxford: Oxford University Press.

Byrne, D. (1981): Integrating skills. In Johnson and Morrow (eds), 108–14.

Byrne, D. (1988): *Teaching Writing Skills.* London: Longman (new edn).

Carrell, F., J. Devine and D. Eskey (eds) (1988): *Interactive Approaches to Second Language Reading.* Cambridge: Cambridge University Press.

Chaix, P. and C. O'Neil (1978): *A Critical Analysis of Forms of Autonomous Learning (Autodidaxy and Semi-Autonomy) in the Field of Foreign Language Learning.* Final Report, UNESCO Doc Ed 78/WS/58.

Clarke, D. F. (1989): Communicative theory and its influence on materials production. *Language Teaching*, 22/2, 73–86.

Collins (1987): *COBUILD English Language Dictionary.* London and Glasgow: Collins.

Cook, G. (1989): *Discourse Analysis.* Oxford: Oxford University Press.

Cook, V. J. (1991): *Second Language Learning and Language Teaching.* London: Edward Arnold.

Cunningsworth, A. (1984): *Evaluating and Selecting ELT Materials.* Oxford: Heinemann.

Day, R. R. (1990): Teacher observation in second language teacher education. In Richards and Nunan (eds), 43–61.

Dickinson, L. (1989): Learning purpose, learning structure and the training of learners for autonomy. In Cecioni, C. (ed.): *Proceedings of the Symposium on Autonomy in Foreign Language Learning.* Florence: Language Centre, University of Florence, 30–42.

Dickinson, L. (1987) *Self-instruction in Language Learning.* Cambridge: Cambridge University Press.

Dubin, F. and E. Olshtain (1986): *Course Design.* Cambridge: Cambridge University Press.

Ellis, B. and G. Sinclair (1989): *Learning to Learn English.* Cambridge: Cambridge University Press.

Freedman, A., I. Pringle and J. Yalden (1983): *Learning to Write: First Language/Second Language.* London and New York: Longman.

Gaies, S. (1980): Classroom-centred research: some consumer guidelines. Paper presented at second annual TESOL summer meeting, Albuquerque, NM.

Gaies, S. and R. Bowers (1990): Clinical supervision of language teaching: the supervisor as trainer and educator. In Richards and Nunan (eds), 167–81.

Gower, R. and S. Walters (1983): *Teaching Practice Handbook.* London: Heinemann.

Grant, N. (1987): *Making the Most of Your Textbook.* London: Longman.

Grellet, F. (1981): *Developing Reading Skills.* Cambridge: Cambridge University Press.

Halliday, M. A. K. and R. Hasan (1976): *Cohesion in English.* London: Longman.

Handy, C. B. (1985): *Understanding Organisations.* London: Penguin Books (3rd edn).

Harmer, J. (1983): *The Practice of English Language Teaching.* London: Longman, (New edition 1992).

Hayes, J. R. and L. S. Flower (1983): Uncovering cognitive processes in writing: an introduction to protocol analysis. In Mosenthal, P., L. Tamor and S. Walmsley (eds): *Research on Writing: Principles and Methods.* New York: Longman, 207–20.

Hedge, T. (1988): *Writing.* Oxford: Oxford University Press.

Hopkins, D. (1985): *A Teacher's Guide to Classroom Research.* Milton Keynes and Philadelphia: Open University Press.

Hymes, D. (1972): On communicative competence. In Pride, J. B. and J. Holmes (eds): *Sociolinguistics*. Harmondsworth: Penguin Books, 263–93.

Jacobs, G. (1988): Co-operative goal structure: a way to improve group activities. *ELT Journal*, 42/2, 97–101.

Johnson, K. (1981): Some background, some key terms and some definitions. In Johnson and Morrow (eds), 1–12.

Johnson, K. (1982): *Communicative Syllabus Design and Methodology*. Oxford: Pergamon Press.

Johnson, K. and K. Morrow (eds) (1981): *Communication in the Classroom*. London: Longman.

Kementerian Pelajaran Malaysia (1979): *The English Syllabus for Forms I–III of Secondary Schools*. Kuala Lumpur.

Kennedy, C. (1983): Video in ESP. In *Video Applications in English Language Teaching*. ELT Documents 114. Oxford: Modern English Publications/The British Council, 95–102.

Kumaravadivelu, B. (1990): Classroom observation: a neglected situation. *TESOL Newsletter*, vol. 24, 6, 5–32.

Littlejohn, A. and S. Windeatt (1988): Beyond language learning: perspectives on materials design. In Johnson, R. K. (ed.) : *The Second Language Curriculum*. Cambridge: Cambridge University Press, 155–75.

Littlewood, W. T. (1981): *Communicative Language Teaching*. Cambridge: Cambridge University Press.

Long, M. H. (1975): Group work and communicative competence in the ESOL classroom. In Burt, M. K. and H. C. Dulay (eds): *On TESOL '75: New Directions in Second Language Learning, Teaching and Bilingual Education*. Washington DC: TESOL, 211–23.

Long, M. H. and P. A. Porter (1985): Group work, interlanguage talk and second language acquisition. *TESOL Quarterly*, 19, 207–28.

Madsen, K. S. and J. D. Bowen (1978): *Adaptation in Language Teaching*. Rowley, MA: Newbury House.

Malamah-Thomas, A. (1987): *Classroom Interaction*. Oxford: Oxford University Press.

McDonough, S. H. (1986): *Psychology in Foreign Language Teaching*. London: Allen and Unwin (2nd edn).

Morrow, K. (1981): Principles of communicative methodology. In Johnson and Morrow (eds), 59–66.

Naiman, N., M. Fröhlich and H. H. Stern (1975): *The Good Language Learner*. Modern Language Centre, Department of Curriculum,

Ontario Institute for Studies in Education.

Nolasco, R. and L. Arthur (1986): Try doing it with a class of forty! *ELT Journal*, 40/2, 100–6.

Nolasco, R. and L. Arthur (1988): *Large Classes*. London and Basingstoke: Macmillan.

Nunan, D. (1988): *The Learner-Centred Curriculum*. Cambridge: Cambridge University Press.

Nunan, D. (1989): *Designing Tasks for the Communicative Classroom*. Cambridge: Cambridge University Press.

Nunan, D. (1990): Action research in the classroom. In Richards and Nunan (eds), 62–81.

Nunan, D. (1991): *Language Teaching Methodology: A Textbook for Teachers*. Hemel Hempstead: Prentice–Hall International.

Nuttall, C. (1982): *Teaching Reading Skills in a Foreign Language*. London: Heinemann.

O'Neill, R. (1982): Why use textbooks? *ELT Journal*, 36/2, 104–11.

Pattison, P. (1987): *Developing Communication Skills*. Cambridge: Cambridge University Press.

Pennington, M. C. (1990): A professional development focus for the language teaching practicum. In Richards and Nunan (eds), 132–52.

Pica, T. and C. Doughty (1985): Input and interaction in the communicative classroom: a comparison of teacher-fronted and group activities. In Gass, S. M. and C. G. Madden (eds): *Input in Second Language Acquisition*. Rowley, MA: Newbury House, 115–32.

Prabhu, N. S. (1987): *Second Language Pedagogy*. Oxford: Oxford University Press.

Pugh, A. K. (1978): *Silent Reading*. London: Heinemann.

Raimes, A. (1983): *Techniques in Teaching Writing*. New York and London: Oxford University Press.

Ramani, E. (1987): Theorising from the classroom. *ELT Journal*, 41/1, 3–11.

Richards, J. C. (1985): *The Context of Language Teaching*. Cambridge: Cambridge University Press.

Richards, J. C. (1990): The dilemma of teacher education in second language teaching. In Richards and Nunan (eds), 3–15.

Richards, J. C. and D. Nunan (eds) (1990): *Second Language Teacher Education*. Cambridge: Cambridge University Press.

Richards, J. C., J. Platt and H. Weber (1985): *Longman Dictionary of*

Applied Linguistics. London: Longman.

Richards, J. C. and T. S. Rodgers (1986): *Approaches and Methods in Language Teaching.* Cambridge: Cambridge University Press.

Richterich, R. and J. L. Chancerel (1980): *Identifying the Needs of Adults Learning a Foreign Language.* Oxford: Pergamon.

Riley, P. (1982): Learners Lib: an experimental autonomous learning scheme. In Geddes, M. and G. Sturtridge (eds): *Individualisation.* Loughborough: Modern English Publications, 61–3.

Rivers, W. and M. Temperley (1978): *A Practical Guide to the Teaching of English as a Foreign or Second Language.* New York: Oxford University Press.

Rixon, S. (1986): *Developing Listening Skills.* London and Basingstoke: Macmillan/Modern English Publications.

Rost, M. (1990): *Listening in Language Learning.* London and New York: Longman.

Rubin, J. and I. Thompson (1982): *The Good Language Learner.* Boston, Mass: Heinle and Heinle.

Sheerin, S. (1989): *Self-Access.* Oxford: Oxford University Press.

Sheldon, L. E. (ed.) (1987): *ELT Textbooks and Materials: Problems in Evaluation and Development.* Oxford: ELT Documents 126; Modern English Publications in association with the British Council.

Sheldon, L. E. (1988): Evaluating ELT textbooks and materials. *ELT Journal,* 42/4, 237–46.

Skehan, P. (1980): Team teaching and the role of the ESP teacher. In *Study Modes and Academic Development of Overseas Students.* ELT Documents 109. London: The British Council, 23–37.

Skehan, P. (1989): *Individual Differences in Second Language Learning.* London: Edward Arnold.

Smith, F. (1978): *Reading.* Cambridge: Cambridge University Press (2nd edn).

Stern, H. H. (1983): *Fundamental Concepts of Language Teaching.* Oxford: Oxford University Press.

Stevick, E. W. (1972): Evaluating and adapting language materials. In Allen, H. B. and R. N. Campbell (eds): *Teaching English as a Second Language.* New York: McGraw–Hill, 102–20.

Stoller, F. (1984): Designing an effective reading lab. *TEAM,* University of Dharan Language Centre, no. 49.

Strevens, P. (1979): Differences in teaching for different circumstances or the teacher as chameleon. In Yorio, C. A., K. Perkins and J. Schachter (eds): *On TESOL '79: The Learner in*

Focus. Washington, DC: TESOL, 2–11.

Stubbs, M. and S. Delamont (eds) (1976): *Explorations in Classroom Observation.* Chichester, New York: John Wiley.

Swan, M. (1985): A critical look at the communicative approach. *ELT Journal*, 39/1, 2–12; 39/2, 76–87.

Thickett, P. (1986): The Use of TLF on an RSA preparatory certificate course. In *English Teaching Information Circular* (ETIC). London: The British Council.

Trim, J. L. M. (1976): Some possibilities and limitations of learner autonomy. In Harding-Esch, E. (ed.): *Self-Directed Learning and Autonomy.* Cambridge and Nancy: mimeo, 1–11.

Underwood, M. (1989): *Teaching Listening.* London: Longman.

Ur, P. (1987): *Teaching Listening Comprehension.* Cambridge: Cambridge University Press.

van Ek, J. A. (1977): *The Threshold Level for Modern Language Learning in Schools.* London: Longman.

van Ek, J. A., L. G. Alexander and M. A. Fitzpatrick (1980): *Waystage English.* Oxford: Pergamon Press (on behalf of the Council of Europe).

van Lier, L. (1988): *The Classroom and the Language Learner.* London: Longman.

Wajnryb, R. (1991): *Classroom Observation Tasks.* Cambridge: Cambridge University Press.

Walker, C. (1987): Individualising reading. *ELT Journal*, 41/1, 46–50.

Wallace, M. J. (1991): *Training Foreign Language Teachers: A Reflective Approach.* Cambridge: Cambridge University Press.

Wenden, A. and J. Rubin (1987): *Learner Strategies in Language Learning.* New York and London: Prentice–Hall International.

White, R. V. (1980): *Teaching Written English.* London: Allen and Unwin.

White, R. V. (1981): Reading. In Johnson and Morrow (eds), 87–92.

White, R. V. (1982): *The English Teachers' Handbook.* Walton-on-Thames: Nelson.

Widdowson, H. G. (1978): *Teaching Language as Communication.* Oxford: Oxford University Press.

Widdowson, H. G. (1979): The simplification of use. In Widdowson, H. G.: *Explorations in Applied Linguistics.* Oxford: Oxford University Press, 185–91.

Wilkins, D. A. (1976): *Notional Syllabuses.* Oxford: Oxford University Press.

Williams, E. (1984): *Reading in the Language Classroom*. London: Macmillan.

Willing, K. (1988): *Learning Styles in Adult Migrant Education*. Adelaide: National Curriculum Resource Centre, Adult Migrant Education Program.

Willis, D. (1990): *The Lexical Syllabus*. London and Glasgow: Collins.

Wright, T. (1987): *Roles of Teachers and Learners*. Oxford: Oxford University Press.

Yalden, J. (1983): *The Communicative Syllabus: Evolution, Design and Implementation*. Oxford: Pergamon Press.

Index